Bills of Lading

BILLS OF LADING
Law and practice

Second edition

ALAN MITCHELHILL

London New York
Chapman and Hall

First published in 1982 by
Chapman and Hall Ltd
11 New Fetter Lane, London EC4P 4EE

Published in the USA by
Chapman and Hall
29 West 35th Street, New York NY10001

Second edition 1990

© *1982, 1990 Alan Mitchelhill*

Typeset in 11/12 Palatino by
Mayhew Typesetting, Bristol

Printed in Great Britain by
The University Press, Cambridge

ISBN 0 412 35750 X

British Library Cataloguing in Publication Data

Mitchelhill, Alan
  Bills of lading: law and practice. – 2nd. ed.
  1. Bills of lading. International law
  341.7'5668
ISBN 0-412-35750-X

Library of Congress Cataloging in Publication Data

Mitchelhill, Alan.
  Bills of lading : law and practice / Alan Mitchelhill. –
  2nd ed.
    p.   cm.
  ISBN 0-412-35750-X
  1. Bills of lading.   2. Contracts, Maritime.   3. Bills
of lading – Great Britain.   4. Contracts, Maritime –
Great Britain.   I. Title.
K1178.M57   1990
343.41'0878–dc20
[344.103878]   89–39184
                                          CIP

Contents

Preface to the second edition   xi

Preface to the first edition   xiii

1   Evolution of the bill of lading   1
    1.1   Historical   1
    1.2   The *Bills of Lading Act* 1855   2
    1.3   Development   4
    1.4   Definition   5

2   Rules governing the bill of lading   6
    2.1   The Hague Rules   6
    2.1.1   Article I – Definitions   6
    2.1.2   Article II – Risks   7
    2.1.3   Article III – Responsibilities and liabilities   8
    2.1.4   Article IV – Rights and immunities   9
    2.1.5   Article V – Surrender of rights and immunities and
          increase of responsibilities and liabilities   12
    2.1.6   Article VI – Special conditions   12
    2.1.7   Article VII – Limitations on the application of the rules   12
    2.1.8   Article IX – Monetary units   12
    2.2   Hague–Visby Rules   13
    2.2.1   Article III   14
    2.2.2   Article IV   15
    2.2.3   Article IVbis   16
    2.2.4   Article IX   16
    2.2.5   Article X   16

3   Conventional and through bills of lading   18
    3.1   The contract of affeightment   18
    3.2   Types of document   19
    3.3   Application as a receipt   19
    3.4   Application as evidence of contract of carriage   19
    3.5   Application as a document of title   19
    3.6   Format on the front of the bill   20
    3.7   Requirement for 'Received' or 'Shipped' bill   22
    3.8   Freight   25
    3.8.1   Freight payable on destination or 'freight collect'   25
    3.8.2   Lump sum freight   25
    3.8.3   Freight paid at port of shipment   25
    3.8.4   Dead freight   25
    3.8.5   Ad valorem freight (according to the value)   26
    3.8.6   Back freight or return freight   26
    3.8.7   Pro rata freight   26

4   Conventional bill of lading terms and conditions   27
    4.1   The Clause Paramount   27
    4.2   Conveyance clause   28
    4.3   Discharge and delivery   28
    4.4   Acknowledgement of weight, quality, marks etc.   28

4.5	Voyage clause	29
4.6	Deck cargo	29
4.7	Carrier's Liberties in the event of blockade, delay etc.	29
4.8	Carrier's Liberties in the event of war etc.	30
4.9	Containers	30
4.10	Port, Customs, Consular and other regulations	30
4.11	Transhipment and forwarding	30
4.12	Dangerous, inflammable, radioactive, damaging or contaminating goods	31
4.13	Claims	32
4.14	Freight	32
4.15	Lien	33
4.16	General Average	33
4.17	Both-to-blame collision clause	33
4.18	New Jason clause	34
4.19	Rights and immunities of all servants and agents of the carrier	34
4.20	Agency clause	35
4.21	Jurisdiction	35

5	Combined transport documents	36
5.1	Warranty	37
5.2	Carrier's responsibility: port-to-port shipment	37
5.3	Carrier's responsibility: combined transport	37
5.4	Special provisions for combined transport	38
5.5	Time-bar	38
5.6	Exclusion of limitation	38
5.7	Amount of compensation: combined transport	38
5.8	Sundry liability provisions	38
5.9	Shipper packed containers	39
5.10	Inspection of goods	39
5.11	Carriage affected by the condition of the goods	39
5.12	Description of the goods	39
5.13	Shipper's and merchant's responsibilities	40
5.14	Freight and charges	40
5.15	Lien	40
5.15.1	Methods and route of transportation	40
5.16	Matters affecting performance	40
5.17	Notification	41
5.18	Variation of the contract	41

6	Variations of conventional and combined transport bills of lading	42
6.1	Bills of lading issued under a charter-party	42
6.2	Bills of lading issued by freight forwarders	43
6.3	Government form bills of lading	44
6.4	Other forms of bills of lading	44
6.5	Short form bill of lading	44

7	Sea waybills and data freight receipts	46

8	A clean bill of lading	48

9	Delivery of cargo under bills of lading and other transport documents which embrace them	50

10	Related documents	52
10.1	The mate's receipt	52

10.2	The National Standard Shipping Note	52
10.3	Ships' delivery orders	53

11 The ship's manifest — 55

12 Documentary credits — 56
12.1	The uniform customs and practice for documentary credits	56
12.1.1	Article 25	56
12.1.2	Article 26	57
12.1.3	Article 27	58
12.1.4	Article 28	58
12.1.5	Article 29	58
12.1.6	Article 30	59
12.1.7	Article 31	59
12.1.8	Article 32	59
12.1.9	Article 33	59
12.1.10	Article 34	59

13 Letters of Indemnity — 61

14 United Nations Conventions — 63
14.1	United Nations Convention on the carriage of goods by sea, 1978: The Hamburg Rules	63
14.1.1	Article 1 – Definitions	63
14.1.2	Article 2 – Scope of application	63
14.1.3	Article 4 – Period of responsibility	64
14.1.4	Article 5 – Basis of liability	64
14.1.5	Article 6 – Limits of liability	65
14.1.6	Article 7 – Application to non-contractual claims	65
14.1.7	Article 8 – Loss of right to limit responsibility	66
14.1.8	Article 9 – Deck cargo	66
14.1.9	Article 10 – Liability of carrier and actual carrier	66
14.1.10	Article 11 – Through carriage	66
14.1.11	Article 12 – Liability of the shipper: general rule	66
14.1.12	Article 13 – Special rules for dangerous cargo	67
14.1.13	Article 14 – Issue of the bill of lading	67
14.1.14	Article 15 – Contents of the bill of lading	67
14.1.15	Article 16 – Bills of lading: reservations and evidentiary effect	67
14.1.16	Article 17 – Guarantees by the shipper	68
14.1.17	Article 18 – Documents other than bills of lading	68
14.1.18	Article 19 – Notice of loss, damage or delay	68
14.1.19	Article 20 – Limitation of actions	68
14.1.20	Article 21 – Jurisdiction	69
14.1.21	Article 22 – Arbitration	69
14.1.22	Article 23 – Contractual stipulation	69
14.1.23	Article 24 – General Average	70
14.1.24	Article 25 – Other conventions	70
14.1.25	Article 26 – Unit of account	70
14.1.26	Article 30 – Entry into force	70
14.1.27	Article 31 – Denunciation of other conventions	70
14.1.28	Article 34 – Denunciation	71
14.1.29	Annex II	71
14.2	UN Convention on international multimodal transport of goods, 1980	71
14.2.1	A summary of the provisions	71

14.2.2	Article 2 – Scope of application	72
14.2.3	Article 5 – Issue of multimodal transport document	72
14.2.4	Article 6 – Negotiable multimodal document	72
14.2.5	Article 7 – Non-negotiable multimodal transport document	72
14.2.6	Article 8 – Contents of the multimodal transport document	72
14.2.7	Article 9 – Reservations in the multimodal document	73
14.2.8	Article 10 – Evidentiary effect of the multimodal document	73
14.2.9	Article 11 – Liability for intentional mis-statements or omissions	73
14.2.10	Article 12 – Guarantee by the consignor	73
14.2.11	Article 13 – Other documents	73
14.2.12	Article 14 – Period of responsibility	73
14.2.13	Article 15 – The liability of the multimodal transport operator for his servants, agents and other persons	74
14.2.14	Article 16 – Basis of liability	74
14.2.15	Article 17 – Concurrent causes	74
14.2.16	Article 18 – Limitation of liability	74
14.2.17	Article 19 – Localized damage	74
14.2.18	Article 20 – Non-contractual liability	74
14.2.19	Article 21 – Loss of the right to limit liability	75
14.2.20	Article 22 – Liability of the consignor – General Rule	75
14.2.21	Article 23 – Special rules on dangerous goods	75
14.2.22	Article 24 – Notice of loss, damage or delay	75
14.2.23	Article 25 – Limitation of actions	75
14.2.24	Article 26 – Jurisdiction	76
14.2.25	Article 27 – Arbitration	76
14.2.26	Article 29 – General Average	76
15	General Average and Particular Average	77
16	The carriage of dangerous goods	79
16.1	Transport by road	79
16.2	Transport by rail	79
16.3	Air	79
16.4	Responsibility for preparation	80
16.5	Container/Vehicle Packing Certificate	80
16.6	Transport emergency information	80
16.7	Bulk tank shipments	81
16.8	HM Customs	81
16.9	Classes of dangerous cargo	81
16.9.1	Class 1 – Explosives	81
16.9.2	Class 2 – Gases	81
16.9.3	Class 3 – Inflammable liquids	81
16.9.4	Class 4 – Inflammable solids and substances	81
16.9.5	Class 5 – Oxidizing substances	82
16.9.6	Class 6 – Poisons and infectious substances	82
16.9.7	Class 7 – Radioactive substances	82
16.9.8	Class 8 – Corrosives	82
16.9.9	Class 9 – Miscellaneous dangerous substances	82
16.9.10	Marine pollutants	82
	The meaning of terms and abbreviations	83

Appendix A   The *Carriage of Goods by Sea Act* 1924. The Hague Rules   95

Appendix B   The *Carriage of Goods by Sea Act* 1971. The Hague-Visby Rules   100

Appendix C   The *Pomerene Bills of Lading Act* 1916 (of the United States of America)   109

Appendix D   The United States *Carriage of Goods by Sea Act* 1936   117

Appendix E   The Hamburg Rules   124

Appendix F   The York-Antwerp Rules 1974   141

Appendix G   An example of through bill of lading conditions   148

Appendix H   A combined transport document   149

Appendix I   BIMCO liner bill of lading   151

Appendix J   BIMCO 'COGENBILL' for use with charter-parties   152

Appendix K   BIMCO 'blank back' liner bill of lading   154

Appendix L   Common short form bill of lading   155

Appendix M   Non-negotiable sea waybill   156

Appendix N   FIATA combined transport bill of lading   157

Appendix O   Dangerous Goods Note (1981)   158

Appendix P   Standard Shipping Note (1981)   160

Appendix Q   Indemnity form   161

Appendix R   Lloyd's Average Bond, Valuation Form and Average Guarantee   162

Appendix S   General average and deposit receipt   165

Index   166

Preface to the second edition

Since the publication of the first edition there have been several changes and developments in shipping documentation including advances in the transmission of information passed from one computer to another by Electronic Data Interchange (EDI), now gradually replacing the conventional methods of document reproduction in international trade between countries where such facilities are available. The dispatch to and receipt of manifests and other freight details at destination ports is just one example of the benefits of EDI, because the arrival of a ship before the manifest is occasionally a serious problem.

The full potential and benefit of the Sea Waybill is also becoming more widely appreciated for marine transportation, when a negotiable document of title is not required, and an international sub-committee of the *Comité Maritime International* (CMI) is drafting a set of Uniform Rules for eventual incorporation in Sea Waybills. Unfortunately, the UK Bills of Lading Act, 1855 was not drafted with such a document in mind, which could cause legal difficulties but the US Pomerene Act does not have this problem. I have therefore expanded the chapter on the subject and also included in this edition both the Pomerene Act and the US Carriage of Goods by Sea Act for the benefit of readers. In this respect I am most grateful to the US Government for permission to reproduce these documents, and the benefit of their library facilities in London for this purpose.

It will be observed that in the general revision of the book I have updated most of the appendices and also included additional chapters on a clean bill of lading, delivery of cargo, manifests and the UN Convention on International Multi-modal Transport of Goods, 1980. The future development of both this Convention and the one governing the Hamburg Rules will be interesting to observe, although quite a lot is likely to happen before either become law.

An interesting aspect in writing on the subject of Bills of Lading is that in most of my shipping career there was little movement or improvement in documentation procedures until the introduction of containerization in the late 1960s and the advent of SITPRO in 1970. Now the situation is constantly under review.

In the preparation of this edition I wish to express my appreciation to Ellerman Lines plc, the Simplification of International Trade Procedures Board (SITPRO), the Baltic and International Maritime Conference (BIMCO), the International Federation of Freight Forwarders Associations (FIATA), Swedish Trade Procedures Council (SWEPRO), and ICC Publishing SA for their kind permission to reproduce once again material from their documents. Also to Sweet & Maxwell Ltd for their permission to again reproduce extracts from *Scrutton on Charterparties*, 18th edn. and to Brian Reeves and Brian Parkinson for their assistance with the latest developments in the field of documentation.

A.M.

Preface to the first edition

This book is an introduction to the way a bill of lading works. It aims to explain in a manner that is hopefully easy to understand, the many aspects for this important document. It is intended as a practical guide for those engaged in the shipping business, and not a study in depth of this immense subject; for this, one must seek one's knowledge from legal and other specialized works of reference. The bill of lading is associated with related documents, some of which are necessary only on special occasions, and I have endeavoured to describe these as they may be used in different ways.

To help the reader understand the development of the bill of lading, the first chapter has been devoted to its historical background. The document has changed substantially in recent times and as one proceeds through the pages, this will be illustrated by the movement from simple to conventional bills and through transport bills to combined transport documents. The document changes with the times to meet the needs of modern conditions and the banking rules of the International Chamber of Commerce.

Sea Waybills have been introduced which, being non-negotiable, do not have to be presented to obtain delivery of the goods at their destination. They can perhaps be described as 'a document of optional simplicity', as they are issued instead of a bill of lading, and they serve the purpose, subject to the credit conditions, of avoiding delay should the cargo arrive before the relevant documentation. When goods move by sea within the EEC countries, various other documents may be used such as Certificates of Shipment and Short Sea (or rail) Consignment Notes. The longer crossings, however, usually require the traditional bills of lading.

With the adoption of new electronic routines, it is possible that bills of lading as we know them today may eventually be replaced by transmitted documents. The problem of dispensing with original signatures would have to be overcome and perhaps changes in the documentary credit procedures will be needed to enable one bank rather than two to complete the transaction. This could be regarded as a futuristic view, but undoubtedly an interesting future lies ahead with the influence of the microchip.

I wish to express my grateful appreciation Ellerman Lines Limited, the Controller of Her Majesty's Stationery Office, the General Council of British Shipping (GCBS), the Simplification of International Trade Procedures Board (SITPRO), the Baltic and International Maritime Conference (BIMCO), the International Federation of Freight Forwarders Associations (FIATA), and ICC Publishing SA for their kind permission to reproduce material from their documents. Also to Sweet & Maxwell Ltd for their permission to reproduce extracts from *Scrutton on Charterparties*, 18th edn. I am also much indebted to Fiona Pellant and David Martin-Clark for their generous help and encouragement during the writing of this book and to Brian Dally and John Griffiths for their valuable comments and advice.

A.M.

1 Evolution of the bill of lading

1.1. Historical

It is not known when bills of lading were first used, although records of cargoes being placed on board ocean-crossing vessels have probably existed for well over a thousand years. Whereas no formal sea code has existed from Greek or Roman times, maritime law grew from the customs and practice of the early seafaring traders. The requirement that every master must take on board a clerk is mentioned in *The Ordonnance Maritime of Trani* (an Italian town) of 1063, and refers to the ship's book or register. This is one of the earliest references to the keeping of records of goods loaded on board ships. The French writer Desjardins in his *Droit Commercial Maritime* says that in a document of 1255, *Le Fuero Real*, it is said that the owners of ships should 'cause to be enrolled in the register all the articles put on board ships, giving their nature and quantity'.

When merchants travelled with their goods, these recorded details formed part of the ship's papers, and the development of a receipt from the master did not come until much later. In Paris a 14th-century manuscript called *Customs of the Sea* has been preserved which is believed to have been drawn up at Barcelona, in which the Register Book which had to be kept by the ship's clerk is mentioned. It further states that the merchants ought to make known to the ship's clerk as soon 'as the ship sets sail' any goods other than those entered in writing, as the owner would not be responsible for damage to goods other than those recorded. This writing, which according to *Customs of the Sea* also included an account of receipts and payments, seems undoubtedly to refer to the rudimentary bill of lading and seems to be in the nature of a document of title as well as the evidence of the merchant's right to the goods entered in his name at the end of the voyage.

These passages show a transitional period in the history of the bill of lading when it seems probable that oral evidence of shipment was replaced by the ship's register which led eventually to the private contract made between the individual merchant and the master. This period also saw a development away from merchants travelling with their goods. They simply dispatched them to a consignee and this necessitated a signed extract from the Register Book as a separate and distinct document of title. It became very difficult to prove title if this single document became lost, as the shippers were in all respects at the mercy of the master who possessed the sole proof of the contract.

In the latter half of the 16th century, the use of the bill of lading was widespread and was defined in *Le Guidon de la Mer* as 'the acknowledgement which the master of the ship makes of the number and quality of the goods on board' and goes on to carefully distinguish it from the Charter Party by saying that 'trois coppies' of it must be drawn up. The words to the effect that 'one of them being accomplished, the others shall be void' also appeared about this time. It is also interesting to note that in the case of *Chapman* v *Peers* (1534), it was expressly stated that it had long been the practice of merchants and the rule of law that no liability attached to the master or owner of the ship for goods not entered in the *Book of Lading*. The need to transfer the title in the goods before they arrived at their destination was brought about by the spread of commerce and the increasing complexity of business, hence the endorsement of the bill of lading to the buyer. The first reported case in which endorsement is actually mentioned in connection with the assignment of a bill of lading is that of *Snee* v *Prescott* (1793), thus the practice was well established by the 18th century and the negotiable bill of lading was in common use.

The earliest bill of lading qualifications used at that time were of a general nature such as 'Act of God', 'dangers of the sea only excepted' or 'inherent vice', but the 18th century judicial decisions caused shipowners to strengthen their bills of lading with provisions known as 'exoneration clauses' or 'negligence clauses'. These not only stipulated the old Common Law exceptions, but also served to protect the shipowners from liability for all perils of the sea and navigation. As this tendency was accentuated throughout the Maritime Nations, shipowners began to exempt themselves from practically every liability, even for their own negligence which led to disputes and complaints from merchants in international trade. As soon as an unfavourable court decision was given, the shipowner's legal advisers were instructed to draft a fresh set of clauses to nullify the result for the future.

The growing dissatisfaction of shippers, bankers and underwriters eventually forced the shipowners to negotiate and improve the situation which in turn led to the adoption, between 1890 and 1901, of model bills of lading mostly in the bulk grain, coal and timber trades. In fact a Conference Form bill of lading was adopted in 1882 at a meeting in Liverpool which was the first to recognize 'due diligence' and to fix a limit of liability of £100 sterling per package. This 'Conference' Form bill formed the basis for the Hamburg Rules adopted at Hamburg in 1885. The text of the 'Hamburg' bill of lading considerably reduced the number of exonerating clauses which had been numerous up to that time although it is understood that Italy was one of the last countries to resist the merchants' pressures for reform.

It was about this time that the problems between shipowning and cargo interests came to a head in the British Dominions and the United States and legislation was demanded to remove the chaotic state of affairs brought about by the shipowners' unlimited freedom of contract. Recommendations followed for the adoption of an international form for all bills of lading in order to highlight and prevent the casual manner in which alterations and additions were introduced without any consideration for the owners of the goods.

Ocean bills of lading were obviously in urgent need of reform because they had by this time acquired qualities other than that of a receipt. Merchants had discovered that by the use of banks and finance houses, it was possible to extend their trade by employing the same capital outlay and spreading the risk of loss by the payment of a simple premium or insurance. Thus in the event of disaster, not uncommon in those days, they were able to remain in business. It became possible for banks to advance cash against the security of bills of lading which in turn made it possible for business to be extended by the purchase and shipment of other consignments. The bank having made the advance was likewise secured as it held the title to documents against payment at the port of discharge.

1.2. The *Bills of Lading Act* 1855

The *Bills of Lading Act* was passed on 14 August 1855 to amend the law relating to bills of lading. Until this time the law was unsatisfactory as contracts were not assignable under Common Law, and when a bill of lading was passed by the shipper to his consignee in order to pass the title in the goods, it did not transfer the rights and liabilities under the contract of affreightment.

Among the principal factors in the introduction of this Act was the decision of the court in the case of *Grant* v *Norway* (1851). This was a case involving the master of a ship who signed a bill of lading acknowledging the shipment of 12 bales of silk, although the goods had never been loaded on board the vessel. The bill had been endorsed over to a third party as security for a debt. When the debt remained unsettled, proceedings were brought against the shipowner as the consignment had never been shipped. The case was dismissed because the court held that the master's action was outside the scope of his authority and therefore did not bind the shipowner. Another difficulty arose from an earlier verdict of a City of London jury in the leading case of *Lickbarrow* v *Mason* (1794) where bills of lading first became 'judicially' recognized as negotiable and transferable documents of title. In this case Lord Loughborough said 'a bill of lading is the written evidence of a contract for the carriage and delivery of goods sent by sea for a certain freight. The contract in legal language is a contract of bailment.' This verdict, however, caused difficulties in cases where goods were lost or damaged at sea, since by the time the goods had arrived, or should have arrived, the buyer would probably have acquired the title to the goods although the contract of carriage had been made with the original shipper.

The introduction of the Act brought about a complete change in the law existing at that time. The Act provides *inter alia* that every consignee named in a bill of lading and every endorsee shall have transferred to him all rights of suit, and that the bill of lading shall be conclusive evidence of shipment. It therefore came to be relied upon for its accuracy and as a truthful representation of the facts.

This Act does not apply unless the endorsement and transfer of the bill of lading has been instrumental in conferring either proprietary or possessory title in the property to the endorsee. For example, the Act does not apply where the property has been passed before the issue of the bill of lading or where the bill of lading ceased to be a document of title before it was transferred to the endorsee. (*Enechem and others* v *Ampelos Shipping* (*The Delfini*) – QBD 24 March 1988 and Court of Appeal 28 July 1989.)

The endorsee of the bill of lading acquires the right to sue for any breach of contract both before and after ownership of the goods was passed to him, a special or 'blank' endorsement being equally acceptable for this purpose. Endorsement to an agent does not relieve the endorser of his liabilities unless the shipowner or ocean carrier specifically agrees to accept the liability of the endorsee in place of the endorser (*Lewis* v *McKee* 1868). It should also be mentioned that the actual sale of the goods does not transfer the liabilities of the bill of lading holder unless the latter document is also transferred, it being held that the consignee named in the bill of lading retained his rights as owner of the goods as against the shipowner until the bill of lading is endorsed to a third party and surrendered (*Fowler* v *Knoop* 1878). The shipper's liability for freight however, is not transferred by endorsement (Section 2 of the Act).

The *Bills of Lading Act* 1855 does not apply to sea waybills.

The *Bills of Lading Act* 1855, which has three Sections only, is reproduced below:

Preamble

Whereas, by the custom of merchants, a bill of lading of goods being transferable by endorsement, the property of the goods may thereby pass to the endorsee, but nevertheless all rights in respect of the contract contained in the bill of lading continue in the original shipper or owner; and it is expedient that such rights should pass with the property: And whereas it frequently happens that the goods in respect of which bills of lading purport to be signed have not been laden on board, and it is proper that such bills of lading in the hands of a bonâ fide holder for value should not be questioned by the master or other person signing the same on the ground of the goods not having been laden as aforesaid:

1. Consignees and endorsees of bills of lading empowered to sue
Every consignee of goods named in a bill of lading and every endorsee of a bill of lading, to whom the property in the goods therein mentioned shall pass upon or by reason of such consignment or endorsement, shall have transferred to and vested in him all rights of suit, and be subject to the same liabilities in respect of such goods as if the contract contained in the bill of lading had been made with himself.

2. Saving as to stoppage *in transitu*, and claims for freight, etc.
Nothing herein contained shall prejudice or affect any right of stoppage *in transitu*, or any right to claim freight against the original shipper or owner, or any liability of the consignee or endorsee by reason or in consequence of his being such consignee or endorsee, or of his receipt of the goods by reason or in consequence of such consignment or endorsement.

3. Bill of lading in hands of consignee, etc., conclusive evidence of shipment as against master, etc.
Every bill of lading in the hands of a consignee or endorsee for valuable consideration, representing goods to have been shipped on board a vessel, shall be conclusive evidence of such shipment as against the master or other person signing the same, notwithstanding that such goods or some part thereof may not have been so shipped, unless such holder of the bill of lading shall have had actual notice at the time of receiving the same that the goods had not been in fact laden on board: Provided, that the master or other person so signing may exonerate himself in respect of such misrepresentation by showing that it was caused without any default on his part, and wholly by the fraud of the shipper, or of the holder, or some person under whom the holder claims.

In the United States of America the Act relating to bills of lading is known as the 'Pomerene' *Bills of Lading Act* 1916. It is much more comprehensive than the British Act and in its 44 sections is in itself a useful guide to bill of lading procedure.

The Pomerene Act relates to interstate and foreign commerce only and applies to bills of lading issued in the United States and provides, *inter alia*, that a Carrier shall be liable to a bill of lading holder for non-delivery or delivery otherwise than in accordance with the description shown on the bill of lading. (Appendix C has the full text.)

1.3. Development

With the development of the bill of lading as a principal commercial document in overseas trade, considerable thought and expertise had to be given to drafting it. Lawyers specializing in maritime affairs, backed by the considerable and hard-headed experience of the shipowners on the variety of risks involved in the operation of a shipping company, were engaged to ensure the protection of their clients' interests. The sea is, however, cruel and so the terms incorporated into the bill of lading became more difficult and harsh for the shipper, almost to the point where the shipowner was 'not responsible for anything apart from the collection of his freight'. Eventually the 'exceptions' led to concern amongst the cargo-owning countries and the first steps taken to control the situation were taken by the United States in the drafting of the *Harter Act* in 1893, which established an important principle by making a distinction between faults in the navigation or management of the vessel and faults in the care and custody of the cargo. It imposed certain regulations on the shipowner and forbade the inclusion of certain types of exception clauses. For instance, the shipowner was unable to contract out of his duty to take every reasonable care in providing a seaworthy ship and in the care of the cargo. This was followed by the *Australian Sea-Carriage of Goods Act* 1904, the *New Zealand and Seamen Act* 1908 and the *Canadian Water Carriage Act* 1910. A start had accordingly been made to put things right, but the field had to be extended. (For most practical purposes the *Harter Act* 1893 was superseded by the United States *Carriage of Goods by Sea Act* 1936 but the *Harter Act* still applies to goods before loading and after discharge, for instance, cargo loaded in USA and delivered at an inland destination in another country.) (See Appendix D.)

The continued dissatisfaction of the cargo-owning countries and the numerous commercial problems caused by the differing terms contained in bills of lading by different ship-owners or even the same owners in a different trade precipitated the British Government's desire to introduce uniform legislation throughout the British Empire. It thus transpired that most of the British Colonies and dependencies enacted measures corresponding to the *Carriage of Goods by Sea Act*, 1924 although some of them took a considerable time to do so. Each country applied the measures only to the carriage of goods by sea from the ports in their own territory and whereas the Australian Act passed in 1924 (the *Sea-Carriage of Goods Act*) is similar to the British Act, it is stipulated in Section 9, that the bill of lading must be subject to the law of the place of shipment. The *Canadian Water Carriage of Goods Act* was passed in 1936 and the *New Zealand Carriage of Goods by Sea Act* 1940, although similar in most respects, does contain a provision making it obligatory for a bill of lading to state that it is subject to the rules.

1.4. Definition

It is interesting to note that neither the *Bills of Lading Act* 1855 nor any other Act of Parliament has defined the meaning of 'Bill of Lading'. However an opportunity should be taken at this juncture to mention that a definition has been given in Article 1 of the new 'Hamburg Rules' adopted at the Diplomatic Conference held at Hamburg in March 1978 as follows:

> 'Bill of Lading' means a document which evidences a contract of carriage by sea and the taking over or loading of the goods by the carrier, and by which the carrier undertakes to deliver the goods against surrender of the document. A provision in the document that the goods are to be delivered to the order of a named person, or to order, or to bearer, constitutes such an undertaking.

Suffice it to say that the Hamburg Rules were a review in 1978 of the Hague Rules by the United Nations Commission on International Trade Law (Uncitral) and may replace all existing legislation on the carriage of goods by sea in future years.

2 Rules governing the bill of lading

2.1. The Hague Rules*

The movement towards the establishment of minimum standards in respect of shipowners' liability came to a head as a result of pressure placed on the British Government by the Dominions which led to discussion amongst the principal shipowners, underwriters and insurance interests, shippers' representatives and leading bankers of the maritime nations. This resulted in a set of rules based on the *American Harter Act* 1893, and known as the Hague Rules, being drafted by the Maritime Law Committee of the International Law Association, and these Rules were recommended for international adoption at the Hague in 1921. After amendment they were eventually presented at the International Diplomatic Conference in Brussels in October 1922 and again in 1923, finally being approved at the International Convention held on 25th August 1924 and recommended for submission to the Governments of the major maritime nations for adoption and enactment into the law of their respective countries. The most important effect of these Rules which, provided a complete code for the carriage of goods by sea, was that the carrier could no longer contract out of certain defined responsibilities. The Rules thus established minimum obligations, maximum immunities and the limit of his liability.

These Rules were applied to most bills of lading issued in the United Kingdom by the *Carriage of Goods by Sea Act* 1924 and they were also adopted or given statutory effect by the then Dominions and Colonies as well as other countries throughout the world.

Whereas the Hague Rules have now been amended by the Brussels Protocol of 1968 and are known as the Hague-Visby Rules, and the *Carriage of Goods by Sea Act* 1924 has been repealed, the Hague-Visby Rules have been ratified by a growing number of States and therefore a working knowledge of the Hague Rules is necessary as they are still applied in many overseas countries. There are nine Articles and these are discussed individually below.

2.1.1. Article I — Definitions

This contains the definitions because it was necessary to define the limits over which the Hague Rules would be effective, as bills of lading vary in character and cover other operations besides carriage by sea. It would have then been an impossible task to draft International Rules dealing with all modes of transport covered by a through bill of lading from an inland place in one country to a town in another part of the world by the use of road, rail, ship and river steamer or barge. The Rules were therefore defined to apply from the time when the goods were received on the ship's tackle to the time when they are unloaded from the ship at port of discharge. The definitions are:

(a) 'Carrier' which includes the owner or the charterer who enters into a Contract of Carriage with a shipper.

*These no longer apply to those countries who are signatories to the 1968 Brussels Protocol.

(b) 'Contract of Carriage' which applies only to contracts of carriage covered by bills of lading or any similar documents of title, in so far as it relates to the carriage of goods by sea, including any similar document issued under, or pursuant to, a charter-party from the moment at which such bill of lading or similar document of title regulates the relations between a carrier and the holder of the same. The contracts mentioned above are those covered by bills of lading. However, a bill of lading may be issued on behalf of a shipowner or on behalf of a charterer but the term 'carrier' has also been used to include either the owner or charterer who contracts with a shipper.

(c) 'Goods' which excludes live animals and cargo stated as being carried on deck and is so carried. The carriage of live animals is always the subject of a special arrangement (for instance they usually need an attendant). When cargo is carried on deck it has to be subject to a special agreement as it is always understood that goods tendered for shipment shall be carried below deck. Where cargo is carried on deck in accordance with the custom of the trade then it is conditional as being at the shipper's risk. However, on those occasions when goods are carried on deck for the carrier's convenience it has to be insured for shipowner's liability because it is technically in breach of contract.

(d) 'Ship' which means any vessel used for the carriage of goods by sea.

(e) 'Carriage of Goods' which covers the period from the time when the goods are loaded on board until the time when they are discharged from the ship. The term 'loaded' is regarded as 'up to the time of loading' or when the goods are under the ship's tackle, and 'discharge' is when the goods are released from the tackle on the quay. In the liner trades the cost of loading and discharge is included in the freight so the real test is the point at which the carrier pays for the loading and discharge operation. This guide may also apply when cargo is handled by chute or pipe.

2.1.2. Article II — Risks

This makes the Rules universally applicable and reads 'subject to the provisions of Article VI (which do not apply to ordinary commercial shipments but which justify a special agreement), under every Contract of Carriage of Goods by Sea, the Carrier, in relation to the loading, handling, storage, carriage, custody, care and discharge of such goods, shall be subject to the responsibilities and liabilities, and entitled to the rights and immunities, hereinafter set forth.'

The Rules being a complete code, neither assuming nor depending on the law of any particular country, define the responsibilities and liabilities to which the ocean carrier shall be subject and the rights and immunities to which the carrier shall be entitled. Thus the Rules when incorporated in a bill of lading constitute the complete basis on which the parties (i.e., the shipper and the carrier) contract with each other. Under English law, any contract for the carriage of goods by sea contains certain undertakings on the part of the carrier, namely, (a) that the ship is seaworthy, (b) that the voyage shall commence and be carried out with reasonable dispatch and (c) that there shall not be any unnecessary deviation from the advertised route except for the saving or attempting to save life or property at sea, Article IV (1). Any failure to carry out any of these undertakings may prevent the carrier from relying on the exceptions from liability under the law.

2.1.3. Article III — Responsibilities and liabilities

In other words the duties of the carrier cover the following:

> Paragraph 1. The carrier shall be bound, before and at the beginning of the voyage, to exercise due diligence to (a) make the ship seaworthy; (b) properly man, equip and supply the ship; (c) make the holds, refrigerating and cool chambers and all other parts of the ship in which the goods are carried, fit and safe for their reception, carriage and preservation.

Let us examine this matter of seaworthiness. If a ship sails in an unseaworthy condition, and this also means uncargoworthy, thus causing loss or damage to goods, the carrier can avoid liability under these Rules by proving that he exercised due diligence at the beginning of the voyage to make the ship seaworthy. However, if the ship is found to be unseaworthy due to a latent defect not discoverable by due diligence, then a cargo-owner would fail in any claim against the carrier. For example, a crack due to metal fatigue not detectable by visual inspection carried out by a competent surveyor.

Subparagraph (c) means that the holds must be in good condition for the reception of cargo, e.g. compartments which had previously carried goods giving off an odour would be unsuitable for the storage of foodstuffs liable to taint.

Paragraph 2 deals with the care of cargo and states 'subject to the provisions of Article IV the carrier shall properly and carefully load, handle, stow, carry, keep, care for and discharge the goods carried'. Whereas the question of discharge has been referred to earlier it may be interesting to note that the operation of delivery to the consignee was analysed in the case of *Petersen* v *Freebody* (1895) when Lord Ester stated that the shipowner acts from the deck or some part of his own ship, but always on board his ship, whereas the consignee's place is alongside the ship where the 'thing' is to be delivered to him. Therefore, if delivery is to be on another ship, he must be on that ship, or if into a barge or lighter, then on that lighter, and if on to the quay, then he must be on the quay. If the shipowner merely puts the goods on the ship's rail, he does not give delivery. He must also put the goods in such a position that the consignee can take delivery of them.

Paragraph 3 states that the carrier after he has received the goods into his charge shall, on demand of the shipper, issue a bill of lading incontestable as to accuracy, stating the leading marks which must remain legible until the end of the voyage, and either the number of packages or pieces or the quantity and the apparent order and condition of the goods. This clause also provides that no carrier shall be bound to state any of the above particulars if he suspects that they do not accurately represent the goods received or which he has no reasonable means of checking. It is for this reason that a qualifying clause 'Quality and contents unknown', 'Said to contain' or 'Quantity said to be' sometimes appears in the body of the bill.

Paragraph 4 is an accessory to the requirements of Clause 3. This is because the shipowner is unable to check the particulars of commodities such as bulk cargo loaded under conditions which leave him in the hands of the shipper, especially in respect of the particulars that are to be stated on the bill of lading. This clause stipulates that a bill of lading shall be *prima facie* evidence of the receipt of the goods described. This means that the carrier is bound to deliver the full amount of goods signed for. The description which the shipper is required to furnish is limited to marks, number, quantity or weight and does not necessarily include the nature and value of the goods. This has been amended in the Hague-Visby Rules.

Paragraph 5, which is also an accessory to Clause 3, states that the *shipper* shall be deemed to have guaranteed these particulars and shall indemnify the carrier against any inaccuracies. This provision does not limit the *carrier's* responsibilities and liabilities to the shipper alone.

Paragraph 6 contains the advantages and disadvantages of a compromise. It is concerned with *prima facie* evidence and not with the ultimate proof of a just claim. The clause provides that the apparent order and condition of the goods should be stated in the act of delivery to the consignee, and if the consignee does not on his receipt of the goods state the apparent order and condition as other than satisfactory, it makes his position more difficult if he endeavours to claim at a later date. The clause deals with the time limit and states that unless notice of loss or damage and the general nature of such loss or damage be given in writing to the carrier or his agent at the port of discharge, before or at the time of the removal of the goods or within three days if the loss or damage is not apparent, such removal shall be deemed *prima facie* evidence of the delivery as described in the bill of lading. If the goods were the subject of a joint survey or inspection, notice in writing need not be given. However, this paragraph also states that 'in any event' the carrier and the ship shall be discharged from all liability unless suit is brought 'within one year after delivery of the goods or the date when the goods should have been delivered'. It is common practice for parties to extend the time limit. When there is a known loss, both the carrier and the receiver must give each other full facilities for inspection and tallying of the goods. Amendments to this are made in the Hague-Visby Rules.

Paragraph 7 was included when the Rules were being drafted because the bankers at the Hague were opposed to 'Received for Shipment' bills of lading. Whereas most of the shipowners disliked them as well, they were aware of instances where shippers demanded the facility and should therefore not be prejudiced by anything done at the Hague. Accordingly, their existence was recognized and this clause therefore provides that after the goods are loaded, the bill of lading, if the shipper demands, shall be a 'shipped' bill of lading provided that any document of title previously issued is surrendered. These days when 'Received for Shipment' bills are in common use with the advent of containerization and the use of depots, it is usual for any such document to be claused 'Shipped on Board' with the date. This rule is also amended by the Hague-Visby Rules.

Paragraph 8 stipulates that any clause relieving the carrier or the ship from liability for loss or damage due to negligence, fault or failure in the duties and obligations provided in this Article, shall be null and void and of no effect. A benefit of insurance is deemed to be a clause relieving the carrier from liability.

2.1.4. Article IV — Rights and immunities

Bearing in mind that the Rules originated as a result of the discontent of merchants with their bill of lading terms, it will be seen that the responsibilities of the shipowner have been clearly defined. However, the owner is clearly entitled to rights and immunities as shown by the *American Harter Act* 1893 previously mentioned, and this article contains a 'catalogue' of those rights and immunities and is therefore extremely important. It commences by stating that 'neither the carrier nor the ship shall be responsible for the loss or damage arising or resulting from' and continues to enumerate in subparagraphs (a) to (q) the specific exceptions. Several of these are now considered to be pointless because they are included in the broader exception of 'perils of the sea' in subparagraph (c) and under the general exceptions included in subparagraph (q). It is unlikely that any of the undermentioned exceptions will now be considered individually: Act of God (d), act of war (e), act of public enemies (f), arrest or restraint of princes, rulers or . . . seizure of people under legal process (g), quarantine restrictions (h), riots and civil commotions (k), or saving or attempting to save life or property at sea (l).

Paragraph 2(a) 'Negligence in Management of the Ship' is probably the most important of all the exceptions because it exempts the carrier for loss or damage arising or resulting from matters outside the control of the shipowner, such as 'Act, neglect or default of the Master, Mariner, Pilot or the servants of the Carrier in the Navigation or in the Management of the ship'. This, therefore, includes personnel both ashore and afloat and has been the subject of much criticism by cargo interests because of its broad interpretation and uncertainty when read in conjunction with Article III (2), between 'Care of the Cargo' and 'Management of the Ship'.

Paragraph 2(b) concerns fire, unless caused by the actual fault or privity of the carrier. In some countries this is interpreted to mean the actual carrier and not one of his servants or agents. The *Merchant Shipping Act* 1894, Section 502(1), also exempts the shipowner from liability for loss of, or damage to, goods by fire on board if such loss is caused without his actual fault or privity. It does not, however, operate under these Rules if the fire was caused by the failure on the part of the owner or master to exercise due diligence to make the ship seaworthy.

Paragraph 2(c) deals with perils of the sea or other navigable waters and is probably the most frequent defence used by carriers as it includes damage to goods caused by sea water which could not be guarded against (i.e., not caused by the want of due diligence). It also covers accidents resulting from the impact of waves or other dangers inherent in the navigation of the vessel such as violent storms and fog. However, the ship must be sufficiently strong to withstand such dangers and the carrier, in order to obtain protection, must prove that loss or damage suffered by the ship or cargo was caused by a marine hazard beyond his control. Cargo underwriters these days have to be satisfied that adverse weather conditions, for instance, were exceptional in their nature and that the loss could not have occurred in ordinary rough seas.

Paragraph 2(j) deals with strikes or restraint of labour. With the high cost of ship operation these days, this is an important defence but must stand the test of reasonableness. For instance the diversion of a ship to another port when the stoppage is only a day or so old, would be considered as inadmissible as more time has to elapse for possible settlement to be reached. There could be an exception if the cargo was perishable and unlikely to withstand delay. Furthermore, it is necessary for the carrier to proceed to the nearest safe and convenient strike-free port in the area that is stipulated in the bill of lading.

Paragraph 2(m) deals with inherent vice and states that the carrier shall not be responsible for 'wastage in bulk or weight or any other loss or damage arising from inherent defect, quality or vice of the goods'. Perishable goods come into this category of 'inherent vice', also bulk commodities which lose weight during the voyage due to evaporation of moisture.

Paragraph 2(n) is another very important exonerating exception. If goods are seen to be packed in such a manner as unlikely to survive the voyage, given normal careful handling, then the bill of lading should be claused 'insufficiently packed – broken bands' or whatever the reason, but it is good practice to give the shipper an opportunity to put the matter right if time permits. It would certainly help in the defence of claims. If goods are packed normally and conform to the custom of the trade, that would be considered sufficient within the meaning of this Article. See Chapter 8 on *Letters of Indemnity* which must not be accepted in exchange for a 'clean bill' if the document should rightly be claused.

Paragraph (q) deals with any other cause arising through no fault of the carrier or his servants. This clause states that 'the burden of proof shall be on the person claiming the benefit of this exception.' The exceptions in paragraphs (a) to (p) were commonly exempted from the previous legislation and are probably more frequently used by carriers because the owner of the goods has to prove negligence on the part of the carrier.

Paragraph 3 stipulates that the shipper shall not be responsible for loss or damage sustained by the carrier arising from a cause which is not his fault.

Paragraph 4 deals with deviation and exempts the carrier from liability for loss or damage resulting from deviation (a) to save life, (b) to save property or (c) if the deviation is 'reasonable'. It is permissible to deviate for the purpose of avoiding danger to the ship and property, also to save life but not for any other purpose. If deviation occurs without reasonable excuse and loss and/or damage occurs, there is no protection from any of the exceptions. It was held in *Scaramanga v Stamp* (1880) that whereas a deviation to save life was justifiable, deviation to save the property of others, was not. Further, if the deviation is not 'reasonable', the immunity of the carrier under Article IV Rule 2(c) from responsibility for loss or damage due to perils of the sea would not apply. In the case of *Stag Line v Foscolo, Mango & Co.* (1932), Lord Buckmaster in the House of Lords said that 'reasonable' meant reasonable in relation to both parties to the contract. The route is the customary or advertised itinerary of the vessel.

Paragraph 5 limits the liability of the carrier to £100 per package or unit of the goods irrespective of the amount of damage sustained by the cargo-owner. However, if the nature and value has been declared by the shipper before shipment and inserted in the bill of lading then liability would be accepted for the stated amount and freight charged accordingly. The reason for limiting the sum to this amount was because the shipowners represented at the Hague Conference held in 1921 required protection against excessive cargo claims. This amount of £100 was raised to £200 for those parties who were signatories to the Gold Clause Agreement, dated 1st August 1950, which was drafted because of the depreciation of world currencies in relation to gold (see Article IX). The 1950 Agreement has subsequently been amended to bring it into line with the provisions of the Hague-Visby Rules. The amended agreement applies to contracts of carriage which are subject to the said Hague or Hague-Visby Rules and are dated on or after 1st July 1977. The package limitation has accordingly been increased from £200 to £400 per package or unit.

Any declaration of value on a bill of lading shall be *prima facie* evidence but not binding or conclusive on the carrier. Neither shall the carrier be responsible for any loss or damage to goods if the nature or value has been knowingly mis-stated by the shipper in the bill of lading. This rule has been amended in the Hague-Visby Rules.

Paragraph 6 refers to goods of an inflammable, explosive or dangerous nature and states that if shipped without the knowledge of the carrier or master of the vessel, they may at any time be discharged or destroyed or rendered innocuous without compensation. If the goods have been shipped with knowledge and consent, but become a danger to the ship or cargo, they may likewise be landed at any place or destroyed or rendered innocuous without liability on the part of the carrier, except to General Average contribution, if any.

2.1.5. Article V — Surrender of rights and immunities and increase of responsibilities and liabilities

This stipulates that a carrier may *surrender* the whole or part of his rights and immunities or *increase* his liabilities under the Rules provided that such surrender or increase is incorporated in the bill of lading. However, he may *not increase* his rights or immunities or *surrender* his liabilities. Such clauses are prohibited under Article III(8). This Article also states that nothing in these Rules shall be held to prevent the insertion in a bill of lading of any lawful provision regarding General Average.

The provisions of these Rules do not apply to charter-parties, and if a bill of lading is issued in the case of a ship under a charter-party it must comply with the terms of these Rules. This is to cover instances where a ship is chartered by a Liner Company to supplement tonnage and then operated on a regular berth under the carrier's regular bill of lading. The Charter-Party Conditions apply to the owner and the charterer only, and the bill of lading conditions apply between the charterer and shipper.

2.1.6. Article VI — Special conditions

This deals with special conditions and states that notwithstanding the previous articles, the carrier, master and his agent, and the shipper, may in regard to particular goods, be at liberty to enter into any agreement in any terms as to responsibilities and liabilities, and as to the rights and immunities or obligations as to seaworthiness, provided that this stipulation is not contrary to public policy and provided that no bill of lading is issued and that the terms agreed are embodied in a non-negotiable receipt and marked as such. This article shall not apply to commercial shipments made in the ordinary course of trade but only to other shipments when the character or condition of the property is such as to reasonably justify a special agreement. The Article also ensures that the shipping documents, if they contain special conditions lessening the carrier's liability, are not in the form of bills of lading in any respect. An example of this is a Parcel Receipt which may limit the carrier's liability to compensation to a small sum for which only a few pounds may be charged as freight.

2.1.7. Article VII — Limitations on the application of the rules

The provisions contained in these rules shall not prevent a carrier or a shipper from entering into any agreement, stipulation, condition or exemption as to the liability of the carrier for the loss or damage in connection with the custody and care of goods prior to loading and subsequent to discharge from the ship on which the goods are carried by sea. It will be observed that when a 'through' bill of lading is issued, the rules apply only to the sea portion of the voyage unless the carrier extends his liability such as when a Combined Transport document is issued (see Chapter VI).

2.1.8. Article IX — Monetary units

Article IX of the 1924 Act provides that the monetary units, namely the shipowner's maximum liability of £100 per package or unit, 'is to be taken to be gold value'. (The present day value of the £100 package limitation was tested in the 'Rosa S' case – QBD (Admiralty Court) 21 July 1988. It concerned a claim in Kenya pounds for £6491 whereby the cargo owners submitted that Article 4 Rule 5 had to be read with the first sentence of Article 9 so that £100 sterling should read £100 sterling Gold Value. Judgment was given in favour of the cargo owners.) Other countries expressed the maximum liability in terms of their currency and not in relation to gold. This lack of uniformity, together with the depreciation of the value of currency in many countries, caused the British Maritime Law Association to draw up an Agreement in 1950 between shipowners' associations, P & I clubs, British Underwriters' Associations and others whereby the shipowner's liability is increased to £200 UK sterling per package or unit. This Agreement is known as the *Gold Clause Agreement*. The Gold Clause Agreement is, generally speaking, now considered redundant. There is a further provision that shipowners will, on request of the cargo interests, extend the twelve months time limit in the Hague Rules by a further twelve months unless Notice of Claim with full particulars available was not given within the twelve month period or there was an undue delay by consignees or underwriters in providing or obtaining the relevant information and formulating the claim.

2.2. Hague-Visby Rules

The Hague Rules were amended by the Brussels Protocol signed on 23 February 1968 and became known as the Hague-Visby Rules. These were brought into effect in the UK on 23 June 1977 by the *Carriage of Goods by Sea Act* 1971 which repealed the Act of 1924. One of the reasons for this amendment was that the existing rules, under modern trading conditions, were considered to be too favourable to the carrier, a view taken particularly by the developing countries.

Visby is an ancient port and the capital of Gotland Island in the Baltic Sea off the Coast of Sweden where the recommendations were signed in 1963. The reason for choosing this place was because in the 13th century it was the centre of a Maritime Association which monopolised the Baltic trade and gave its name to the *Laws of Visby*, a Maritime Legal Code generally known as the *Sea Laws*. It was thus an appropriate place to select for this occasion.

The Rules became operative after being ratified by ten states, namely Denmark (but not the Faroes), Ecuador, France, Lebanon, Norway, Singapore, Sweden, Switzerland, Syria and the UK. Some contracting states apply these rules to both inward and outward voyages but the UK has not done this. What the UK has done is to apply the rules to two other classes of voyage not covered by the compulsory provisions of the Protocol, namely, (a) all coastal voyages within the UK, and (b) all voyages, whether international or domestic where the contract evidenced by the bill of lading expressly provides that the Hague-Visby Rules shall govern the Contract of Carriage.

Section 1(vii) of the Act provides that the Rules shall apply to 'deck cargo' or live animals where the bill of lading or non-negotiable receipt covering such carriage is expressly made subject to the Rules, whereas the Protocol does not alter the position with regard to deck cargo and live animals; i.e., deck cargo and live animals are excluded from the definition of goods. Thus, in order to avoid potential liability for these types of cargo under English law, it would appear necessary to make specific reference to deck cargo or live animals in the clause paramount or to draft the clause in some other qualified or restricted manner.

It is proposed that these Rules be dealt with as enacted by the *Carriage of Goods by Sea Act* 1971 because the provisions 'as set out in the Schedule to this Act, shall have the force of law' where the port of shipment is a port in the UK. The liability for loss or damage to the goods in Article IV(a) was amended by the *Merchant Shipping Act* 1981 to replace Gold francs by amounts equivalent to Special drawing rights (SDRs) of the International Monetary Fund. This amendment came into force on 4th February 1984 when 10 000 gold francs per package or unit was changed to 666.67 units of account and 30 gold francs per kilogramme of gross weight was changed to 2 units of account per kilogramme. These amounts are converted into national currency published daily. The equivalent amount is approximately £500 and £1.50 respectively.

The principle differences between the 1924 and the 1971 Acts are as follows:

2.2.1. Article III

Whereas the bill of lading is still *prima facie* evidence of the receipt by the carrier of the goods, there has been added, in Paragraph 4, 'However, proof to the contrary shall not be admissible when the bill of lading has been transferred to a third party acting in good faith'. The effect of this provision in the bill of lading as to leading marks, numbers of packages or quantity or weight, also the apparent order and condition of the goods is equally operative when the bill of lading has been transferred to a third party, provided that the third party has acted in good faith. The importance of this amendment is that if a claim is made against a shipowner under a correctly signed bill of lading and transferred to a third party, the owner will be unable to resist a claim for shortage by proving that the number of packages stated was incorrect or had been short shipped.

Paragraph 6, the third paragraph of this section, has been amended to read:

> Subject to Paragraph 6bis* the carrier and the ship shall in any event be discharged from all liability whatsoever in respect of the goods, unless suit is brought within one year of their delivery or of the date when they should have been delivered. This period may, however, be extended if the parties so agree after the cause of action has arisen.

The effect of this is that the one year time limit now applies to all claims 'in respect of the goods' and not just to claims for loss or damage. For instance, claims for misdelivery may be included.

Paragraph 6bis states that

> An action for indemnity against a third person may be brought even after the expiration of the year provided for in the preceding paragraph if brought within the time allowed by the law of the Court seized of the case. However, the time allowed shall be not less than three months, commencing from the day when the person bringing such action for indemnity has settled the claim or has been served with process in the action against himself.

This amendment means that the carrier is not discharged from liability within the one year time limit provided by Article III, Paragraph 6(4) in the case of claims for indemnity by, for instance, another carrier who has paid a claim for loss or damage to goods. The carrier who has paid the claim has at least another three months from the time of settlement to pursue his right of indemnity against the other carrier.

---

*The expression 'bis' means another paragraph below referring to the same subject matter.

2.2.2 Article IV

Paragraph 5 is now in six sections and deals with limitations of liability and introduces a commodity exchange price and what is referred to as 'the normal value' of the goods.

5.(a) Unless the nature and value of such goods have been declared by the shipper before shipment and inserted in the bill of lading, neither the carrier nor the ship shall in any event be or become liable for any loss or damage to or in connection with the goods in an amount exceeding the equivalent of 666.67 units of account per package or unit or 2 units of account per kilo of gross weight of the goods lost or damaged, whichever is the higher.

5.(b) The total amount recoverable shall be calculated by reference to the value of such goods at the place and time at which the goods are discharged from the ship in accordance with the contract or should have been so discharged.

The value of the goods shall be fixed according to the commodity exchange price, or, if there be no such price, according to the current market price, or, if there be no commodity exchange price or current market price, by reference to the normal value of goods of the same kind and quality.

5.(c) Where a container, pallet or similar article of transport is used to consolidate goods, the number of packages or units enumerated in the bill of lading as packed in such article of transport shall be deemed the number of packages or units for the purpose of this paragraph as far as these packages or units are concerned. Except as aforesaid such article of transport shall be considered the package or unit.

The effect of this Provision is that packages or units, shown on a bill of lading as being packed into a container, will then be adopted as the package or unit basis otherwise the container itself will form the basis.

5.(d) Neither the carrier nor the ship shall be entitled to the benefit of the limitation of liability provided for in this paragraph if it is proved that the damage resulted from an act or omission of the carrier done with intent to cause damage, or recklessly and with knowledge that damage would probably result.

The effect of this sub-paragraph is that the carrier and the ship will be deprived of the benefit of limitation where it is proved that damage resulted from an intentional act or omission on his part done with intent to cause damage or recklessly knowing that damage would probably result.

5.(e) The declaration mentioned in sub-paragraph (a) of this paragraph, if embodied in the bill of lading, shall be *prima facie* evidence, but shall not be binding or conclusive on the carrier.

5.(f) By agreement between the carrier, master or agent of the carrier and the shipper other maximum amounts than those mentioned in sub-paragraph (a) of this paragraph may be fixed, provided that no maximum amount so fixed shall be less than the approximate maximum mentioned in that sub-paragraph.

5.(g) Neither the carrier nor the ship shall be responsible in any event for loss or damage to, or in connection with, goods if the nature or value thereof has been knowingly mis-stated by the shipper in the bill of lading.

The above paragraphs are similar to those in Article IV of the Hague Rules.

2.2.3. Article IVbis

There are four additional paragraphs to those already in the Hague Rules, namely,

> 1. The defences and limits of liability provided for in these Rules shall apply in any action against the carrier in respect of loss or damage to goods covered by a contract of carriage whether the action be founded in contract or in tort.

This confirms that the carrier is entitled to rely on all the defences and limits of liability irrespective of whether the action is in contract or in tort.

> 2. If such an action is brought against a servant or agent of the carrier (such servant or agent not being an independent contractor), such servant or agent shall be entitled to avail himself of the defences and limits of liability which the carrier is entitled to invoke under these Rules.

This has the effect of providing the carrier's servants and agents (but not independent contractors) with the same defences and limits of liability as those stated in the bill of lading. Stevedores will not therefore be protected unless they are direct employees (i.e. servants or so closely connected as to be regarded, in law, as servants of the carrier). This new provision will probably only assist where damage is caused by the Master or members of the crew. Therefore the presence of the 'Himalaya' clause in the bill of lading will continue to be necessary in order to protect independent contractors such as stevedores.

> 3. The aggregate of the amounts recoverable from the carrier, and such servants and agents, shall in no case exceed the limit provided for in these Rules.
>
> 4. Nevertheless, a servant or agent of the carrier shall not be entitled to avail himself of the provisions of this Article, if it is proved that the damage resulted from an act or omission of the servant or agent done with the intent to cause damage or recklessly and with knowledge that damage would probably result.

The provisions of Paragraph 4 are similar to Paragraph 5(e) above except that it refers to servants or agents of the carrier.

2.2.4. Article IX

This states that 'These Rules shall not affect the provisions of any international Convention or national law governing liability for nuclear damage.' This replaces Article IX in the Hague Rules which deals with monetary units as gold value.

2.2.5. Article X

This states that:

> The provisions of these Rules shall apply to every bill of lading relating to the carriage of goods between ports in two different States if:
> (a) the bill of lading is issued in a contracting State, or
> (b) the carriage is from a port in a contracting State, or
> (c) the contract contained in or evidenced by the bill of lading provides that these Rules or legislation of any State giving effect to them are to govern the contract, whatever may be the nationality of the ship, the carrier, the shipper, the consignee, or any other interested person.

This new Article also provides that a contracting state shall not be prevented from applying the Rules to bills of lading not included in the preceding paragraph. Therefore any country which is a contracting state can apply the Convention to both inward and outward bills of lading although such provision is not made compulsory. Care must accordingly be exercised if a carrier or agent is asked to issue a bill of lading by means of commercial convenience for cargo loaded in a non-contracting state, because it is the place of issue rather than the port of loading which determines whether the Hague Rules limit of £100 or the Hague-Visby limit of say £500 applies to the contract of carriage.

3 Conventional and through bills of lading

A closer look at this document will show that it has three important elements, namely that it is:

(a) Evidence of the contract of affreightment i.e. it contains all the essential terms;

(b) *prima facie* evidence of the receipt by the carrier that the goods are shipped or received for shipment; and

(c) a 'quasi negotiable' document which by endorsement or by contract in pursuance of which the endorsement is made, passes the title in the goods.

3.1. The contract of affreightment

In the case of ordinary general cargo carried on regular liner terms, the contract of affreightment is usually made when space is booked for the goods which require shipment by a named vessel for a particular destination, i.e., the goods are offered to the carrier and accepted either in writing or by telephone or when receipt at the docks or terminal is acknowledged or when the goods are actually loaded on board the carrying vessel. Generally speaking, space booked over the telephone for conventional or less than container load (LCL) cargo is not confirmed in writing unless especially requested. However, full container loads (FCL) which may require transport facilities are usually confirmed in writing and so also are hazardous cargoes and goods requiring special stowage.

The terms of any contract must be definite but not necessarily set out in detail at the time when the contract is made, and it is also necessary that they are readily accessible if required, for instance, in the event of a dispute at a later date.

Whereas a written contract in the past took precedence over any verbal agreement this is no longer the law. It has been held that a shipper is entitled to rely on a verbal promise given by a ship's agent that the vessel will proceed direct to the named port of discharge and shall not deviate, although the bill of lading which was subsequently issued actually contained a clause giving the ship liberty to do so (*Ardennes* v *Ardennes* 1951). It may be difficult to prove what was actually said in the event of a dispute, and it is accordingly good practice to keep a paper record at the time of the transaction. Article 1(b) of the Hague-Visby Rules states:

'Contracts of carriage' applies only to contracts of carriage covered by a bill of lading or any similar document of title, in so far as such document relates to the carriage of goods by sea, including any bill of lading or any similar document as aforesaid issued under or pursuant to a charter-party from the moment at which such bill of lading or similar document of title regulates the relations between a carrier and a holder of the same.

3.2. Types of document

There are various kinds of bill of lading dependent upon their function:

1. Those issued with printed clauses for conventional or through traffic on liner terms.

2. Those issued for goods accepted under 'Combined Transport' conditions.

3. 'Short form' or 'blank back' documents.

4. Bills of lading issued under a charter-party.

5. Bills of lading issued by a freight forwarder.

3.3. Application as a receipt

We know that the prime function of a bill of lading is as a receipt, usually issued by or on behalf of the Master or contracting carrier for goods either loaded on board or received for shipment by a vessel for carriage by sea and for delivery at the place of destination nominated by the shipper against the surrender of one 'original' endorsed bill by the consignee or his agents. It is usual commercial practice for bills of lading to be made out in sets of two or three originals, all of equal validity, any one of which being accomplished, i.e., surrendered in exchange for the goods, the others stand null and void. As all the 'originals' forming the set have equal value it follows that they must not be marked 'original', 'duplicate', etc., as this will automatically destroy the validity of all but the original one.

It also acknowledges that the goods were received in apparent good order and condition, which has the effect of preventing the carrier from alleging (if the goods out-turned damaged) that they were damaged prior to shipment. Any damage sustained before acceptance by the carrier must be noted on the face of the bill of lading; this is known as issuing a 'claused' document.

The position is different in the case of a vessel chartered by a merchant when the terms of the contract are contained in the charter-party. Such a document is a receipt only and not negotiable in the usual sense, nor is it subject to the Hague or Hague-Visby Rules.

3.4. Application as evidence of contract of carriage

The conditions on which goods are accepted by the carrier for shipment constitute the terms of the contract of carriage between the shipper and the carrier except when, as mentioned above, the shipper has entered into a charter-party.

The bill of lading is, technically speaking, only evidence of a contract which has already been made. It is however permissible in law to submit evidence to prove that the terms agreed were different from those contained in the bill of lading if such is the case. Such a situation is unusual because any major changes would make the transaction in practice subject to the overriding conditions of a Booking Note, in other words a special agreement.

3.5. Application as a document of title

The special verdict in the case of *Lickbarrow* v *Mason* (1794) recognized the custom and practice of merchants that a bill of lading, which makes goods deliverable to the order of the shipper named thereon, is a document of title, and that the shipper can pass the title which he possesses to someone else by endorsing and handing over the bill of lading to that other person. This endorsement may be made in the following manner, namely,

(i) by a special endorsement to a named person such as 'Deliver to the order of John Smith' and then signed. The property can then pass to that person; or

(ii) by means of a general endorsement whereby the shipper signs only his name on the back of the bill of lading, this being the usual method with an 'order' bill, which automatically passes the property with the delivery of the document.

(iii) There are however instances in everyday business when 'order' bills are presented unendorsed at destination and there are two ways of handling this situation to avoid delay and storage charges. Either a letter of indemnity is obtained from the consignee countersigned by a bank whilst the bill is returned to the shipper for signature or the shipper can authorize a third party to endorse on his behalf. It is unwise to accept on trust that a particular office has authority to sign and written confirmation is necessary on each and every occasion.

When a bill of lading has been made out to 'order' it is known as 'negotiable' and the shipper passes the document only upon payment by the buyer or consignee. Care must be exercised to avoid words such as 'without recourse' appearing among the endorsements as this may be unacceptable to the carrier and therefore cause delay as the delivery of the cargo can only be performed after a correctly endorsed bill of lading is presented to the carrier.

The delivery of goods without the original bill of lading often as a result of 'commercial pressure' can result in many difficulties, and whereas the availability of cargo before the bill of lading at destination is a frequent and recurring problem, delivery should be given only against the duly endorsed bill or against a legally worded Letter of Indemnity which should contain both the signature of the party requesting delivery of the cargo and the countersignature of a reputable bank (see Chapter 13 and Appendix Q on Letters of Indemnity).

The P and I Associations repeatedly draw attention of their members to this matter and have issued warnings about the acceptance of a special Charter-party clause sometimes demanded to the effect that should the bill of lading not arrive at the discharging port in time then owners agree to release the entire cargo without presentation of the bill.

A clause of this nature purports to transfer consequential liabilities and risks to the shipowner which are in direct conflict with the essential legal basis of all maritime transport. It is however unlikely that the shipowner's P and I cover would be available in the event of a dispute, thus causing the entire risk to be borne by the shipowner or ocean carrier concerned.

Commercial problems are recognized both in the liner and bulk trades, especially where large consignments of bulk oil are concerned and substantial administrative expenses, delays, demurrage charges and possible financial loss may be incurred because of missing or defective documents.

3.6. Format on the front of the bill

The bills themselves are printed usually on the international A4 size paper aligned to the SITPRO Board bill of lading format which conforms to the recommendations of the International Chamber of Shipping, a design which is widely used by shipping lines throughout the world. They are generally available for purchase from stationers specializing in the sale of shipping documents. On the front or face of the bill, the following data have to be completed in the correct position.

A. Name and address of shipper or agent acting on his behalf. If an agent is employed it should be indicated as such to avoid the acceptance of full legal responsibility as a principal.

B. Name and address of consignee or made out to the 'order' of the shipper if so required. An 'order' bill must be endorsed by the shipper before despatch to the consignee. It is also desirable to indicate the telex number of the notify party if possible, to assist notification on arrival at the destination. The requirement to notify is not however obligatory and this is usually emphasized in the clauses of the bill, it being assumed that other advices would be available to the party who is purchasing the goods. But when a bill has been made out to 'order' it is desirable to complete the 'Notify Party' box as this should help in prompt clearance and delivery of the goods.

An 'order' bill is a negotiable document when endorsed.

C. When a 'Through' bill is required either from an inland collection point to port of destination or from the port of loading to an inland destination overseas or right through from and to the inland points, then the 'Pre-Carriage by' box should show the method to be applied.

D. The place of acceptance, the ports of loading and discharge, also if required at an inland destination abroad (assuming that the carrier can offer suitable facilities), the name of the final place of delivery. Sometimes the word 'Intended' appears on 'Received for shipment' bills.

Cargo collected away from the docks or loading terminal may be subject to schedule changes for operational reasons after the bill has been issued. The document may be amended and the word 'Intended' deleted after shipment has taken place but this does not necessarily apply to the port of discharge. It is important that this information is completed and correct as it forms part of the contract of carriage.

E. The name of the carrying vessel must be shown. This is one aspect that may be changed to the name of a substituted ship should operational difficulties arise, and the carrier has the liberty to do this. On some 'Received for Shipment' through bills or Combined Transport documents the words 'Intended Vessel' may be shown. This is because cargo may be received either on a 'House' basis or consolidated at an inland depot where the bill is issued. By the time that the goods arrive at the loading terminal it is possible that the sailing schedule may have changed although the intention to ship on the named vessel remains. Such wording on this type of document is recommended by the principal P and I Associations. The word 'Intended' can be deleted when loading has taken place; this to conform to Letter of Credit requirements.

F. The details that follow such as Marks and Numbers of the goods to be carried are a statutory requirement under Article iii(3) of the *Carriage of Goods by Sea Act* 1971 (Hague-Visby Rules) which states:

3. After receiving the goods into his charge the carrier or the master or agent of the carrier shall, on demand of the shipper, issue to the shipper a bill of lading showing among other things:
(a) The leading marks necessary for identification of the goods as the same are furnished in writing by the shipper before the loading of such goods starts, provided such marks are stamped or otherwise shown

clearly upon the goods if uncovered, or on the cases or coverings in which such goods are contained, in such a manner as should ordinarily remain legible until the end of the voyage.

(b) Either the number of packages or pieces, or the quantity, or weight, as the case may be, as furnished in writing by the shipper.

(c) The apparent order and condition of the goods.

Provided that no carrier, master or agent of the carrier shall be bound to state or show in the bill of lading any marks, number, quantity or weight which he has reasonable ground for suspecting not accurately to represent the goods actually received, or which he has no reasonable means of checking.

and

5. The shipper shall be deemed to have guaranteed to the carrier the accuracy at the time of shipment of the marks, number, quantity and weight as furnished by him, and the shipper shall indemnify the carrier against all loss, damages and expenses arising or resulting from inaccuracies in such particulars. The right of the carrier to such indemnity shall in no way limit his responsibility and liability under the contract of carriage to any person other than the shipper.

G. If the goods are presented as a full container load (FCL) then the Container Number must be shown but the inclusion of Seal Numbers may cause problems because the carrier and the Customs have the right to open and inspect contents. It is stated in Article IV(c) of the *Carriage of Goods by Sea Act* 1971:

(c) Where a container, pallet or similar article of transport is used to consolidate goods, the number of packages or units enumerated in the bill of lading as packed in such article of transport shall be deemed the number of packages or units for the purpose of this paragraph as far as these packages or units are concerned. Except as aforesaid such article of transport shall be considered the package or unit.

The effect of the provision is that if packages or units are enumerated in the bill of lading as being packed in the container, then the package or unit basis will be adopted; otherwise the container itself will be the basis.

H. The weight or measurement of cargo in bulk or for individual packages (although not a legal requirement) is necessary for freighting, operating liability and statistical purposes. It will be asked for if not provided.

3.7. Requirement for 'Received' or 'Shipped' bill

I. Then follows usually at the bottom, a clause which stipulates the actual type of document issued (i.e., 'Received for shipment' or 'Shipped on board'). This clause which forms an essential link with the printed clauses on the reverse side, usually takes the following form, although there may be variations according to individual company requirements.

(a) Received the goods in apparent good order and condition and, as far as ascertained by reasonable means of checking, as specified above unless otherwise stated. The carrier, in accordance with the provisions contained in this document, and with those of the applicable tariff conditions (copies of which are available on request)

(i) undertakes to perform or to procure the performance of the entire transport from the place of acceptance to the place of delivery.

(ii) assumes liability as prescribed in this document for such transport. In accepting this bill of lading the shipper, consignee and owners of the goods, and the holder of this bill of lading, agree to be bound by all of its conditions, exceptions and provisions whether written, printed or stamped on the front or back hereof.

or in the case of a 'Shipped' bill

(b) Shipped either on board the above local vessel in or off the local port named above or (if no local vessel is named above) on board the above ocean vessel in apparent good order and condition (unless otherwise stated herein) and to be carried direct or by transhipment and subject to the exceptions, terms and conditions of this bill of lading and to those of the applicable tariff conditions (copies of which are available on request) to the extent that the latter do not conflict with the exceptions, terms and conditions of this bill of lading, to the above-named port of discharge or such other alternative port or place as is provided hereunder (or as near thereto as she may safely get, lie and discharge) and there to be delivered subject as aforesaid in the like good order and condition. Delivery to be made to the consignee named above or to his or their assigns.

Weights as shown in this bill of lading as declared by shippers, and the Master is unable to check same. In accepting this bill of lading the shipper, consignee and owners of the goods and the holder of this bill of lading, agree to be bound by all of its conditions, exceptions and provisions whether written, printed or stamped on the front or back hereof.

A 'Received for Shipment' bill can be made into a 'Shipped' document after loading on board, by a rubber stamp endorsement reading 'Shipped on board' showing the date and then signed over the Company stamp.

The relevant Article III(7) of the 1971 Act states that:

7. After the goods are loaded the bill of lading to be issued by the carrier, master, or agent of the carrier, to the shipper shall, if the shipper so demands, be a 'shipped' bill of lading, provided that if the shipper shall have previously taken up any document of title to such goods, he shall surrender the same as against the issue of the 'shipped' bill of lading, but at the option of the carrier such document of title may be noted at the port of shipment by the carrier, master or agent with the name or names of the ship or ships upon which the goods have been shipped and the date or dates of shipment, and when so noted, if it shows the particulars mentioned in paragraph 3 of Article III, shall for the purpose of the article be deemed to constitute a 'shipped' bill of lading.

It should be stressed that bills of lading must not be issued before cargo is in the possession of the carrier. It cannot be assumed that the quantity stated by the shipper is correct unless the cargo is properly tallied and the bill of lading claused for any damage or discrepancy (*Van Ekris* v *'Rio Paraguay'* – 573 F. Supp. 1475–1983, United States).

J. It is necessary to show the place where the ocean freight is payable, i.e., loading port, destination or where required by special arrangement.

K. The number of original bills forming the set must always be shown. If the documents are passed through a bank it follows that they require all the 'negotiable' title documents.

L. The date of a bill of lading is a most important element, and shipowners and their agents must exercise every care to show: (a) the date the goods were 'Received for Shipment' (when such a document is issued), (b) the date that the goods were actually loaded on board, (c) the date of sailing, or (d) the date of issue of the bill if provision is made for this.

It is important to remember that what is said must be factual and the truth, and the issuing office must never knowingly make a false statement to perhaps help a shipper through a letter of credit problem. A 'Shipped' bill must not show a date earlier than the day the cargo was placed on board. In some ports it is customary to date all the bills with the last day of loading because an individual hatch tally is not taken, which is an acceptable practice provided that *all* the goods are on board. Should a date be shown knowing that it is incorrect or 'not quite the truth' it is a deliberate act of deception and can make the document invalid in the hands of a bank or other financial institution. It was established in the case of *Stumore* v *Breen* (1886) that a master who signs a bill of lading showing the incorrect date of shipment is personally liable for any damages that may result.

More recently, in the case of the *'Saudi Crown'* – QBD (Admiralty – 1985), the shipowner was held liable as principal for the action of his loading agents who falsely or erroneously dated bills of lading 15 July when loading of the cargo was not completed until 26 July. In this instance an unsuccessful endeavour was made by the defendant to rely on the decision in *Grant* v *Norway* (1851) that a bill of lading signed for goods not on board did not bind the shipowner. The admiralty judge quoted a principle cited in *Lloyds* v *Grace Smith & Co* (1912) that an innocent principal is civilly responsible to the same extent as if it was his own fraud.

The Baltic and International Maritime Conference (BIMCO) warn that 'The Captain who agrees, for whatever reason it may be, to antedate bills of lading commits a very grave fault because of the considerable importance of this document in matters of documentary Credit and because of the necessity to be able to have faith in the document.'

M. The place of issue is shown alongside the date.

N. A full signature is placed on all 'original' bills 'for the Master' or 'for the Carrier' in the following manner.

> In witness whereof the Master, Owner or Agent of the ship has affirmed to the number of Bills of Lading stated above, all of this tenor and date, one of which being accomplished, the others to stand void. This means that if the shipowner acts upon one of them in good faith he will have 'accomplished' his contract and not be liable or answerable to any of the others.

O. The bill must of course be numbered by the carrier. In addition it is now a convenient practice in the UK for the Customs Registered Number (CRN) and the shippers' or Freight Forwarders' reference to be stated.

P. Freight is usually charged according to a tariff drawn up by the Shipping Company or the Conference particular to the trade. It may be calculated as the gross weight (kilogrammes) or gross measurement or volume measured in cubic metres. In the case of high valued goods for which an invoice is usually required, it is calculated on the declared value, known as *ad valorem*. Article IV 5(a) of the Hague-Visby Rules states:

> 5(a) Unless the nature and value of such goods have been declared by the shipper before shipment and inserted in the bill of lading, neither the carrier nor the ship shall in any event be or become liable for any loss or damage to or in connection with the goods in an amount exceeding the equivalent of 666.67 units of account per package or unit or 2 units of account per kilo of gross weight of the goods lost or damaged, whichever is the higher.

The rules governing the payment of freight are complex and which custom and practice over a great many years have determined for the most part. There are various methods which may be used but in most instances freight is deemed earned on shipment, ship and/or cargo lost or not lost. Under charter-party conditions, it is usually payable on discharge of the cargo or concurrent with discharge.

3.8. Freight

3.8.1. Freight payable at destination or 'freight collect'

Whereas it is a *prima facie* rule that freight is payable on delivery of the goods, it is nowadays usually payable in accordance with the appropriate tariff, and the bill of lading generally provides that it has been earned by the carrier on receipt of the goods. Furthermore, responsibility for payment remains that of the shipper (Article 2 *Bills of Lading Act* 1855), any transfer of the document or of the ownership of the goods notwithstanding, until payment in full has been made.

This does not seem to be generally understood, especially when the consignee does not take delivery of the cargo at destination, but the collection of freight and charges is in accordance with the contract of carriage which remains between the shipper and the carrier and has no relation with the sale contract for the goods. Whereas the carrier has a possessory lien on the cargo for any outstanding freight and charges, he is often reluctant to exercise this liberty unless all other efforts have failed; he usually prefers to give extended credit facilities, which by custom and usage are still free of interest. When cargo is sold by the carrier, it has be subject to a national press notice before disposal, and is usually sold because the consignee is not known or has rejected the consignment and/or the shipper abroad is no longer 'available' or in communication.

3.8.2. Lump sum freight

This is a gross amount of freight agreed for the use of the entire ship or a portion thereof and it is not necessary for the full quantity of the cargo to arrive. It is sufficient for only a part of the cargo to be delivered for the full freight to be due. This method is adopted only occasionally under normal 'Liner' terms, more often under charter-party or Booking Note conditions.

3.8.3. Freight paid at port of shipment

This is usually known as prepaid freight and stamped as such on the bill of lading before issue. If the bill is marked 'paid' when this is not the position and the document has passed into the hands of a third party in good faith, the carrier has probably lost his right to recovery. This is not an unknown occurrence. Where actual money has not passed, it is usual practice to accept a Banker's Guarantee agreeing to pay within a given period of time.

3.8.4. Dead freight

The term dead freight is usually used in chartering when a charterer fails to provide the agreed quantity of cargo and under the provisions of the charter-party the owner may have recourse to action against him for freight on that portion of the space not used. If, however, the carrier fills some of the unused space with other cargo, he may only claim damages for the portion remaining vacant. This is rarely resorted to under Liner terms.

3.8.5. Ad valorem freight (according to the value)

This is calculated on the value of the goods rather than on the weight or measurement. In such cases the carrier may ask for evidence such as an invoice, especially if he has reason to query the value of the cargo declared by the shipper.

3.8.6. Back freight or return freight

This is freight charged for the return of cargo which has not been accepted at the port of delivery. There are usually special arrangements made in this respect such as an agreement to collect a lesser sum calculated on the outward amount less a given percentage.

3.8.7. Pro rata freight

A method of remuneration which is rarely used but means that only part of the ocean freight is payable. An example is when only part of the bill of lading quantity is delivered and the amount due is calculated on the balance handed over to the consignee, or if cargo is discharged at an intermediate port for operational or other reasons and the carrier is unable to onforward the goods to their final destination.

4 Conventional bill of lading terms and conditions

The conventional 'long form' bill of lading usually contains about 30 numbered clauses which are fairly standard in their content, but there may be variations depending on the requirements of the carrier and the trade concerned. These clauses evidence the contract of carriage and must be read in conjunction with any conditions which are stamped or printed on the front. Stamped or written clauses also take precedence over those that are printed. As judicial attitudes change quite quickly these days, it is a wise precaution to consult lawyers to ensure as far as possible, that the clauses are legally sound and will hopefully be upheld by the courts in the event of a dispute. Let us therefore examine some of the more important clauses (see Appendix G).

4.1. The Clause Paramount

It is usual for most bills of lading to contain a clause known as the 'Clause Paramount' which specifies the law to be applied to the contract of carriage. Section 3 of the *Carriage of Goods Act* 1924 provides that every 'outward' bill of lading shall contain an express statement that it is to have effect subject to the provisions of the Act. Section 1(6)a of the 1971 *Carriage of Goods by Sea Act* and Article X(c) of the Hague-Visby Rules set out the principle that even a voluntary Clause Paramount will attract the statutory application of the rules. An example of a Clause Paramount incorporating both the Hague Rules and the Hague-Visby Rules is set out below:

'Text of Clause Paramount'
The Force of Law
The 1924 Act provided that the Hague Rules were to 'have effect' in relation to the stipulated carriage. The 1971 Act provides that the amended Rules 'shall have the force of law'. It is submitted that this change in terminology has two results (see *Scrutton on Charterparties*, 18th edition, Sweet and Maxwell, London).

1. It demonstrates that the statutory implied terms take effect, not merely as part of the proper law, where that law is English, but as part of the statute law of England, to which an English court must give effect, irrespective of the proper law.

2. The 1971 Act for the first time gives statutory force to the Rules irrespective of the termini of the voyage, where there is an express incorporation clause. This means that whereas under the previous legislation the incorporation of the Hague Rules in cases falling outside the Act gave them merely contractual effect, so that they had to be construed in conjunction with the other terms in the bill of lading, under the 1971 Act incorporation of the Amended Rules causes them to override any contradictory provisions of the bill.

An example of a Clause Paramount which incorporates both provisions is shown hereunder:

1. CLAUSE PARAMOUNT

IT IS MUTUALLY AGREED that this bill of lading shall have effect subject to the provisions of the International Convention relating to bills of lading dated Brussels 25th August 1924 (hereinafter called the Hague Rules), except where legislation giving effect to the Hague Rules as amended by the Protocol signed in Brussels 23rd February 1968 (hereinafter called the Hague-Visby Rules) is compulsorily applicable, in which case this bill of lading shall have effect subject to the provisions of such legislation. Neither the Hague Rules nor the Hague-Visby Rules shall apply where the goods carried hereunder are live animals or cargo which is stated on the face hereof as being carried on deck and is so carried. Provided that nothing contained in this bill of lading shall deprive the carrier of any limitations of or exemptions from liability conferred on the carrier or the ship by any statute or enactment whatsoever (whether of the United Kingdom or otherwise).

4.2. Conveyance clause

This clause stipulates where the carrier's responsibility shall commence and terminate and points out that loss or damage occurring before or after that time is not admissible. In relation to 'through transport' it also contains a reference to any amount recoverable for damage while the goods are in the hands of an agent or sub-contractor.

4.3. Discharge and delivery

In this clause the carrier expresses his liberties to commence discharge on arrival without notice to the consignee and to continue unloading on the quay or into shed, warehouse, depot, etc. until completion.

It is usually stipulated that the receiver shall receive the goods as fast as the ship can deliver, irrespective of the custom of the port. Discharge overside into consignee's lighters or craft is invariably at the ship's option and subject to prior permission being given. It may not be operationally possible, for instance. It is here too that reference will be made in respect of sorting to marks and to the provisions applicable to the declaration of optional cargo, i.e., for discharge at one of a range of ports in the ship's itinerary. This declaration usually has to be made not later than 48 hours before the vessel's expected time of arrival.

4.4. Acknowledgement of weight, quality, marks etc.

The carrier does not accept any responsibility for information supplied by the shipper as to the quantity, weight or quality of goods nor for the weight of cargo shipped in bulk where it has been ascertained by a third party other than the carrier. He is responsible only for leading marks, provided that they are clearly shown on the packages and of a specified height, usually two inches, and does not acknowledge the contents of packages or other containers. That is why such information is shown as 'Said to Contain'.

4.5. Voyage clause

This is where reference is found whereby the ship may sail without tugs or pilots, adjust compasses, tow or be towed or sail at reduced speed. It will also state that the ship may proceed by any route at the carrier's or Master's discretion and sail before or after the advertised sailing dates. Such liberties shall all be deemed to be part of the contractual voyage.

4.6. Deck cargo

Reference is usually made here to the carriage of live animals and to responsibility not being accepted for cargo which is 'stated to be carried on deck and is so carried'. If goods are stowed on deck and an under-deck bill is given, then the carrier has to accept full liability and insure accordingly. This could also apply to containers loaded on the deck of a conventional ship, i.e., not a container or cellular ship. Cargo so carried shall contribute to General Average.

4.7. Carrier's Liberties in the event of blockade, delay etc.

This is also known as the 'Caspiana' clause and is the clause which gives the shipowner and/or Master certain important liberties as stated below to:
1. proceed to such convenient port as the carrier shall in his absolute discretion select and there discharge the goods;
2. carry the goods back to the country of shipment and discharge them there;
3. retain them on board the ship and return and discharge them at the original port of discharge in the same or substituted ship at the sole risk and expense of the shipper, consignee and/or owner of the goods;
4. abandon the carriage of the goods by land at such convenient place as the carrier may select and there discharge the goods from the container.

When the goods have been abandoned or discharged they shall thereafter be at the sole risk and expense of the consignee and such discharge shall constitute full and final completion of the contract of carriage, the carrier or Master giving notice of such discharge to the consignee of the goods as far as he is known.

Full freight and charges shall be deemed earned together with all extra expense that may have been incurred, for which the carrier retains his lien on the goods.

These liberties are exercised in case of war, hostilities, strikes, port congestion, lock-outs, civil commotions, quarantine, ice, storms or any other cause beyond the carrier's control which may result in damage to or loss of the vessel or give rise to risk of capture, seizure or detention of the vessel or cargo.

With trouble in so many ports and places throughout the world in recent years, this clause is frequently used when ships are diverted from the intended port of unloading, but it should be stressed that such liberties are exercised with extreme caution as there must always be a sound reason in the interests of all concerned.

This clause is known as 'The Caspiana' clause as a result of the case of *Renton* v *Palmyra* (1957) where the vessel *Caspiana*, homeward-bound from Canadian ports to London, was diverted to Hamburg due to strikes preventing her from entering the port and sailing again safely and without delay in accordance with the bill of lading.

The shipowners and/or Master had liberty under the bill in such circumstances to proceed to any safe and convenient port, and the ship proceeded to Hamburg because the strike had already spread to Hull. The action was brought to recover the costs and expenses incurred by the consignees in the return of the cargo to London. It was held that the shipowners were protected by the bill of lading conditions in taking the actions stated.

It is in clauses of this nature that words may appear such as 'strikes, port congestion, lock-outs' *or any other cause beyond the carrier's control,* or similar instances where specific words are followed by the addition of general words. The interpretation that has to be given to this is known as *ejusdem generis* or 'matters of a similar nature'. So the general words 'or any other cause' are confined in the application to things of the same kind such as 'strike, port congestion or lock-outs'. This is a subject which has given rise to several legal cases over the years.

4.8. Carrier's Liberties in the event of war etc.

It is in this clause that the ship has the liberty to comply with the orders, directions or recommendations of the Government of the Nation under whose flag the vessel sails. The compliance with such orders shall not be deemed a deviation and delivery in accordance therewith shall be a fulfilment of the contract voyage.

4.9. Containers

Most modern bills of lading now contain a clause on this subject which incorporates terms and conditions applicable to 'Shipper Packed Containers'. The carrier is also entitled to open and inspect the contents of a shipper packed container and may abandon the transportation if they are considered to be unsafe for any reason. Provision is made for the repositioning of containers, this is to ensure that they are cleaned before return, and for compliance with container equipment interchange conditions. The latter is to ensure that any shipper or consignee in possession of a container shall be responsible for any loss or damage.

4.10. Port, Customs, Consular and other regulations

It is necessary that shippers furnish all particulars necessary to enable the bill of lading to be made out in accordance with the prescriptions and regulations of Port, Customs and Consular Authorities and warrant that the goods are not only lawful merchandise at the port of loading *but remain so throughout the voyage.* This clause also covers the requirement for Consular, Health and other certificates and payment of any penalties if they are required but not provided.

4.11. Transhipment and forwarding

This is one of the important clauses which distinguish a through bill from a Combined Transport document, the main difference being one of liability. Firstly, the carrier has the liberty to discharge the goods either before or after sailing from the port of loading and/or store them either ashore or afloat; secondly the goods may be transhipped and forwarded by another vessel or vessels or by other means such as overland or by air. Occasionally it is necessary to implement this clause for operational reasons but more usually it is the intention to tranship and forward the cargo and is reflected as such on the front of the bill.

In all of the above mentioned circumstances on a conventional through bill of lading one bill only is issued to the shipper, the contracting carrier acting from the point of transhipment from the ocean vessel only as a forwarding agent. The carrier may also make contracts for storage or on-carriage on the terms and subject to the limitations of liability in use by the persons with whom such contracts are made.

From the point that he accepts the goods he also takes responsibility for them in the following manner. Should loss or damage occur before loading on board or after discharge from the ocean vessel the contracting carrier will, on behalf of the shipper, recover the necessary monetary amount from the party held liable within the prescribed limits according to whether the contract is under the RHA, CMR or CIM conditions. However if the loss occurred at sea then the Hague or the Hague-Visby Rules would apply in the normal way. An important point to remember is that a road haulier may not be insured for loss or damage thus making any recovery difficult, and it may not be as much as desired or anticipated. The contracting ocean carrier on a through bill acts as agent only in this matter on behalf of the shipper. However the haulier usually insures against liability for loss or damage to the goods that he carries.

Other circumstances may occur under this clause, such as cargo discharged overside to craft for eventual loading aboard an on-carrying ship at another part of the port but several days' delay occurs as the second ship is not available, resulting in demurrage on the craft. This demurrage may be for account of the owner of the goods. Where the cargo has to be forwarded by two separate ships or conveyances the consignee is required to take delivery as presented.

The on-carrying bill of lading would be made out showing the ocean contracting carrier as shipper and his agent at destination as consignee, claused: 'Delivery to be given to the holder of the original through bill of lading by vessel ——— from ——— dated ———'. This ensures effective control of the contract of carriage under the *Bills of Lading Act* 1855.

4.12. Dangerous, inflammable, radioactive, damaging or contaminating goods

It is both statutory and by the Common Law of England that a shipper shall not tender for shipment any goods in this category without giving written notice of their nature to the carrier, and he is liable for the warranty that is given. This is a very important undertaking because any loss, damage or expenses incurred as a result of a misdeclaration (and these could be considerable) will fall entirely on the shipper or the person making such declaration on his behalf, nor would the shipowner be liable to make any General Average contribution for the goods in question in such circumstances.

If the goods were to become dangerous or unstable, inflammable, radioactive, damaging or contaminating after shipment the owner of the goods may be required to pay for the cost of rendering them harmless by unloading or jettison or destruction. The appropriate section in the *Carriage of Goods by Sea Act* 1971, Article IV Rule 6 reads:

> Goods of an inflammable, explosive or dangerous nature to the shipment whereof the carrier, master or agent of the carrier has not consented with knowledge of their nature and character, may at any time before discharge be landed at any place, or destroyed or rendered innocuous by the carrier without compensation and the shipper of such goods shall be liable for all damages and expenses directly or indirectly arising out of or resulting from such shipment.
>
> If any such goods shipped with such knowledge and consent shall become a danger to the ship or cargo, they may in like manner be landed at any place, or destroyed or rendered innocuous by the carrier without liability on the part of the carrier except to general average, if any.

4.13. Claims

This clause stipulates the limits of liability for loss or damage in accordance with the Hague-Visby Rules as scheduled to the *Carriage of Goods by Sea Act* 1971 and usually states the position when goods are shipped in bulk, or without marks, or goods with the same marks are shipped to more than one consignee. Furthermore it is usually here that the carrier states that he does not undertake to arrive at the place of delivery by a particular time, neither is he liable for any direct, indirect or consequential loss caused by delay.

In respect of claims, Article IV(b) of the 1971 Act states:

> The total amount recoverable shall be calculated by reference to the value of such goods at the place and time at which the goods are discharged from the ship in accordance with the contract or should have been so discharged.
>
> The value of the goods shall be fixed according to the commodity exchange price, or, if there be no such price, according to the current market price, or if there be no commodity exchange price or current market price, by reference to the normal value of goods of the same kind and quality.

This introduces for the first time the notion of a commodity exchange price and what is referred to as 'the normal value' of the goods.

The one year time limit now applies to all claims 'in respect of the goods' and not merely to claims for 'loss or damage'. The intention is to apply the time limit to claims which might not strictly speaking, come within the term 'loss or damage' and thus includes claims for wrong delivery but the extent to which the amendment will be effective in achieving its object is open to argument. This period may, however, be extended if the parties so agree after the cause of action has arisen.

Article III paragraph 6bis of the 1971 Act refers to an action for indemnity against a third person, i.e., another carrier, who has to pay a claim for loss which occurred whilst the goods were in his care.

4.14. Freight

A clause is usually included stipulating that freight shall be deemed earned on shipment, whether the vessel and/or the goods are lost or not lost, and further that it shall be paid in freely transferable currency. Reference is also made to penalty charges in respect of misdeclaration of weights, measurement, value or contents. If it is agreed that freight may be payable elsewhere than at the port of shipment, the shipper will nevertheless remain responsible until it is paid (*Bills of Lading Act* 1855).

4.15. Lien

This clause states that the carrier, his servants or agents shall have a lien on the goods and the right to sell them for freight, demurrage, salvage, general average contributions and other charges or expenses, and also for previously unsatisfied debts.

At Common Law a lien for freight applies to goods consigned to the same consignee on a particular voyage but does not apply to different contracts of carriage on various voyages.

4.16. General Average

There are two clauses that may appear relating to general average or they may all be included under one heading. The two are general average and the New Jason Clause. Whereas the Hague-Visby Rules contain no provisions relating to general average, Article V does include the following paragraph:

> Nothing in these Rules shall be held to prevent the insertion in a bill of lading of any lawful provision regarding general average.

This clause stipulates that general average shall be payable and adjusted according to the York-Antwerp Rules 1974 and may continue by stating that the port or place of the adjustment and the currency thereof shall be selected by the carrier. General Average is explained briefly in Chapter 15.

4.17. Both-to-blame collision clause

The aim of this clause is to divide between the carrier and the owner of the goods damages resulting from loss of cargo in the event of a collision through the common fault of the carrying ship and another vessel. The wording of this clause is standard and reads as follows:

> If the ship comes into collision with another ship as a result of the negligence of the other ship and any act, neglect or default of the Master, Mariners, pilots or the servant of the Carrier in the navigation or in the management of the ship, the Owners of the goods carried hereunder will indemnify the carrier against all loss or liability to the other non-carrying ship or her Owners in so far as such loss or liability represent loss of, or damage to, or any claim whatsoever of the Owners of the said goods, paid or payable by the other or non-carrying ship or her Owners to the Owners of the said goods and set off, recouped or recovered by the other or non-carrying ship or her Owners as part of their claim against the carrying ship or Carrier. The foregoing provisions shall also apply where the Owners, Operators or those in charge of any ship or ships or objects other than or in addition to the colliding ships or objects are at fault in respect to a collision or contact.

The clause forms an essential part of all American bills of lading and most ocean contracts of carriage because of the special principles governing collision at sea under American law. Shipowners throughout the world insert this clause in the bills of lading to modify the rules on the subject of collision which are contained in American legislation, in the event of any litigation being conducted according to American Law. Shipowners' worry in this respect is because the United States has not ratified the 1910 Brussels Collision Convention, which may have the following effect.

Let us suppose that a non-American ship comes into collision with an American vessel resulting in legal action, it would be possible for the American shipowner to arrest a ship belonging to the non-American owners upon her arrival in an American port and this is irrespective of where the collision had taken place.

The effect of this clause is to restore the position as if the law of countries other than the United States had applied, so that, if the ship is held only partly to blame, a proportion of the other vessel's damage would be payable and nothing in respect of her own cargo.

4.18. New Jason clause

This is another clause that is required because Rule D of the York-Antwerp Rules 1974 is not valid in the United States. It is inserted to give the equivalent effect and reads as follows:

> In the event of accident, danger, damage or disaster before or after the commencement of the voyage, resulting from any cause whatsoever, whether due to negligence or not, for which, or for the consequences of which, the Carrier is not responsible, by statute, contract or otherwise, the goods, Shippers, Consignees and/or Owner of the goods shall contribute with the Carrier in General Average to the payment of any sacrifices, losses or expenses of a general average nature that may be made or incurred and shall pay salvage and special charges incurred in respect of the goods.

4.19. Rights and immunities of all servants and agents of the carrier

This is also known as the 'Himalaya' Clause. It is a fundamental principle of English Law that only a person who is party to a contract may sue on it. Similarly, the protection afforded by the terms of a contract can only be relied upon by the parties to that contract. Thus, the benefit of any exception or limitation clauses in a contract of affreightment cannot be relied upon by a person who is not a party to the contract, e.g., a Master, crew member or independent contractor, even though he may have participated in the performance of the contract; see the case of *Midland Silicones* v *Scruttons* (1962).

It is necessary, therefore, for a shipowner who wishes to protect his Master, crew or independent contractors, to insert in a charter-party and more particularly in a bill of lading appropriate express words exempting such persons from liability. The clause which is commonly used in this respect is called a 'Himalaya' clause; named after the case of *Adler* v *Dickson* (1954) involving a personal injury claim on board the SS *Himalaya* and where the clause had been inserted in the passenger ticket.

The wording of the Himalaya clause is as follows:

> No servant or agent of the carrier (including every independent contractor from time to time employed by the carrier) shall in any circumstances

whatsoever be under any liability whatsoever to the shipper, consignee or owner of the goods or to any holder of this bill of lading for any loss, damage, or delay of whatsoever kind arising resulting directly or indirectly from any act neglect or default on his part while acting in the course of or in connection with his employment and, but without prejudice to the generality of the foregoing provisions in this clause, every exemption, limitation, condition and liberty herein contained and every right, exception from liability, defence and immunity of whatsoever nature applicable to the carrier or to which the carrier is entitled hereunder shall also be available and shall extend to protect every such servant or agent of the carrier acting as aforesaid and for the purpose of all the foregoing provisions of this clause the carrier is or shall be deemed to be acting as agent or trustee on behalf of and for the benefit of all persons who are or might be his servants or agents from time to time (including independent contractors as aforesaid) and all such persons shall to this extent be or be deemed to be parties to the contract in or evidenced by this bill of lading.

By virtue of Article IVbis (2) of the Hague-Visby Rules, for the first time in relation to the carriage of goods by sea the benefit of statutory exceptions afforded to the carrier are extended to 'a servant or agent of the carrier (such servant or agent not being an independent contractor)'. Despite the Privy Council decision in the 'Eurymedon' (1974), it remains questionable whether a stevedore, who is an independent contractor, will be able to rely on a Himalaya clause in a bill of lading which is subject to the Hague-Visby Rules.

4.20. Agency clause

Also known as the 'demise' clause, this provides that if the carrying ship is not owned by or chartered by demise, in other words it is 'leased' to the shipping line by whom the bill of lading is issued, then the bill is effective only as a contract with the owner or demise charterer and means that the person issuing the bill acts as an agent only.

It works in this way. If a cargo-owner suffers damage or loss resulting from negligence of the shipowner, he may be asked to refer his claim to the shipowner direct for settlement. However, in practice he is unlikely to be inconvenienced in this way and the contracting carrier (who issued the bill) will deal with the matter in the usual manner rendering his own claim on the owner in due course.

The demise clause was originally designed to protect time charterers from becoming liable as parties to a bill of lading as they were unable to claim protection or limit their liability under Sections 502 and 503 of the *Merchant Shipping Act* 1894. However, the position has been changed by the *Merchant Shipping (Liability of Shipowners and Others) Act* 1958 which seems to have removed the necessity for this clause as far as English Law is concerned, although it still remains in common use.

4.21. Jurisdiction

This clause is the one which stipulates under whose jurisdiction any claims shall be settled. Sometimes it states that they shall be determined according to English Law or maybe the law of the country of the carrier's principal place of business.

5 Combined transport documents

As previously mentioned the difference between a 'through' and a 'combined transport' bill of lading is generally speaking one of responsibility for the land portion of the contract of carriage. On a through bill of lading the ocean carrier accepts responsibility as an agent from the place of acceptance, if expressly stated on the face of the bill of lading to the point of loading and subsequently after discharge from the carrying vessel and the responsibility for the sea voyage is in accordance with the Hague-Visby Rules. However, the position under combined transport documents is different because the carrier accepts 'through liability' as a principal for the contracts that he makes with sub-contractors. Furthermore, the clauses are constructed differently from those on a conventional through bill of lading as some lines express their contracts so as to conform to English Case Law. An ambiguity in the wording of a contract in English Law would be construed against the party tendering the document. For example, on a printed bill of lading an ambiguity would be construed against the carrier who issued the bill. When drafting these documents, every care is taken to avoid the use of words which could have an uncertain construction. The rapid expansion of combined transport, also known as intermodal or multimodal transport, i.e., the through movement of goods from the place of acceptance to the final destination by the successive use of more than one mode of transport, resulted in BIMCO deciding in 1971 to issue the COMBICONBILL, Combined Transport Bill of Lading, as a means of facilitating documentary requirements in international commerce.

The fact that there was not at that time an international convention applicable to combined transport resulted in the development of a multitude of different documents for combined transport, and prompted the ICC to publish in 1973 a set of Uniform Rules for a Combined Transport Document. This led BIMCO, in consultation with INSA, whose headquarters are in Gdynia, to prepare and issue a document known as the COMBIDOC, Combined Transport Document, which could be placed at the disposal of BIMCO members who might be asked by their customers to issue documents subject to the ICC Rules.

Another feature is that if the combined transport includes transport by sea the bill of lading will be accepted by a bank even though it does not contain a 'Shipped on Board' endorsement unless the letter of credit specifically requires one. This is recognized by the provision in Article 27 of the Uniform Customs and Practice referred to earlier.

Many combined transport documents issued by other individual shipowners or container consortia are based on the ICC Rules for Combined Transport Documents (ICC brochure No. 298), and the general provisions indicating their scope are mentioned in Chapter 12.

In examining some of the clauses in a combined transport document it will be noticed that there is no transhipment clause as found in a conventional bill. The inclusion of a 'No Transhipment' clause in a Letter of Credit is designed to prevent transhipment of a merchant's cargo at his risk but without his knowledge, but where a full liability document is issued this problem is to a large extent avoided.

Buyers or others who normally require 'Shipped on Board' bills of lading are recommended to use in their Letter of Credit a qualification such as 'Shipped on Board bill of lading' or 'Combined Transport Document'.

In discussing some of the clauses set out below it should be stated that the best protection for any shipper, exporter or buyer is the reputation of the carrier that he chooses and the attitude or policy of the company in the application of the respective terms and conditions.

An important aspect of a modern bill of lading is that it has to be fair to the merchant in its conditions as well as giving adequate and comprehensive protection to the carrier. The clauses must be drafted in clear and uncomplicated language thus preventing disputes and misunderstandings from arising. Merchants are now taking an increasing interest in the conditions of carriage, whereas this was not always the position in the past. Another development is the inclusion of the United States *Carriage of Goods by Sea Act* 1936 Clause Paramount in British and Continental Consortia bills of lading because of the increasing amount of US multimodal traffic now moving via European ports, which may involve the application of American law.

The format on the front of the document is different from the conventional type. This is because the CTO requires several additional data elements. However, within these contracts there is much conformity in the design of both types of document. In this bill of lading, it will be noticed that 'Merchant' replaces 'Shipper' as the title holder of the goods.

It will also be observed that there is not a Clause Paramount as such, similar to a conventional bill, because the provisions of the Hague-Visby Rules are incorporated elsewhere and the list of clauses usually commences with definitions of certain words used in the document. This is necessary to avoid confusion.

5.1. Warranty

This states that the merchant entering into the contract of carriage has the authority of the person owning the goods. It is necessary to protect the Carrier from any suggestion of complicity if the presenter of the goods has no right to give orders in respect of them. The warranty is also designed to create a contractual link between the shipowner and all parties interested in the goods, through the agency of the shipper.

5.2. Carrier's responsibility: port-to-port shipment

It is stated here that liability of the carrier for loss or damage occurring from and during loading into any sea-going vessel up to and during discharge shall be determined according to the Hague or the Hague-Visby Rules, whichever shall apply.

5.3. Carrier's responsibility: combined transport

This is usually a long clause and covers important items such as: where the state of carriage at which loss or damage occurred *is not* known, the carrier shall be relieved of liability if such loss was due to an act or omission of the merchant or insufficiency of packing or other similar reasons for which the carrier cannot be held liable. There is then provision for where the stage of carriage where any loss or damage occurred *is* known. It covers a variety of eventualities which may be encountered during a combined transport movement and covers air, road, rail, canal or sea carriage and becomes subject to any international convention or national law which would apply in the place where the loss occurred.

5.4. Special provisions for combined transport

This clause covers two or three special provisions such as: *notice of loss or damage*. This inclusion is necessary because whereas the Hague and Hague-Visby Rules stipulate three days, the ICC Rules for Combined Transport (Rule 10) allows seven consecutive days within which time any notice must be given in writing to the carrier stating the general nature of the loss or damage.

5.5. Time-bar

It is usual for the carrier to state that his liability will be considered as discharged unless suit is brought within a period of nine months. This limit would however be overridden by the time limit in any international convention which may be applicable.

5.6. Exclusion of limitation

If it can be proved that loss or damage resulted from any act or omission of the carrier done with intent to cause damage he would not be entitled to rely on any benefit from the limitation of liability clause.

5.7. Amount of compensation: combined transport

It is here stipulated how compensation shall be calculated, such as the value at the time and place of delivery; also that the value shall be determined according to the commodity exchange price or by reference to the normal price for such goods.

It is also stated that the maximum liability shall not exceed a given amount per kilo of gross weight of the goods lost or damaged.

5.8. Sundry liability provisions

These would apply to combined transport and port-to-port shipments and include such items as:

Delay – the carrier does not undertake that the goods shall arrive at a destination by a given time. This is a provision in most bills of lading.

Supply of containers – the terms of the bill of lading govern the responsibility of the carrier in this respect.

Ad valorem – where the value of the goods is stated on the bill of lading, a higher rate of compensation is payable for loss or damage, paid on a *pro rata* basis. This is not peculiar to combined transport bills.

Hague Rules limitation – it is usual to stipulate the amount where these rules are applicable.

Scope of application – unless provided for in the document a carrier does not accept liability for consequential loss except where it is mandatory by an international convention.

5.9. Shipper packed containers

The shipper has considerable responsibility under this clause because the carrier does not accept any liability for the method by which the container is packed, or the unsuitability of the goods for carriage in a container or the unsuitability of the container or its defective condition, unless caused by the want of due diligence by the carrier when supplying the same.

This clause will usually include a reference to indemnity whereby the merchant indemnifies the carrier against loss, damage, liability or expense mentioned in the previous paragraph. This is very important and is sometimes not generally understood, and could involve the merchant in substantial amounts of money for which adequate insurance cover should be provided so as to afford the required protection. For instance, in addition to liability for expenses incurred as a result of bad packing or stowing goods in an unsuitable container there is also the indemnity for merchants or shippers of hazardous cargo and this includes such matters as misdescription, misdeclaration or inadequate packing. This indemnity also embraces loss, damage and personal accident, and extends to damage to the ships, hauliers' vehicles and terminal installations both at home and abroad.

5.10. Inspection of goods

It is necessary in the interests of all concerned that the carrier should have the right to open any container if considered necessary. There may be many reasons for this when the permission or attendance of the shipper may not be possible. The refrigeration machinery in a reefer container may break down, requiring the cargo to be transferred to another unit or undeclared hazardous goods may cause trouble such as the escape of gas or liquid, and there are other examples such as misdeclaration of weight.

5.11. Carriage affected by the condition of the goods

This clause states that if the goods cannot safely or properly be carried or carried further the carrier may abandon them into safe custody at the sole risk and expense of the owner of the goods. Whereas it is desirable to notify the said owner as quickly as possible, the necessity for prompt action may prevent this and the carrier cannot contractually commit himself to so doing before implementing this clause. Further, this clause implies a duty to exercise due diligence, which again emphasizes the importance of choosing a carrier of good reputation.

5.12. Description of the goods

It is stipulated here that the bill of lading is *prima facie* evidence of receipt of the goods in apparent good order and condition unless otherwise stated. The number of containers or packages should be shown on the front of the document and any proof to the contrary is not admissible when the bill of lading has been transferred to a third party in good faith (Hague-Visby Rules Article III (4)).

5.13. Shipper's and merchant's responsibilities

Some carriers incorporate this clause which warrants that the particulars given by the shipper are correct, as he is the only one who knows the precise nature of the goods. The shipper also indemnifies the carrier against any fines or other expenses incurred by misdescription or inadequacy of marks and numbers leading to problems with Customs and other Authorities. A similar provision is incorporated in a conventional bill. This clause means exactly what it says and applies to requirements anywhere on the vessel's itinerary.

5.14. Freight and charges

This is similar to the clause in other bills of lading and is a contractual stipulation which applies to all freight which may be defined in the Definitions clause as 'all charges payable to the carrier in accordance with the applicable tariff'. In a clause of this nature there is usually provision for penalty where cargo has been misdeclared so as to deceive. Such a provision has to be considered in conjunction with the Lien clause.

5.15. Lien

The carrier has a lien on any goods or documents for outstanding charges whether freight, demurrage, General Average or any other expenses. The above reference to documents means that the carrier will usually withhold a 'freight paid' bill until payment is made, i.e., will exercise his lien on it.

There are the usual clauses for stowage, dangerous goods, General Average and the both-to-blame collision clause and Jurisdiction clause already mentioned earlier, but one or two other clauses may be given in greater detail than in a conventional bill such as:

5.15.1. Methods and route of transportation

This gives the carrier freedom of action to use any means of transport or conveyance or to proceed by any route, load or unload the goods at any place and otherwise to be free to discharge his responsibilities to care for the cargo according to whatever circumstances that may arise. Carriers are, however, always conscious of their customers' position and do not exercise their rights in this respect except with great care.

5.16. Matters affecting performance

This clause deals with matters where the carriage may be affected by hindrance or delay and the carrier provides that he may have to take action to abandon or place the goods at the merchant's disposal at a place other than that shown on the bill of lading, all additional charges being for account of the owner of the goods. It should however be stated that any action taken in this respect is in the merchant's interests and would usually be in accordance with his wishes in the circumstances, it being appreciated that the carrier will avoid any inconvenience to his customers except in the most serious circumstances.

5.17. Notification

There is no obligation on the part of the carrier to notify the consignee of the arrival of the goods; indeed it is not always possible. It is the responsibility of the consignee to keep himself informed about ships' arrivals and usually he is in receipt of documents in this respect. Whereas carriers invariably dispatch arrival notices, the notify address is regarded only as 'information' and no liability is accepted for any failure to inform, as may be the position with ordinary break-bulk shipping.

5.18. Variation of the contract

This stipulates that the terms and conditions of the bill of lading cannot be varied by any servant or agent without written consent of the carrier. The reason for this is that an ocean carrier has complicated insurance arrangements covering liability. He cannot therefore take the risk of allowing an agent or other person liberty to amend a carefully drafted document for which special insurance is arranged which could perhaps lead to a fundamental breach of contract. Permission must, therefore, always be obtained from Principals. The general provisions incorporated in the ICC Uniform Rules for Combined Transport Documents (brochure 298) include: (a) a definition of the document and its acceptability as a negotiable or non-negotiable document; and (b) it lays down the responsibilities and liabilities of a CTO and the rights and duties of the parties concerned with the transaction.

Provision is also made for liability for loss or damage when the stage of transport where loss of damage occurred *is known* and *is not known*. The above-mentioned rules also include under Rule 15 a provision covering failure to effect delivery within 90 days after the expiry of a time limit expressed in combined transport documents or, when no time limit is agreed, after the elapse of a period of time that it would be reasonable to allow for the completion of the combined transport operation.

There is also a rule concerning the time-bar which is given as a period within nine months after delivery of the goods, or the date when the goods should have been delivered.

6 Variations of conventional and combined transport bills of lading

6.1. Bills of lading issued under a charter-party

This is a bill of lading which is different from those mentioned previously; it is basically a receipt for cargo loaded on board the vessel and is still frequently signed by the Master or by the specific agreement of the Master or owners. The terms and conditions are in accordance with those incorporated in the charter-party (normally governed by the rules of Common Law) and only a few clauses are enumerated on the document which include the Both-to-blame Collision clause, the General Average and the New Jason clause, a War Risk clause, Demise clause and in the case of voyage charters, probably the Chamber of Shipping Voyage Charter Clause Paramount 1958 in respect of the Hague Rules. Whereas the Rules scheduled to the *Carriage of Goods by Sea Act* 1924 or 1971 do not apply to charter-parties, its provisions may be incorporated by a clause known as a Clause Paramount. This may give rise to difficulties where the charterer is also the shipper of his own goods and issues himself with a bill of lading. In such instances the Hague Rules would apply as a matter of contract under the charter-party but not under the bill of lading, unless and until the bill of lading was negotiated to a third party. However where a shipowner 'charters-in' tonnage to supplement his fleet, then he would issue his normal bills of lading for any cargo loaded without reference to the charter-party and a contract of carriage would then exist between the shipper and the charterer.

A bill of lading issued subject to the terms of the charter-party may be negotiated in the same way as a liner bill, the endorsee being deemed aware of the charter-party terms to the extent that they are incorporated by reference in the bill of lading. This is very important, because a separate undertaking will emerge between the shipowner and the bill of lading holder if the third persons are unaware of the charter-party conditions.

When a bill of lading is signed by the Master under a Demise charter, he does so, generally speaking, on behalf of the Charterer and not his owners. If however a ship is *not* chartered by demise then a bill of lading signed by the Master usually represents a contract with the shipowners. However, it would be misleading to assume that he personally signs because in practice it is usually done on his behalf. There would be a clause in the charter-party to the effect that 'The Master, Charterers and/or their Agents are hereby Authorized by *owners* to sign on Master and/or owners' behalf Bills of Lading as presented in accordance with Mates' and/or Tally Clerks' receipts without prejudice to this Charter-Party', or there would be a separate letter or Authority to similar effect signed by the Master or owners. This has a direct bearing on the Demise clause in the bill of lading which reads 'If the ship is now owned or chartered by demise to the shipping line by whom this bill of lading is issued, this bill of lading shall take effect only as a contract with the owner or demise charterer'.

The BIMCO 'Congenbill' is an excellent example of a bill of lading widely used with charter-parties for which no specific bill of lading form is prescribed. This document incorporates a Clause Paramount similar to that found in the BIMCO 'Conlinebill' liner bill of lading.

As far as bills of lading for use in voyage chartering are concerned, BIMCO have been instrumental for many years in preparing a variety of bill of lading forms. For instance, there are specific forms for specific trades, such as the POLCOALBILL bill of lading to be used for shipments chartered on the POLCOALVOY charter in the Polish coal export trade for both deep sea and short sea voyages. There is also the SOVORECONBILL for shipments under the SOVORECON, soviet ore charter-party, used for the carriage of ores and ore concentrates from USSR ports. There are, of course, other bills of lading designed for use with specific charter-parties.

6.2. Bills of lading issued by freight forwarders

Many freight forwarders issue a document known as a 'contract bill of lading' acknowledging a contract of carriage between themselves as principals and their customers. However, a separate contract of affreightment is to be entered into between the freight forwarder and the carrier evidenced by a bill of lading signed by or on behalf of the Master or the carrier.

In addition to the standard conditions of the Ocean Carrier's bill of lading, there is also another type which must be mentioned. The International Federation of Freight Forwarders Associations (FIATA) introduced a (new) Combined Transport Bill of Lading in January 1988 – in short, FIATA FBL. It is a carrier type document which is acceptable as a marine bill of lading provided that all the requirements of UCP Article 26 (see Chapter 12) are met. For this purpose the document has to show the additional information of 'Port of Loading', 'Ocean Vessel' and 'Port of Discharge'.

The freight forwarder when issuing it acts as a 'Contractual Carrier', because he concludes a contract for transport. This is in contrast to the 'actual' carrier, who carries the cargo, but it does not mean that a freight forwarder cannot carry the cargo for a part or for the total transport distance himself. The FBL is based on and complies with the Uniform Rules for a Combined Transport Document (ICC publication No. 298), and it bears the ICC symbol alongside that of the National Freight Forwarders Association on the front of the document. It can be issued as either a negotiable or as a non-negotiable document, but in the latter case it would have to be marked as such. The FIATA FBL was created to serve as a combined or multimodal transport document, involving more than one mode, e.g., road and sea, rail and road, etc.

A freight forwarder acting as Combined or Multimodal Transport Operator and issuing the FIATA FBL is responsible for the cargo and for the performance of the transport. He assumes not only responsibility for delivery of the goods at destination but also for all carriers and third parties engaged by him for the performance of the whole transport.

When the freight forwarder becomes liable for compensation in respect of loss of or damage to the goods, such compensation is calculated by reference to the value of such goods at the place and time of delivery to the consignee. The value of the goods is fixed according to the current commodity exchange price, or, if there is no such price, according to the current market price, or if there is no commodity exchange price or current market price, by reference to the normal value of goods of the same kind and quality. However, compensation shall not exceed two Special Drawing Rights (SDR) (approx. £1.50) per kilogramme of gross weight of the goods lost or damaged (unless the merchant has declared a higher value).

Arrival times are not guaranteed, but if the freight forwarder is held liable in respect of delay, other than loss or damage to the goods, his liability is limited to double the freight for the transport covered by the bill of lading or the value of the goods, whichever is the less.

This FIATA FBL is uniform throughout the world and is easily recognizable by its distinctive blue colour. It is copyright by FIATA (Zurich-Switzerland) and a specimen is reproduced with their kind permission as Appendix M. It should be mentioned that only freight forwarders who are members of FIATA and have proper authorization may issue the document.

It is a convenient commercial document which allows a freight forwarder to collect a quantity of clients' goods for one destination and ship them under one ocean (groupage) bill for delivery to one consignee at a destination for distribution to the holders of the respective 'house' bills.

6.3. Government form bills of lading

This is a convenient and standardized document designed to meet the requirements of the Department of Trade and Industry or the Crown Agents. It is a normal short form or 'blank back' bill of lading, printed as a Government Form and subject to the *Carriage of Goods by Sea Act* 1971 and York-Antwerp Rules 1974. Only a few clauses are included such as those relating to freight, the New Jason and the Both-to-blame Collision clauses, Demise and War clauses, a Port Restriction (Caspiana) clause and a Voyage clause. The Crown Agents form incorporates all the terms and conditions of the carrier's bill of lading.

However, in view of the nature of the document, there is usually a provision in respect of non-disclosure of the contents under the Official Secrets Act.

Some Government forms of foreign countries may be unacceptable to the carrier and require a superimposed notation to include all the terms and conditions of the contracting carrier before they can be issued.

6.4. Other forms of bills of lading

There are various other bills of lading forms for use in the liner trades including those of BIMCO who have been actively engaged for many years in preparing suitable documents and clauses for use by shipowners. A notable example of this is the *Conlinebill*, a Liner bill of lading, originally drafted and issued in 1949 for use by those BIMCO members operating regular liner services, and this document incorporates Liner Terms duly approved by this body. The *Conlinebill* is printed with French, German and Spanish translations, and to illustrate its popularity a quantity of over one million copies are sold each year.

6.5. Short form bill of lading

'Short form' or 'blank back' bills of lading have been in general use in Canada, the United States of America and Scandinavia for a number of years and recently in the European trade where their use is increasing. It was not until 1978, however, that a 'Common' document was introduced into the British shipping scene by the General Council of British Shipping (GCBS) who hold the copyright for the design of the form and the text.

This GCBS document is printed on one side of the paper only and can be used for shipments by any shipping company from the United Kingdom which has accepted the scheme. The principal benefit is that instead of using the carrier's own pre-printed form, the shipper has only to type the name of the contracting carrier in the space provided. The terms and conditions of the carrier's bill of lading are applied to the contract of affreightment by means of an 'Incorporation' clause which also reflects the Hague-Visby Rules. The text of this clause appearing on the document is common to a number of carriers who will individually provide, on request, full details of their standard terms and conditions. In general, it is no different from any other bill except that the conditions are not printed on the reverse side and it is acceptable within the ICC Rules mentioned earlier.

Another example of blank backed liner bills of lading is the BIMCO document introduced at the end of 1978 which is very similar in all respects to the GCBS version except for the wording of the Incorporation clause.

The Incorporation clause on the GCBS form was carefully drafted by legal experts from P and I Clubs and Defence Associations working in committee with representative bodies.

Apart from commercial convenience, these documents were developed to combat the growing number of copies of bills of lading that are requested for each consignment by taking advantage of new techniques such as reproduction by photostating and thus enabling a merchant not only to reproduce extra copies for domestic use, but also to print his own blank forms under licence and avoid the inconvenience of maintaining substantial stocks of individual long forms of bills of lading for many different ocean carriers.

7 Sea waybills and data freight receipts

The 'company' waybill has been in general use for many years for the carriage of goods by sea in the North Atlantic, West African and Scandinavian trades. In the North Atlantic the reduced voyage time also brought about the development of a Data Freight Receipt which is a similar document. It can be said that the North Atlantic trade was one of the pioneers in modern electronic data transmission, as such methods are now in general use in a variety of other services brought about by the installation of compatible computers in the offices of principals and their overseas agents. The Data Freight Receipt is a document which is produced in an office at the port of destination from cargo details entered into a computer at the port of shipment. The benefit to be gained is that it is very quickly available to the consignee thus overcoming the problem of postal delays brought about by faster voyage times. However, as such facilities are not generally available or indeed suitable for all trades throughout the world, other standard methods will remain in use for the foreseeable future.

The progress toward the introduction of a common non-negotiable sea waybill for use in the export trade from the United Kingdom began with a SITPRO recommendation in 1970 that shippers should be offered the choice of alternative transport documents that did not require production to obtain possession of the goods at destination. It developed as a document of optional simplicity and as an alternative to the bill of lading.

Following considerable study and discussion with the major national trade interests, including the banks and underwriters, the common short form sea waybill scheme was launched by the General Council of British Shipping in January 1977. It has been defined as follows:

> Non-negotiable document which evidences a contract for the carriage of goods by sea and the taking over or loading of the goods by the carrier, and by which the carrier undertakes to deliver the goods to the consignee named in the document.

A short form or blank back document is one which does not have any terms or conditions printed thereon; they are incorporated by means of a standard clause printed on the front or face of the waybill known as an 'Incorporation clause'. The sea waybill incorporates the Hague-Visby Rules and the normal terms and conditions of the contracting carrier's bill of lading. However, the sea waybill is not a negotiable document of title to the goods and has to be made out to a named consignee to whom the goods are to be delivered. The benefit of the document is that is does not necessarily have to be produced to obtain physical transfer, adequate proof of identity of the named person being all that is required.

It should be stressed that it is not intended as a replacement for other non-negotiable documents, such as the parcel receipt, which is not covered by the Hague-Visby Rules nor is it suitable for use with shipments of live animals or deck cargo which are specifically excluded from the rules. The shipper should obtain insurance cover in the same manner as for cargo consigned under a bill of lading and the underwriters duly advised that the shipment has been effected under a waybill. The principal benefits, therefore, are that:

(a) it does not have to be produced to obtain the goods and obviates postal delays particularly when fast transit times are involved, thus avoiding demurrage charges and shed-rent;

(b) it is suitable for 'in-house' documentation where no financial risk is involved, i.e., household and personal effects, samples and goods of no commercial value or shipments between companies or branches of a single multi-national organization;

(c) it is suitable for open account trading where absolute confidence exists between the parties to the transaction;

(d) it is generally possible, should the necessity arise, to convert a bill of lading into a non-negotiable waybill or vice versa, provided that the cargo is still in the possession of the ocean carrier, and subject of course to the surrender of the complete set of original documents. The clerical procedure is different from that of a bill of lading because the consignment should be manifested on a separate sheet and an arrival notice sent by the ship's agents at destination to the named consignee stating that the consignment has been effected under a waybill thus indicating that a bill of lading was not issued for the shipment. It is this notification or other suitable means of identification which should be presented by the named consignee, together with any collection charges that have been incurred so as to obtain delivery of the goods.

The sea waybill is acceptable when documents are transmitted through a bank for collection unless the bank actually finances the transaction or the Letter of Credit does not permit its use.

As mentioned in Chapter 1, the UK *Bills of Lading Act* 1855 does not apply to sea waybills but will doubtless be amended to cater for this modern document so as to alleviate the problem as to whether a consignee can sue or be sued on the contract of carriage.

The US Pomerene Act (Appendix C) provides that a consignee named in a 'straight bill of lading' can sue the carrier once he has become the owner of the goods – a 'straight' bill of lading being a non-negotiable document and therefore indistinguishable from a waybill. It accordingly avoids the difficulty that the UK has yet to overcome.

The Baltic and International Maritime Council (BIMCO) of Copenhagen, Denmark and the Swedish Trade Procedures Council (SWEPRO) of Gothenburg have also developed a series of sea waybills. The BIMCO documents include a 'GASTANKWAYBILL' a Gas Tank Waybill for use in the LPG trade and a 'CHEMTANKWAYBILL 85' which is a Chemical Tank Waybill. These specialized documents are subject to the terms and conditions of the Voyage Charter Party as well as incorporating the Hague/Hague-Visby Rules, General Average, New Jason and Both-to-blame Collision clauses. The SWEPRO Sea Waybill contains a unique NODISP declaration under which the shipper can expressly assign his right of disposal over the goods to the named consignee. This declaration enables the buyer to pay against documents and the Letter of Credit issuing bank to obtain security in the goods transported. If however, the shipper wishes to retain the right of disposal, the word NODISP is deleted.

8 A clean bill of lading

There have been differing definitions by learned Judges for over a century as to what constitutes a 'clean' bill of lading, from *Arrospe* v *Barr* (1881) until *Golodetz* v *Czarnikow-Rionda* – *'The Galatia'* (1980), but the most modern and accepted one was given in the case of *British Imex Industries* v *Midland Bank Ltd* (1958) when the judge stated that 'I incline to the view . . . that a clean bill of lading is one that does not contain any reservations as to the apparent good order or condition of the goods or the packing.' It will be observed from Article 34(a) of the Uniform Customs and Practice for Documentary Credits (ICC No. 400) 1983 revision (in Chapter 12) that their definition is similar to that of the British Imex case, namely 'A clean transport document is one which bears no superimposed clause or notation which expressly declares a defective condition of the goods and/or the packaging.'

The subject concerns the payment of goods in international trade which is generally financed by a system of credit, the conditions of which usually stipulate that the ocean carrier is required to issue a bill of lading or transport document acknowledging that the goods were received or shipped in apparent good order and condition. The seller or shipper is under an obligation to deliver his goods to the carrier in sound condition, suitably packed to withstand the voyage. The buyer or consignee relies on the assurance provided by the bill of lading.

It is the duty of the carrier to inspect the goods when they are received into his charge although this is necessarily limited to a reasonable external inspection, and care must therefore be exercised to ensure that the packages are not damaged, torn or stained, evidencing pre-shipment damage. This is both for his own protection, to avoid unnecessary claims, and for that of his customers, who will rely on the authenticity of the document.

It is unnecessary to stipulate in a letter of credit that a bill of lading should be endorsed 'clean on board' because such a request indicates that the expression has been misunderstood. Ocean carriers discourage superfluous clauses.

If cargo is loaded on board a ship or taken in charge, and then becomes damaged, it is necessary for a *clean* bill of lading to be issued. It is only cargo damaged *before* being received by the carrier that warrants a claused document.

This problem was the subject of a law case between *Golodetz* v *Czarnikow-Rionda 'The Galatia'* (1980). Briefly, *The Galatia* was chartered to carry a cargo of sugar from Kandla, India to Bandar Shahpour, Iran. However, four days after arrival at Kandla when the sugar was partially loaded, a fire broke out and 2008 bags (200 tons) became damaged by fire and water, and were discharged and condemned as it was not commercially practicable to recondition it. One of the conditions of the contract of sale was that payment for the sugar would be made against a full set of 'clean on board' bills of lading and that the Master was required to issue Mate's receipts acknowledging receipt of the cargo on board. On this occasion *two* sets of bills were signed, namely, one for the main quantity and another for the damaged balance of 200 tons. This latter bill contained a typewritten clause saying 'cargo covered by this bill of lading has been discharged Kandla view damaged by fire and/or water used to extinguish fire for which General Average declared.' This latter bill of lading was rejected by the buyers and a dispute arose as to who was to bear the loss for the damaged portion of the consignment as a clean Mate's Receipt had been issued. The outcome depended on whether the bill was clean or claused. The Court applied two tests to ascertain the character of the bill of lading namely, the commercial or practical test to establish whether the bill was acceptable to the banks as 'clean' and the legal test because the damage occurred after the cargo had been loaded in apparent good order and condition. The conclusion was that the bill of lading had to be regarded as 'clean'. This decision was upheld by the Court of Appeal.

It will be noted that the *post shipment damage clause* should *not* have been inserted on the bill of lading but made by another statement in a Survey Report or other document.

Another case, *British Imex Industries* v *Midland Bank Ltd* (1958) involved the shipment at Antwerp of 520 tons of steel bars on board the *Nordstern* for Aquaba. The bill of lading stated 'Shipped at Antwerp in apparent good order and condition, weight, measure, marks, numbers, quality, contents and value unknown'. There was also an additional clause on the reverse side of the bill of lading which stated 'Iron and steel . . . Vessel not responsible for correct delivery and all expenses incurred at port of discharge consequent upon insufficient securing or marking will be payable by consignees unless every piece is distinctly and permanently marked with oil paint and metal-tagged, so that each piece or bundle can be distinguished at port of discharge.'

The Bank refused to pay when the documents were presented to them by the sellers, alleging that the bills of lading were not 'clean' or were otherwise defective because they contained no express acknowledgement by the shipowners that the goods were marked and secured in the manner prescribed. The sellers concluded that the additional clause went no further than Article IV rule 2(n) and (o) of the Hague Rules which provide that 'Neither the carrier nor the ship shall be responsible for loss or damage arising from (n) Insufficiency of packing and (o) Insufficiency or inadequacy of marks.'

It was held that the bills of lading presented were in this case 'clean' as they contained no reservations by way of endorsement, clausing or otherwise to suggest that the goods were defective and that the Letter of Credit did not require the bill of lading to be endorsed with any acknowledgement that the additional clause had been complied with and as such the bank could not insist on such an acknowledgement before payment.

It will be observed from the above that only notations that refer to the *defective condition* of the goods or the packaging will render the bill of lading or transport document unclean. An 'insufficiency of packing' or other 'disclaimer' clauses such as 'Secondhand drums', 'Paper bags' or 'Unprotected' do not by themselves cause the document to be unclean as the items may not be defective, but the carrier has noted the fact just in case they do not stand up to the voyage.

9 Delivery of cargo under bills of lading and other transport documents which embrace them

A shipowner or ocean carrier is generally required to deliver goods upon presentation of one original bill of lading to a named consignee or to the person who is entitled to them as the rightful owner. In this respect it is necessary to stress the importance of endorsements mentioned in paragraph 3.5. Occasionally conflicting claims of ownership to the goods arise which necessitate particular care in avoiding delivery to anyone other than the rightful owner. Should this occasion arise, it is advisable to regard the cargo as 'in dispute' – withholding delivery until the matter has been investigated with the shipper with whom the contract of carriage was made. For instance, the shipper may 'stop' delivery to the consignee named in the bill (unless of course the document has already been negotiated) and give instructions that the goods are to be delivered to some other person. The bill of lading and the manifest would then have to be amended. Delivery to anyone who is not entitled to the goods and without the production of the bill is *prima facie* a conversion of the goods and a breach of contract (*Skibsaktieselskapet Thor* v *Tyrer* (1929) and *Sze Hai Tong Bank* v *Rambler Cycle Co* (1959)).

Whereas the issue of bills of lading in sets of two or three originals is still common practice, modern methods of documentation highlight this as an outdated procedure. In due time this practice will probably be discontinued thus leading to the issue of only one original document. However, until such an occasion arises it is usual for all the bills in the set to be kept and negotiated together except where merchants do not require external finance from a bank or other financial institution.

In certain trades there has survived the old practice whereby a shipper or charterer entrusts the Master of the carrying vessel with one of a set of three original bills of lading contained in an envelope addressed to the consignee or to the party to whom delivery should be given, in exchange for the same bill. This practice may occur with oil cargoes where there could be intervening transactions involving the negotiation of bills between various buyers and sellers through their banks, although none of them would actually possess the full set of documents.

Although the simplicity of the arrangement has many attractions from a commercial point of view, it does expose the shipowner or carrier to serious risks. It has been pointed out by the *Comité Maritime International* that in some jurisdictions the courts may award damages to an innocent holder of a negotiated bill of lading if it appears that the cargo has already been delivered to someone else with the 'complicity of the Master'. The delivery of cargo *without* the production of the bills of lading or other document of title is dealt with in Chapter 13.

The delivery of refrigerated cargo may cause problems if the bill of lading is not presented at the time of discharge, particularly if suitable facilities are unavailable, as such cargo cannot be left in the open unattended, awaiting collection. In major ports and container berths this situation should not arise because clip-on and other suitable facilities are available. However, where this is not the case, arrangements would probably be made by the carrier for the cargo to be delivered to a convenient cold store and held there 'to the order of the carrier' until the original bill of lading is duly presented.

However, if cold store facilities have been requested by the consignee or his representative because the bill of lading is not available then a suitable bank-countersigned indemnity should be obtained by the carrier before delivery.

When a merchant sells his goods on one bill of lading to several different receivers the bill has to be 'split' to the required amounts. This procedure is for one of the original bills to be presented to the shipowner or carrier with a letter detailing the splitting requirements and the *full* amount of freight and charges.

Separate delivery orders are then issued, each one of which must be correctly endorsed before presentation at the discharging berth. Freight must not be paid on a pro-rata basis per delivery order as any dispute or query has to be made direct to the holder of the delivery order to the seller of the goods, and not the carrier.

When bulk oil is carried the amount shown on the bill of lading should always be shown as 'quantity said to be' and care exercised when delivery is required to several receivers as the quantity in the ship's tanks is not exact and the last merchant to arrange collection may be short on quantity. Any problems arising from this situation should also be referred to the bill of lading holder who gave the delivery instructions, and not to the carrier.

Requests for sampling of goods before the presentation of the bills of lading should be resisted as a very unsound practice. It is not the shipowner's business to become involved in such matters as it may lead to a contract of sale dispute between buyer and seller, rejection of the cargo, and numerous other problems for which the shipowner could be held responsible.

10 Related documents

10.1. The mate's receipt

The mate's receipt is a document upon which the particulars contained in
the bill of lading are based and it is necessary that the information on both
documents is substantially the same. It is not a document of title to the
goods shipped as it does not contain a contract of carriage and its possession is therefore not equivalent to possession of the goods, nor does its
endorsement or transfer pass any title. However, it is *prima facie* evidence
that the person named therein is entitled to receive the bill of lading in
exchange. It occasionally happens that ownership of the goods is transferred before the bill is issued, in which case due notice of the transaction
should be given by the shipper to the ocean carrier. A mate's receipt may
be subject to the carrier's bill of lading terms and conditions and has now
been generally replaced in the United Kingdom by the Standard Shipping
Note which must accompany all goods to the docks or terminal. It is on this
document that any notation will appear such as 'frail cases' or 'dented
drums' which is transmitted to the bill of lading before issue. In those ports
where a mate's receipt is used, it is usual for it to be exchanged for the bill
of lading.

10.2. The National Standard Shipping Note

The National Standard Shipping Note (NSSN) has replaced the mate's
receipt in most United Kingdom ports and unlike the latter is a document
which forms part of the SITPRO aligned series. They hold the copyright and
it is administered by them. It is compiled by the supplier of the goods or
the shipper/freight forwarder, giving full details of the goods similar to
those shown on the bill of lading, against which it is matched before issue.
It is necessary in most ports for the NSSN to accompany the goods to the
docks or terminal.

The NSSN comprises a six part set, copies of which are retained by those
parties handling the goods until they are finally on board, from which a
'shipped' bill of lading is eventually issued. The note is not acceptable for
the shipment of hazardous cargo from the United Kingdom as the SITPRO
Dangerous Goods Note (DGN) should be used for that purpose.

A consignment under an NSSN is defined as one or more pieces, packages, containers, tanks, barges or rail wagons moved at the same time to the
same consignee or 'Notify Party'.

In the case of multi-vehicle deliveries, it is necessary to prepare separate
notes for each vehicle *provided that the documents are linked in some way*, or
one note may be prepared for the total consignment *provided that according
to local port practice it is lodged either before the arrival of the goods or it is carried
by the first driver to arrive at the reception point.*

10.3. Ships' delivery orders

These documents, which must not be confused with merchants' delivery sub-orders, are issued at the port of destination in exchange for an original endorsed bill of lading and they have been accepted by the courts as 'the token of an authority to receive possession'. It is customary for the delivery order to be subject to all the terms and conditions of the carrier's bill of lading and it must not contain any reservations or clauses other than those appearing in the bill of lading except where increased obligations or extra costs may be incurred in giving delivery beyond the bill of lading. A delivery order has several uses, for instance, a bill of lading holder may wish to sell part or all of the consignment to several different merchants. Alternatively, he may not wish his buyer to know the identity of the supplier abroad for trade reasons and therefore when exchanged for the bill of lading, the delivery order can be a useful document. It must be endorsed by the party to whom it is made out, but if issued in one port for delivery in another and freight is payable at destination, the order would then be 'consigned' to the carrier's agent to ensure that it would have to be presented and released before collection of the goods is authorized.

A consignee may require his bill of lading to be 'split' into several lots for different buyers for which the procedures are as follows:

Where the actual quantity is stated on the bill of lading (e.g. 400 cartons), the buyer's name would appear on the order and in practice he would have recourse to the carrier in the event of loss or damage. However, where the actual quantity is not accurately known, such as a tank of bulk vegetable oil, a more cautious attitude should be taken. Commodities shipped in bulk are subject to ullage due to evaporation and therefore should be acknowledged as 'a quantity said to be'. The delivery order in this case should only be made out in the name of the consignee of the bill of lading, who in turn would issue his own sub-orders. The reason for this is that the last person to collect the commodity may receive a short delivery which was beyond the control of the carrier and accordingly the claim for this loss would correctly be directed against the seller rather than the shipowner.

A ship's delivery order should be directed to the Master of the vessel and not to the cargo superintendent or other authority since the Master is the person in possession of the goods under the bill of lading, and an order to him to deliver would give rise to a delivery under that bill.

Whereas the commercial procedure works very well and without difficulty, the legal position is rather more obscure. For instance, a shipowner may not have any contractual relationship with the person named in the delivery order if he is not the bill of lading consignee. Consequently, if the goods are lost or damaged after they have been sold to the person named by the consignee, that person could, at least in theory, sue the shipowner in tort, who may have difficulty either limiting his liability or relying on any of the defences in the bill. The Receiver must, however, show that he was the owner of the goods when the loss or damage occurred; *Margarine Union* v *Cambay Prince Steamship Co*. (1967). In other words, the shipowner is bailee of the goods owned by the person named in the delivery order and, therefore, if these goods are lost or damaged, then the shipowner would have to disprove negligence in order to escape liability. Another aspect is where a delivery order is given for an undivided bulk cargo because the Receiver named therein does not acquire a legal or possessory title to his goods until his parcel is separated from the bulk or after discharge from the vessel. The receiver would not have a claim against the shipowner for loss or damage prior to that time; at least his chances of a successful action would be remote.

Another aspect is that of lien where a shipowner issues a delivery order to a Dock or Harbour Authority prior to the arrival of the vessel, instructing them to release goods to a named person. Having done so, General Average expenses are then incurred. The position in this instance is that in addition to any rights of lien that the carrier may have at Common Law, he would also derive additional rights of lien from the bill of lading.

11 The ship's manifest

The ship's cargo manifest contains information required by customs authorities at ports throughout the world, and as such is an important document and must be accurate in all details.

The particulars that it contains include the name of the ship and that of the Master, the nationality of the vessel, port of loading and port of discharge. The cargo has to be detailed carefully such as marks, numbers, contents, kind and numbers of packages, weight, measurement, container numbers, names of shippers and Receivers and full freight details. The freight particulars are usually detached before being handed to customs authorities as it does not concern them.

The information on the manifest is arranged in order of port of loading and port of discharge, also numerically to bill of lading on one sheet and container number on another sheet.

It should be stressed that *all* packages should be included on the manifest especially privileged freight free or similar items of goods because their omission could lead to a charge of attempted smuggling thus placing the Master of the ship and/or his owners in serious difficulties including penalties being levied such as a heavy fine or even imprisonment. Penalties may also be imposed for clerical errors or omissions in the cargo details, and all these fines usually have to be paid or a bond deposited in order that the ship may leave port.

The number of copies produced depends on the local needs of the ship's agents at the ports of loading and discharge, as customs and port authorities vary their requirements from country to country. Copies should also be in the agent's possession before the arrival of the ship so as to avoid any delay in the commencement of discharge. Further, a complete manifest should be placed on board the vessel as soon as practicable for use by the Master. In troubled areas a copy may be demanded by the Naval Authorities.

The information contained on the manifest is used for a variety of purposes including company trade statistics, accountancy and by customs and port authorities for the collection of taxes and dues. The data are also required to check merchants' import and export customs entries, and by Government departments for trade and other returns. It is this document which is examined by Government Investigation departments to ensure compliance with the regulations when sanctions have been imposed against another country.

The transmission of readable computer data between shipping lines and their overseas agents has now eased many of the problems mentioned provided that compatible equipment is installed, or by the physical transfer of magnetic tape by airmail services for the long distance routes where more voyage time is available. It should be mentioned that in addition to the manifest, the Master should also have in his possession a complete set of 'Captain's copies' of bills of lading for 'on board' reference purposes.

12 Documentary credits

12.1. The uniform customs and practice for documentary credits

If a bill of lading as one of the negotiable documents has to be presented through a bank against a Letter of Credit for payment of the sale contract price, it is necessary that all the details conform to the Letter of Credit requirements, otherwise the bank may refuse acceptance or withhold payment. Problems of this nature arise if the shipper delays examination of the terms of the Letter of Credit until the bill is issued or about to be issued, as anxiety then exists over expiry dates or perhaps the bill cannot be issued as 'clean on board' because of pre-shipment damage. The interpretation of Letter of Credit terms has often caused problems and disagreement, which has been eased to a considerable extent by a set of rules known as the Uniform Customs and Practice for Documentary Credits. These Rules were originally adopted by the International Chamber of Commerce in 1933 and have been updated at regular intervals by the ICC Banking Commission since its introduction. They form an internationally accepted set of standards for guidance and assistance in international trading operations in every part of the world, and have been adopted by most of the principal banks in 156 countries. Each revision takes into account the changing circumstances of commercial practice and the latest 1983 revision, published as Brochure ICC No. 400 (which came into force on 1st October 1984) applies to all documentary credits and is binding on all parties thereto unless otherwise expressly agreed. The 1983 revision notes the continuing revolution in transport technology, and the geographical extension of containerization and combined transport; the increasing influence of trade facilitation activities on the development of new documents and new methods of producing them; the communications revolution, replacing paper as a means of transmitting information (data) relating to a trading transaction by methods of automated or electronic data processing; and the development of new types of documentary credits, such as the deferred payment credit and the stand-by credit.

Those Articles which refer in particular to bills of lading and transport documents are dealt with in section D.1. of the Rules which are reproduced as follows:

12.1.1. Article 25

Unless a credit calling for a transport document stipulates as such document a marine bill of lading (ocean bill of lading or a bill of lading covering carriage by sea), or a post receipt or certificate of posting:

a. banks will, unless otherwise stipulated in the credit, accept a transport document which:

i appears on its face to have been issued by a named carrier, or his agent, and

ii indicates dispatch or taking in charge of the goods, or loading on board, as the case may be, and

iii consists of the full set of originals issued to the consignor if issued in more than one original, and iv meets all other stipulations of the credit.

b. Subject to the above, and unless otherwise stipulated in the credit, banks will not reject a transport document which:

i bears a title such as 'Combined transport bill of lading', 'Combined transport document', 'Combined transport bill of lading or port-to-port bill of lading', or a title or a combination of titles of similar intent and effect, and/or

ii indicates some or all of the conditions of carriage by reference to a source or document other than the transport document itself (short form/blank back transport document), and/or

iii indicates a place of taking in charge different from the port of loading and/or a place of final destination different from the port of discharge, and/or

iv relates to cargoes such as those in Containers or on pallets, and the like, and/or

v contains the indication 'intended', or similar qualification, in relation to the vessel or other means of transport, and/or the port of loading and/or the port of discharge.

c. Unless otherwise stipulated in the credit in the case of carriage by sea or by more than one mode of transport but including carriage by sea, banks will reject a transport document which:

i indicates that it is subject to a charter-party, and/or

ii indicates that the carrying vessel is propelled by sail only.

d. Unless otherwise stipulated in the credit, banks will reject a transport document issued by a freight forwarder unless it is the FIATA Combined Transport Bill of Lading approved by the International Chamber of Commerce or otherwise indicates that it is issued by a freight forwarder acting as a carrier or agent of a named carrier.

12.1.2. Article 26

If a credit calling for a transport document stipulates as such document a marine bill of lading:

a. banks will, unless otherwise stipulated in the credit, accept a document which:

i appears on its face to have been issued by a named carrier, or his agent, and

ii indicates that the goods have been loaded on board or shipped on a named vessel, and

iii consists of the full set of originals issued to the consignor if issued in more than one original, and

iv meets all other stipulations in the credit.

b. Subject to the above, and unless otherwise stipulated in the credit, banks will not reject a document which:

i bears a title such as 'Combined transport bill of lading', 'Combined transport document', 'Combined transport bill of lading or port-to-port bill of lading', or a title or a combination of titles of similar intent and effect, and/or

ii indicates some or all of the conditions of carriage by reference to a source or document other than the transport document itself (short form/blank back transport document), and/or

iii indicates a place of taking in charge different from the port of loading and/or a place of final destination different from the port of discharge, and/or

iv relates to cargoes such as those in Containers or on pallets, and the like.

c. Unless otherwise stipulated in the credit, banks will reject a document which:

i indicates that it is subject to a charter-party, and/or

ii indicates that the carrying vessel is propelled by sail only, and/or

iii contains the indication 'intended', or similar qualification in relation to

- the vessel and/or the port of loading – unless such document bears an on board notation in accordance with article 27 (b) and also indicates the actual port of loading, and/or

- the port of discharge – unless the place of final destination indicated on the document is other than the port of discharge, and/or

iv is issued by a freight forwarder, unless it indicates that it is issued by such freight forwarder acting as a carrier, or as the agent of a named carrier.

12.1.3. Article 27

a. Unless a credit specifically calls for an on board transport document, or unless inconsistent with other stipulation(s) in the credit, or with article 26, banks will accept a transport document which indicates that the goods have been taken in charge or received for shipment.

b. Loading on board or shipment on a vessel may be evidenced either by a transport document bearing wording indicating loading on board a named vessel or shipment on a named vessel, or, in the case of a transport document stating 'received for shipment' by means of a notation of loading on board on the transport document signed or initialled and dated by the carrier or his agent, and the date of this notation shall be regarded as the date of loading on board the named vessel or shipment on the named vessel.

12.1.4. Article 28

a. In the case of carriage by sea or by more than one mode of transport but including carriage by sea, banks will refuse a transport document stating that the goods are or will be loaded on deck, unless specifically authorized in the credit.

b. Banks will not refuse a transport document which contains a provision that the goods may be carried on deck, provided it does not specifically state that they are or will be loaded on deck.

12.1.5. Article 29

a. For the purpose of this article transhipment means a transfer and reloading during the course of carriage from the port of loading or place of dispatch or taking in charge to the port of discharge or place of destination either from one conveyance or vessel to another conveyance or vessel within the same mode of transport or from one mode of transport to another mode of transport.

b. Unless transhipment is prohibited by the terms of the credit, banks will accept transport documents which indicate that the goods will be transhipped, provided the entire carriage is covered by one and the same transport document.

c. Even if transhipment is prohibited by the terms of the credit, banks will accept transport documents which:

i incorporate printed clauses stating that the carrier has the right to tranship, or

ii state or indicate that transhipment will or may take place, when the credit stipulates a combined transport document, or indicates carriage from a place of taking in charge to a place of final destination by different modes of transport including a carriage by sea, provided that the entire carriage is covered by one and the same transport document, or

iii state or indicate that the goods are in a Container(s), trailer(s), 'LASH' barge(s), and the like and will be carried to the place of taking in charge to the place of final destination in the same Container(s), trailer(s), 'LASH' barge(s), and the like under one and the same transport document.

iv state or indicate the place of receipt and/or of final destination as 'CFS' (container freight station) or 'CY' (container yard) at, or associated with, the port of loading and/or the port of destination.

12.1.6. Article 30

If the credit stipulates dispatch of goods by post and calls for a post receipt or certificate of posting, banks will accept such post receipt or certificate of posting if it appears to have been stamped or otherwise authenticated and dated in the place from which the credit stipulates the goods are to be dispatched.

12.1.7. Article 31

a. Unless otherwise stipulated in the credit, or inconsistent with any of the documents presented under the credit, banks will accept transport documents stating that freight or transportation charges (hereinafter referred to as 'freight') have still to be paid.

b. If a credit stipulates that the transport document has to indicate that freight has been paid or prepaid, banks will accept a transport document on which the words clearly indicating payment or prepayment of freight appear by stamp or otherwise, or on which payment of freight is indicated by other means.

c. The words 'freight prepayable' or 'freight to be prepaid' or words of similar effect, if appearing on transport documents, will not be accepted as constituting evidence of the payment of freight.

d. Banks will accept transport documents bearing reference by stamp or otherwise to costs additional to the freight charges, such as costs of, or disbursements incurred in connection with, loading, unloading or similar operations, unless the conditions of the credit specifically prohibit such reference.

12.1.8. Article 32

Unless otherwise stipulated in the credit, banks will accept transport documents which bear a clause on the face thereof such as 'shippers load and count' or 'said by shipper to contain' or words of similar effect.

12.1.9. Article 33

Unless otherwise stipulated in the credit, banks will accept transport documents indicating as the consignor of the goods a party other than the beneficiary of the credit.

12.1.10. Article 34

a. A clean transport document is one which bears no superimposed clause or notation which expressly declares a defective condition of the goods and/or the packaging.

b. Banks will refuse transport documents bearing such clauses or notations unless the credit expressly stipulates the clauses or notations which may be accepted.

c. Banks will regard a requirement in a credit for a transport document to bear the clause 'clean on board' as complied with if such transport document meets the requirements of this article and of article 27 (b).

13 Letters of Indemnity

A Letter of Indemnity is a document of both legal and commercial convenience and should always be handled with care. Its purpose in connection with bills of lading is *inter alia* to enable cargo to be released to a consignee without production of the original endorsed bill or to permit the issue of a duplicate set of documents when the originals have been lost or mislaid in transit. In view of the risk involved in giving delivery of cargo without an original bill of lading or in issuing a duplicate set, the countersignature of a reputable bank is necessary, and an example of the usual form is shown in Appendix Q.

It is sound practice, when an indemnity is presented for the release of cargo, for the carrier or his agent to confirm with the shipper that it in order to give delivery, and whereas this may not be absolutely necessary as adequate protection has been given, it nevertheless avoids problems arising through possession of goods before payment and an unfortunate dispute between seller and buyer with the carrier in the middle.

If a duplicate set of bills is issued to the shipper who has lost the originals, it is usual to mark them to indicate that they are duplicates issued against an indemnity or to number the new set in red, with the ship's agent at the destination being advised accordingly.

Letters of Indemnity submitted on behalf of a national Government do not require a banker's countersignature for obvious reasons.

The period of validity of a Letter of Indemnity before becoming time-barred under English Law is subject to the *Limitation Act* 1939 which under Section 2(i) provides that an action 'shall not be brought after the expiration of six years from the date on which the cause of action accrued.'

The question that therefore needs answering is when does a cause of action accrue on a Letter of Indemnity? It is reasonably well accepted that the cause of action accrues when the plaintiff's (e.g. shipowner or carrier's) liability to a third party is sufficiently established to allow the plaintiff to institute proceedings on the indemnity and from that time he has a further six years in which to do so. It is therefore possible for a bank to be at risk for any time up to twelve years although this period is unusual.

Shipowners or carriers must be cautious about issuing misleading documents where, for instance, a shipper in order to obtain a clean bill of lading is prepared to offer a Letter of Indemnity. A Letter of Indemnity must not therefore be accepted from a shipper to avoid the issue of a claused or 'dirty' bill where goods have been accepted or loaded in a damaged or unsound condition. Such a document represents an act of deception, namely, to obtain payment for goods knowing them to be unsound. In such instances it is not only the buyer or consignee but the bank and the cargo underwriters who are also deceived. A dangerous practice, not unknown but certainly undesirable and not recommended, as the issue of a clean bill of lading for 'dirty' or damaged goods may expose the shipowner to heavy claims from parties such as banks and buyers who have bought the goods on the strength of the clean bill.

There is no P and I Club cover against such claims and the Letter of Indemnity would be unenforceable against the shipper in English Law, (see also Article 17 paragraphs 2, 3 and 4 of the Hamburg Rules, which deals with this problem).

Letters of Indemnity may therefore be accepted to assist merchants or shippers for a variety of reasons some of which are:

(a) Release of goods when the original bill is lost by the receiver.

(b) The issue of duplicate bills when the originals have been lost by the shipper or mislaid in transit to the consignee.

In respect of (a) and (b) above it should be made clear that whereas these cases are enforceable any resulting claims would *not* be recoverable under the rules of the Carriers P and I Association.

(c) If a material alteration is required such as a change in the name of the consignee when the full set is not available.

(d) Some other amendment required by a shipper after issue of the bill and dispatch of the manifest to the discharge port. Carriers are frequently fined by customs authorities abroad if documents do not agree.

(e) Delivery to a different consignee other than the one named on the original bill when for instance the first named is unobtainable due to civil disturbance and the goods sold to another buyer.

This would be an indemnity given by the original shipper. However, sometimes this is not possible and as an alternative the shipper is advised to exercise his right of stoppage *in transitu* at Common Law which effectively cancels the position of the first consignee and substitutes someone else.

Whereas it is advisable for a Letter of Indemnity to be unlimited as to value, there are occasions when this may not be commercially possible and a limit is required by the carrier to be placed on the liability thereunder. In such circumstances it has been recommended that the monetary limit must not be less than 150 per cent of the CIF value of the relevant cargo.

There are in addition other types of indemnity which have to be automatically accepted by shippers, such as those incorporated in the conditions of the bill of lading. The most important of these involves the shipment of hazardous cargo where the shipper accepts responsibility for the consequences of inadequate packing, misdeclaration, misdescription or the mismarking of any dangerous cargo. This includes shipments by conventional or containerized means. The importance of this is not always fully appreciated; shippers of FCL cargo, for example, indemnify the carrier not only for loss, damage, expenses or other liabilities resulting from these consequences but also for personal accident and damage to the carrying vessel, hauliers' vehicles, terminal installations etc., not only in the country of shipment but also abroad. It will be seen that care must be exercised to ensure that adequate liability insurance is available.

14 United Nations Conventions

14.1. United Nations Convention on the carriage of goods by sea, 1978: The Hamburg Rules

A United Nations Conference on the Carriage of Goods by Sea was held at Hamburg in March 1978 when the Diplomatic Conference adopted new Rules to be known in the future as the 'Hamburg Rules'.

The conference was attended by 78 states and the convention provides that the new Rules will come into operation one year following the twentieth state to ratify or accede to it. Further, there is no requirement that a state ratifying or acceding to the convention should be required to represent a particular amount of gross tonnage similar to that laid down by previous conventions.

It will have been noted from the foregoing chapters that the history of the law relating to contracts of carriage shows a series of pendulum swings between excessive protection of the carrier and excessive protection of the shipper. This convention appears to benefit shippers and consignees in user countries rather than those who are providing the shipping services, and therefore the cost of transport by sea is expected to rise considerably when these rules are adopted and form part of the legislation of the maritime nations. In addition, the transfer to the ship of a significant part of the liability at present borne by cargo interests means that it will have an effect on the insurance market in some countries due to a reduction in cargo insurance premiums as the risk is absorbed in the freight rates.

The main differences between the Hague-Visby Rules and the Hamburg Rules are described as follows.

14.1.1. Article 1 – Definitions

The definitions of 'goods' and 'carrier' are modified from those given in the Hague-Visby Rules and it will be observed that 'goods' now includes live animals. The definition 'Contract of Carriage' has also been substantially altered to mean any contract whereby the carrier undertakes against payment of freight to carry goods by sea from one port to another; however, a contract which involves carriage by sea and also carriage by some other means is deemed to be a contract of carriage by sea for the purposes of this convention only in so far as it relates to the carriage by sea. There are additional definitions such as 'actual carrier', 'shipper', 'consignee' and 'bill of lading'. As previously mentioned this is the first time in history that the meaning of a 'bill of lading' has been defined within an international convention.

14.1.2. Article 2 – Scope of application

This article includes various provisions for the application of the convention including its application to all contracts of carriage by sea whether they are contained in a bill of lading or some other document evidencing the contract of carriage. The provisions do not apply to charter parties except that, where a bill of lading is issued pursuant to a charter party, the provisions of the convention apply to such a bill of lading if it governs the relations between the carrier and any holder of the bill of lading other than the charterer. Further, the provisions are also applicable when the actual port of discharge is located in a contracting state.

14.1.3. Article 4 – Period of responsibility

This article governs the duration of the carrier's responsibility which is extended to the entire period during which the goods are in the carrier's charge, at the port of loading, during the carriage and at the port of discharge, and accordingly greatly increases the liability of the carrier. For instance, under the existing Hague-Visby Rules the carrier accepts responsibility from ship's tackle on loading to ship's tackle on discharge, whereas under this convention the carrier is deemed to be 'in charge' of the goods from the time that he has taken them over from the shipper or other third party who is handling the goods for shipment. Secondly the period of the carrier's responsibility continues until he has delivered the goods by either handing them over to the consignee at the port of discharge or transferring them to an authority or other third party to whom the goods must be handed over.

The effect of this will be a shift from the cargo insurer to the ship's liability insurer. It is thought that this will bring about a state of uncertainty and considerable expensive legislation in the future, particularly as it is by no means certain that the litigation in the various countries will produce the same result.

The main purpose of placing liability on the carrier was probably to ensure good performance.

14.1.4. Article 5 – Basis of liability

The general principle set out under this article places the liability, based on the presumption of fault, on the sea carrier and as such he may exempt himself by proof to the contrary. This principle is to be read in conjunction with the Common Understanding contained in Annex 2 of the Convention. However, such proof will be difficult to provide because of the wide difference of interpretation by the courts in different countries.

Under this Article the carrier shall be liable for a claim resulting from loss of or damage to the goods as well as from delay in delivery if the occurrence which caused the loss or delay took place while the goods were in his charge (as defined under Article 4) unless the carrier can prove that he, his servants and agents took all measures that could reasonably be required to avoid such an occurrence.

Delay is a type of damage, and delay in delivery occurs when the goods have not been delivered at the port of destination in accordance with the contract of carriage within the time expressly agreed to or, in the absence of such an agreement, within a reasonable time bearing in mind the circumstances of the case.

A person entitled to make a claim for the loss of goods may treat the goods as lost when they have not been delivered as specified in Article 4, 2(b), namely,

(i) by handing over the goods to the consignee; or
(ii) in cases where the consignee does not receive the goods from the carrier, by placing them at the disposal of the consignee in accordance with the contract or with the law or with the usage of the particular trade, applicable at the port of discharge; or

(iii) by handing over the goods to an authority or other third party to whom, pursuant to law or regulations applicable at the port of discharge, the goods must be handed over.

Also, in accordance with Article 5(3)

> The person entitled to make a claim for the loss of goods may treat the goods as lost if they have not been delivered as required by Article 4 within 60 consecutive days following the expiry of the time for delivery according to paragraph 2(b) above.

With regard to live animals, the carrier is not liable for loss, damage or delay in delivery resulting from any special risks inherent in that kind of carriage. If the carrier proves that he has complied with any special instructions given to him by the shipper and in the circumstances of the case the loss, damage or delay in delivery could be attributed to such risks, it is to be presumed that such loss or delay was so caused unless there is proof that the fault rests with the carrier, his servants or agents.

In the case of fire on board a ship affecting the goods, the carrier shall be liable providing that the claimants prove that the fire arose from the fault or neglect on the part of the carrier. In other words the onus of proof is on the shipper.

The carrier shall not be liable except in General Average where any loss or delay results from measures to save life or property at sea.

It should also be mentioned that Article 5 (7) has no counterpart under the Hague-Visby Rules and states the ordinary rule on contributory negligence. Thus, where fault or neglect on the part of the carrier, his servants or agents combine with other causes to produce loss, damage or delay the carrier is only liable to the extent that such loss, damage or delay is attributable to such fault or neglect.

14.1.5. Article 6 – Limits of liability

The provisions in this article are similar to those given in the Hague-Visby Rules providing for a dual system for limitation purposes. However the figures are no longer given in poincaré francs as in the 1968 Protocol but in Special Drawing Rights (SDRs). The corresponding amounts are:

(a) The amount equivalent to 835 SDRs (approx. £640) per package or other shipping units, or
(b) 2.5 SDRs (approx. £1.90) per kilogramme of gross weight, whichever is higher.
(c) Liability for delay in delivery is limited to an amount roughly equivalent to 2.5 times the freight payable for the goods delayed.

Whilst dealing with this subject reference should be made to Article 26 which provides that the date of conversion into national currency is the date of judgement or the date agreed upon by the parties.

14.1.6. Article 7 – Application to non-contractual claims

This article extends the carrier's defences and limits of liability to his servants or agents. It also makes clear that the carrier has the right to plead his Hamburg Rules defences and limits even where he is sued in tort rather than contract. In the event of an action being brought against a servant of the carrier and he proves that he acted within the scope of his employment, then he is entitled to avail himself of the defences and limits of liability which the carrier is entitled to invoke under this convention.

14.1.7. Article 8 – Loss of right to limit responsibility

These conditions are similar to those provided in the 1968 Rules except that specific reference to 'delay' is now made.

14.1.8. Article 9 – Deck Cargo

This article stipulates the instances on which the carrier has the right to carry goods on deck. In this respect the carrier shall be entitled to carry the goods on deck only if such carriage is in accordance with an agreement with the shipper or with the usage of the particular trade or is required by statutory rules or regulations.

Where the carrier and the shipper have agreed that the goods shall be carried on deck, the carrier is required to insert a clause to that effect in the bill of lading. In the absence of such a clause the carrier will have the burden of proving that the agreement for carriage on deck had been entered into; however, the carrier would not be entitled to invoke such an agreement against a third party who had acquired the bill of lading in good faith.

The carriage of goods on deck contrary to the express agreement of the shipper would be deemed to be an act or omission of the carrier within the meaning of Article 8.

14.1.9. Article 10 – Liability of the carrier and actual carrier

This is an entirely new provision and therefore no comparison can be made with the Hague-Visby Rules. The effect of this article is to make the actual carrier of the goods an agent of the contracting carrier. This rule also provides that the carrier shall, in relation to the carriage performed by the actual carrier, be responsible for the acts and omissions of the actual carrier and of his servants and agents acting within the scope of their employment. Where and to the extent that both the carrier and the actual carrier are liable their liability is joint and several.

14.1.10. Article 11 – Through carriage

This is also a new rule, there being no similar provision in previous conventions. It will be seen that whereas Article 10 deals with transhipment of cargo carried under ordinary bills of lading, Article 11 covers on-carriage under the 'through' bill of lading where suitable provision is made on the front of the bill of lading for such movement. Where a contract for carriage provides explicitly that a specified part of the carriage shall be performed by a named person other than the carrier, the contract may also provide that the carrier shall not be liable for any loss, damage or delay in delivery due to an occurrence whilst the goods are in the charge of the actual carrier during that part of the carriage. Nevertheless the burden of proving that such loss was caused by such an occurrence rests with the carrier, the actual carrier being responsible in accordance with the provisions of Article 10.

14.1.11. Article 12 – Liability of the shipper: general rule

This article covers the basic responsibility of the shipper similar to the provisions contained in Article 4 of the Hague-Visby Rules whereby the shipper shall not be liable for loss sustained by the carrier or for damage to the ship unless such loss or damage has been caused by the fault or negligence of the shipper, his servants or agents.

14.1.12. Article 13 – Special rules for dangerous cargo

This article is similar to that contained in the Hague-Visby Rules.

14.1.13. Article 14 – Issue of the bill of lading

This article is to some extent an expansion of the Hague-Visby Rules. The carrier shall be obliged to issue to the shipper a bill of lading on demand when the goods are received into the charge of either the carrier or the actual carrier. There is no requirement to issue a bill of lading other than on demand. The article also gives various means by which the bill of lading may be authenticated such as in handwriting, perforation, rubber stamp, symbols or by any other mechanical or electronic means provided it is not inconsistent with the law of the country where the bill of lading is issued.

14.1.14. Article 15 – Contents of the bill of lading

This article sets out a list of particulars to be included in a bill of lading. This includes, among other things, the general nature of the goods, the leading marks necessary for identification of the goods, the number of packages or pieces, *and* (this is very important because under the 1971 Act (Article III(3)) this requirement is in the alternatives) the weight of the goods or their quantity otherwise expressed; all such particulars should be provided by the shipper. However, it should be noted that Article 15(3) provides that the absence of one or more of the particulars listed shall not invalidate the bill of lading. This article also provides that after the goods are loaded on board and *if the shipper so demands* the carrier shall issue to the shipper a 'shipped' bill of lading which in addition to the particulars mentioned above shall state that the goods are on board a named ship and the date or dates of loading. If the carrier has previously issued a bill of lading or other document of title in respect of the goods to the shipper, the shipper shall be required to surrender such document in exchange for a 'shipped' bill of lading. The previously issued document may be amended accordingly. It should also be pointed out that under this article:

> (a) There are fifteen items of particulars which must be included in the bill of lading of which nine are always to be included and the remaining six are to be included only in appropriate circumstances.
>
> (b) Notwithstanding the word 'must' in the first line of the article compliance is not mandatory because of the absence of penalties for failure to comply and indeed Article 15(3) even stipulates that the absence of one or more of the particulars in the bill of lading will not affect the 'legal character' of the document.

14.1.15. Article 16 – Bills of lading: reservations and evidentiary effect

This article provides that if the particulars furnished by the shipper on the bill of lading are thought not actually to represent the goods taken over, or if the carrier has no reasonable means of checking such particulars, he may insert in the bill of lading a reservation specifying these inaccuracies or grounds of suspicion or the absence of reasonable means of checking. Failure to state on the bill of lading the apparent condition of the goods means the carrier is deemed to have noted that the goods are in apparent good condition.

Article 16(3) deals with the evidential value of a bill of lading without reservation and with the exception of two points is the same as under the

Hague-Visby Rules, i.e., that such a bill of lading is *prima facie* evidence of receipt of the goods described except when it has been transferred to a *bona fide* third party, when it becomes conclusive evidence. The two new points are:

(a) The third party is required to have relied upon the statements in the bill of lading.

(b) When referring to a third party the text of the Rules provides that this 'includes a consignee' thus dispelling any doubts as to whether or not a consignee is a third party for the purposes of a contract of carriage.

14.1.16. Article 17 – Guarantees by the shipper

This article provides that the shipper is deemed to have guaranteed to the carrier the accuracy of all the statements made to him for insertion in the bill of lading. The shipper shall indemnify the carrier against all loss resulting from any inaccuracy in such particulars and shall remain liable even if the bill of lading has been transferred by him to a third party.

14.1.17. Article 18 – Documents other than bills of lading

This provides that where a document other than a bill of lading is issued by the carrier it shall be *prima facie* evidence of the taking over of the goods.

14.1.18. Article 19 – Notice of loss, damage or delay

There are three allowable periods stipulated in this article for notice of the general nature of the loss or damage;

(a) For apparent loss or damage notice of the general nature of such loss to be given in writing not later than the working day after the day of delivery.

(b) For loss or damage which is not apparent at the time of delivery, notice has to be given within 15 consecutive days.

(c) Any loss resulting from delay, notice has to be given within 60 days after delivery to the consignee.

The above mentioned periods are substantially greater than those laid down by previous legislation. It will be recalled that the period given under Article III, Rule 6 of the Hague-Visby Rules in respect of non-apparent loss or damage, is within three days of delivery.

The lack of valid notice in the case of apparent or non-apparent damage does not prevent recovery but creates a presumption in favour of the carrier. In the case of delay, lack of valid notice does bar recovery.

14.1.19. Article 20 – Limitation of actions

It is stipulated here that any action relating to the carriage of goods under this convention is time barred if proceedings have not been instituted within a period of two years.

The limitation period commences on the day that the carrier has effected delivery of the goods, but where no goods have been delivered it then commences on the last day on which the goods should have been delivered. In this respect the day on which the period of limitation commences shall not be included in the period.

14.1.20. Article 21 – Jurisdiction

This article, which has no counterpart under the Hague-Visby Rules, lists the places where, at the plaintiff's option, proceedings may be brought under the convention. They are: (a) the principal place of business or the original residence of the defendant; or (b) the place where the contract was made, provided that the defendant has a place of business there; or (c) the port of loading or the port of discharge; or (d) any additional place designated for that purpose in the contract of carriage.

By virtue of paragraph 3 this list is exclusive. Paragraph 2, however, allows action to be brought in any place in a contracting state where proceedings for the arrest of the ship or sister ship have been brought subject to the defendant's right to restore the action to one of the places listed in paragraph 1. Paragraph 5 allows other places to be designated by agreement of the parties after a cause of action has arisen.

The provisions of this paragraph do not constitute an obstacle to the jurisdiction of the contracting States for provisional or protective measures. (Not really known until recently in English law.)

Whereas neither the Hague Rules nor the Hague-Visby Rules contain a jurisdiction provision, the widely drafted jurisdiction clause is found here and, unusually, jurisdiction is conferred on non-contracting States whose courts would not be bound to apply to the convention.

One of the positive aspects of the jurisdiction provision is that it leaves the parties free to agree, after a claim under the contract of carriage has arisen, on a place of their own designation where the action may be instituted.

14.1.21. Article 22 – Arbitration

There are no similar provisions in the Hague-Visby Rules. This article provides that if an arbitration clause is included in a charter-party but there is no similar clause in the bill of lading, then arbitration cannot be invoked against an innocent third party bill of lading holder.

The claimants in a dispute over a contract of carriage are granted the same wide choice in deciding where to bring arbitration proceedings as given in Article 21.

14.1.22. Article 23 – Contractual stipulation

Any stipulation which is not in accordance with this convention shall be null and void. The nullity of such a stipulation shall not affect the validity of the other provisions of the contract of which it forms a part. Further, a clause assigning benefit of insurance of the goods in favour of the carrier or any similar clause shall also be null and void.

The carrier may increase his responsibilities and obligations under this convention. A form of 'Clause Paramount' is required where a bill of lading or other document evidencing the contract of carriage is issued. Where a claimant has incurred loss as a result of a stipulation which is null and void under this article or as a result of the omission of a Clause Paramount, then the carrier must pay compensation to the extent required in order to give the claimant compensation in accordance with the provisions of this convention for any loss of or damage to the goods as well as for delay in delivery.

It will be seen therefore that there is no possibility of contracting out of any of the provisions of the convention and the carrier will be under an obligation to insert a statement to that effect in his bills of lading or other documents evidencing the contract of carriage.

14.1.23 Article 24 – General Average

Nothing in this convention shall prevent the application of provisions in the contract of carriage or national law regarding the adjustment of general average.

In paragraph 2 under this article the carrier will no longer be entitled to a contribution from cargo in general average situations brought about by error in navigation or any of the other matters from which he is exonerated by the Hague or Hague-Visby Rules. This may lead to a change in the structure of insurance and may even affect the institution of general average itself.

14.1.24. Article 25 – Other conventions

This Article (paragraph 1) is similar to Article VIII of the Hague-Visby Rules in so far as it shall not modify the rights or duties of the carrier, the actual carrier or their servants or agents in relation to the limitation of liability of owners of sea-going ships.

However paragraph 3 expands the 1968 Rules (Paragraph IX) and excludes from the convention liability for damage caused by nuclear incident if the operator of a nuclear installation is liable for such damage.

No liability shall arise under the provisions of this convention for any loss of, or damage to, or delay in delivery of luggage when such liability is governed by any international convention or other national law relating to the carriage of passengers and their luggage by sea.

The Article therefore keeps distinct from this convention other conventions with which it might come into conflict, for example, the Athens Convention on the International Carriage of Passengers and their Luggage and the Limitation of Liability Conventions.

14.1.25. Article 26 – Unit of account

The unit of account in this convention is the Special Drawing Right (SDR) as defined by the International Monetary Fund (IMF). Any State which is not a member of the IMF and whose law does not permit the use of the SDR may use the poincaré franc as long as the conversion into the national currency is made in such a manner as to express in the national currency of the state, as far as possible, the same real value for the amounts expressed in the SDRs stipulated in the convention.

14.1.26. Article 30 – Entry into force

This article provides that the convention shall enter into force one year after twenty States have ratified it.

14.1.27. Article 31 – Denunciation of other conventions

This article is necessary in order to phase out the Hague and Hague-Visby Rules once the Hamburg Rules become operational and to minimize the confusion if three separate legal regimes are in action at the same time. Provision is made however for a contracting state to defer denunciation of the Hague and Hague-Visby Rules for a maximum period of five years from the entry into force of this convention.

14.1.28. Article 34 – Denunciation

This article provides that a contracting state may denounce this convention at any time by means of notification in writing.

14.1.29. Annex II

It is stated in this annex that it is the main understanding that the liability of the carrier under this convention is based on the principle of presumed fault or neglect. This means that, as a rule, the burden of proof rests on the carrier, but there are provisions to modify this rule.

14.2. UN Convention on international multimodal transport of goods, 1980

14.2.1. A summary of the provisions

This Convention and the Hamburg Rules will eventually come into force and replace existing legislation, and it is useful to mention them.

This Convention (a Convention binds States, not private persons) was concluded under the auspices of the United Nations Conference on Trade and Development (UNCTAD). It was adopted on 24 May 1980 and will enter into force twelve months after it has been ratified by 30 States. This Convention (which is constructed on similar lines to the Hamburg Rules and has clauses which are similar in content) imposes an agreed system of liability over existing unimodal regimes in order to govern the contractual relation between a consignor and the multimodal transport operator (MTO) for the entire transport of the goods from the time the MTO takes them in charge until delivery, irrespective of the different modes of transport that will be involved.

The Convention has eight parts and contains 40 Articles plus an annex dealing with provisions on Customs matters.

Part	I	Articles	1–4	General provisions
	II		5–13	Documentation
	III		14–21	Liability of the multimodal transport operator
	IV		22–23	Liability of the consignor
	V		24–27	Claims and Actions
	VI		28–31	Supplementary provisions
	VII		32	Customs matters
	VIII		33–40	Final clauses

Article I contains ten definitions. Special mention should be made of the following:

'International multimodal transport' is defined as meaning 'the carriage of goods by at least two different modes of transport on the basis of a multimodal transport contract from a place in one country at which the goods are taken in charge by the MT operator to a place designated for delivery situated in a different country'. Two conditions are therefore necessary; (a) that the goods are carried by two modes of transport and (b) between two different countries.

'Multimodal transport operator' is defined as meaning any person who on his own behalf or through another person acting on his behalf concludes a multimodal transport contract and who acts as a principal, not as an agent, or on behalf of a consignor or of the carriers' participating in the multimodal transport operations and who assumes responsibility for the performance of the contract. In other words the operator may not own or control the modes of transport. He may be a non-vessel operating carrier (NVO), or a non-vessel owning common carrier (NVOCC). The operator may enter into agreements with sub-contractors and it should accordingly be noted that he is a principal acting on his own behalf and not on behalf of others.

'Consignee' is defined as 'the person entitled to take delivery of the goods'.

'Goods' includes any Container, pallet or similar article of transport or packaging, if supplied by the consignor.

'Writing' means *inter alia* telegram or telex.

14.2.2. Article 2 – Scope of application

The provisions of the Convention apply to all contracts of multimodal transport between places in two States provided (a) that the place for the taking in charge of the goods is located in a Contract State or (b) that the place of delivery is located in a Contracting State.

14.2.3. Article 5 – Issue of multimodal transport document

This Article stipulates that the MT document shall be signed by the operator or by a person on his behalf and may be in either negotiable or non-negotiable form at the option of the consignor. This document is to be issued when the operator takes charge of the goods. The signature on the document may be in handwriting, printed in facsimile, perforated, stamped, in symbols or by any other mechanical or electronic means provided that it is not inconsistent with the law of the country where it is issued.

14.2.4. Article 6 – Negotiable multimodal transport document

The legal effect of the negotiable MT document is given here. Delivery of the goods would be made against its production and the operator would be discharged from his obligation by delivering the goods to the person holding it. The document shall be transferable by endorsement if made out to 'order' but endorsement is not required where the MT document is made out to 'bearer'.

14.2.5. Article 7 – Non-negotiable multimodal transport document

The name of the consignee must be indicated where a non-negotiable document is issued and the operator would be discharged from his obligation to deliver when he makes such delivery to the consignee named.

14.2.6. Article 8 – Contents of the multimodal transport document

This follows the lines of Article 15 of the Hamburg Rules on the particulars to be included in the document giving the date or the period of delivery of the goods at the place of delivery, if expressly agreed upon between the parties. This is particularly relevant to Article 16 which makes delay one of the bases of liability. Another provision is that the absence of one or more of the particulars in the document shall not effect the legal character of the MT document.

14.2.7. Article 9 – Reservations in the multimodal document

This Article corresponds with Article 16 of the Hamburg Rules in that it states that the MT operator has the right to insert reservations in the MT document if he has reasonable grounds to suspect the accuracy of the particulars or if he has no reasonable means of checking such particulars, he shall insert a reservation in the document specifying the inaccuracies, the grounds of suspicion or the absence of reasonable means of checking. Failure to make such a note would indicate that the goods were in apparent good condition.

14.2.8. Article 10 – Evidentiary effect of the multimodal document

Under this Article the MT document shall be *prima facie* evidence of the taking in charge of the goods as described and proof to the contrary by the MT operator shall not be admissible if the MT document is issued in negotiable form and has been transferred to a third party, including a consignee, who has relied in good faith on the description of the goods.

14.2.9. Article 11 – Liability for intentional mis-statements or omissions

This Article states that where an operator with intent to defraud gives false information concerning the goods or omits any information from the document, he will lose the right of limitation and be liable for any loss, damage or expenses to a third party, including a consignee who relied on the accuracy of the document. It deals only with the case where there is an intention of fraud and obviously the burden of proof is on the claimant.

14.2.10. Article 12 – Guarantee by the consignor

A consignor shall be deemed to have guaranteed the accuracy of the particulars inserted in the MT document which includes the marks, numbers, weight and quantity and, if applicable, the dangerous nature of the goods, There is no duty on the part of the operator to ensure the accuracy of the particulars. It also states that if the document is transferred, the operator remains liable to the holder of the document and the consignor still remains liable for any loss resulting from inaccuracies of the particulars.

14.2.11. Article 13 – Other documents

The issue of the MT document does not preclude the issue, if necessary, of other documents relating to transport or other services involved in international multimodal transport in accordance with applicable international conventions or national law, and the issue of such other documents shall not affect the legal character of the MT document.

14.2.12. Article 14 – Period of responsibility

This Article deals with the period from the time the MT operator takes the goods in his charge to the time of their delivery. In this article, reference to the MT operator shall include his servants or agents or any other person of whose services he makes use for the performance of the contract. Reference to the consignor or consignee shall also include their servants or agents.

14.2.13. Article 15 – The liability of the multimodal transport operator for his servants, agents and other persons

The operator shall, subject to Article 21, be liable for the acts and omissions of his servants or agents when such servant is acting within the scope of his employment and when such person is acting in performance of the contract.

14.2.14. Article 16 – Basis of liability

The liability of the operator is based on the principle of fault or neglect as he shall be liable for loss resulting from loss of or damage to the goods, as well as from delay in delivery, if the occurrence which caused the loss, damage or delay in delivery took place while the goods were in his charge as defined in Article 14, unless the multimodal transport operator proves that he, his servants or agents or any other person referred to in Article 15 took all measures that could reasonably be required to avoid the occurrence and its consequences. If the goods have not been delivered within 90 days following the date when they should have been delivered then the claimant may treat the goods as lost.

14.2.15. Article 17 – Concurrent causes

Where there are combined faults which produce loss, damage or delay in delivery, the operator shall be liable only for that part which is attributable to his fault or neglect provided he can prove his part which attributed to the loss, damage or delay.

14.2.16. Article 18 – Limitation of liability

The limit is higher than that stipulated in the Hamburg Rules, being 920 units of account per package or other shipping unit or 2.75 units of account (SDRs) per kilogramme of gross weight of the goods lost or damaged. (approx. £704 and £2.10 respectively). This amount will not apply however, if the MT document does not include sea or inland waterways. The liability is then limited to an amount not exceeding 8.33 units of account per kilogramme of gross weight of the goods lost or damaged. The liability for loss resulting from delay according to the provisions of Article 16 shall be limited to an amount equivalent to 2½ times the freight payable for the goods delayed.

14.2.17. Article 19 – Localized damage

This Article deals with loss or damage which has occurred during one particular stage of the multimodal transport in respect of which an applicable international convention or mandatory law provides a higher limit of liability than the limit stipulated in Article 18, then the limit of the MT operator's liability would be determined by reference to the provisions of such convention or mandatory national law.

14.2.18. Article 20 – Non-contractual liability

The defences and limits of liability under this Article shall apply in any action against the operator for loss or damage to the goods whether the action is founded in contract, tort or otherwise. Furthermore, in any action brought against a servant or agent he shall be entitled to avail himself of the defences and limits of liability to which the operator himself would be entitled.

14.2.19. Article 21 – Loss of the right to limit liability

The MT operator would not be entitled to the benefit of the limitation of liability if it is proved that the loss, damage or delay in delivery resulted from an act or omission of the MT operator which was intentional or reckless knowing that such loss would probably result.

14.2.20. Article 22 – Liability of the consignor – General Rule

The consignor would be liable for loss sustained by the operator if caused by his fault or neglect or that of his servants or agents acting within the scope of their employment.

14.2.21. Article 23 – Special rules on dangerous goods

This Article is identical to Article 13 of the Hamburg Rules stipulating that

(a) that the consignor shall mark and label the goods in a suitable manner as dangerous and
(b) inform the operator of the dangerous nature of the goods and if necessary, the precautions to be taken.

Failure to do so will make him liable to the MT operator for all loss resulting from the shipment and the goods may at any time be unloaded, destroyed or rendered innocuous without payment of compensation.

14.2.22. Article 24 – Notice of loss, damage or delay

The notice of any loss or damage shall be given in writing by the consignee indicating the general nature of the loss or the damage not later than the working day after the day 'when the goods were handed over to the consignee'.

Where the loss or damage is not apparent, the consignee must give notice within six consecutive days of delivery to the MT operator. The time for giving notice for loss resulting from delay in delivery is to be given within 60 consecutive days after the day of delivery. Where there has been a joint survey or inspection by the parties concerned, no notice is needed. However, any failure to give timely notice is considered to be *prima facie* evidence that no loss or damage was sustained.

14.2.23. Article 25 – Limitation of actions

Any action under this convention shall be time-barred if judicial or arbitral proceedings have not been instituted within a period of two years. Where notification of a claim is not given in writing within six months starting after the day when the goods are delivered or should have been delivered, the action shall be time-barred at the expiry of this period. During the running of the limitation the period may be extended by a further declaration in writing.

14.2.24. Article 26 – Jurisdiction

In judicial proceedings under this Convention, the Plaintiff, at his option may institute an action in a court according to the law of the state where the court is situated in one of the following places:

1) the principal place of business of the defendant (i.e., the operator); or

2) the place where the contract was made provided the defendant has there a place of business, branch or agency through which the contract was made; or

3) the place of taking the goods in charge or place of delivery; or

4) any other place agreed in the contract or evidenced in the MT document

14.2.25. Article 27 – Arbitration

This Article allows disputes to be referred to arbitration which can be instituted at those places listed in 1–4 under Article 26. Any clause on arbitration which is inconsistent with paras 2 and 3 will be null and void.

14.2.26. Article 29 – General Average

The concept of General Average is still applicable to the sea transport element of the MT contract.

15 General average and particular average

As special reference to this subject is always included in the bill of lading clauses, some explanation may be useful because there is considerable authority to support the principle that General Average exists independently of the contract of carriage.

Average means loss, particular average being applicable to an individual or particular loss such as 'two cases crushed and contents missing'. However, *General Average* refers to circumstances much more serious and affects all the interests connected with the voyage including that of the shipowner.

The definition of particular and general average according to the *Marine Insurance Act* 1906 is 'A particular average loss is a partial loss of the subject matter being insured, caused by a peril insured against, and which is not a general average loss.' 'A general average loss is a loss caused by or directly consequential on a general average act.' It includes a general average expenditure as well as a general average sacrifice. There is a general average act where any extraordinary sacrifice or expenditure is voluntarily and reasonably made or incurred in time of peril for the purpose of preserving the property imperilled in the common adventure.

The origin of General Average dates back to ancient times beyond record, but it is considered to have been in use for over 4000 years and since merchandise has been carried by sea in ships. It formed part of the Rhodian Law and reference to this law is found in the Digest of the Emperor Justinian which decreed that 'if, in order to lighten a ship, merchandise is thrown overboard, that which has been given for all shall be replaced by the contribution of all.'

Although laws were lost and forgotten during the Dark Ages after the fall of the Roman Empire, customs of the sea were remembered and were later formulated in various codes mentioned in the Rolls or Judgments of Oleron which were influential in the foundation of maritime law.

In the case of *Birkley* v *Presgrave* (1801), one of the earliest in which the principle of General Average was recognized, the definition by Mr Justice Lawrence included reference to sacrifices made or expenses incurred for the preservation of ship and cargo, similar to that mentioned in the Digest of Justinian centuries earlier.

In France, a different definition was given in the Ordinance of Louis XIV in 1681 as 'extraordinary expenses incurred and damage suffered, for the common good and safety of the merchandise and the vessel'.

It will be seen that confusion was beginning to arise and accordingly by the middle of the 19th century a movement was begun for a uniform international set of rules to establish exactly what constitutes a General Average act. A conference was held in York in 1864 formulating a set of eleven rules, known as The York Rules, followed in 1877 by another conference in Antwerp using the earlier rules as a basis of discussion, hence the name York-Antwerp Rules. These have been duly revised over the years in 1890, 1924, 1950 and 1974 and General Average is adjusted accordingly.

The York-Antwerp Rules 1974 were adopted by the International Maritime Committee at the Hamburg Conference of April 1974 and consist of lettered (since 1924) and numbered rules, the text of which is given in Appendix D.

General Average is adjusted according to the lettered rules unless otherwise provided in the numbered rules.

Whereas a shipowner has a lien on the cargo at Common Law for its share of General Average, he is also under an obligation to the cargo interests for the goods sacrificed, to ensure that a contribution is made towards their loss. The shipowner advises the shipper and/or the consignee of the circumstances of the causality enclosing copies of the Lloyd's Average Bond and/or Underwriter's Guarantee in respect of the contribution and/or deposit, which are signed by the insurance company concerned before being returned to the Average Adjusters and also before release of the cargo. It will be observed that the security required is in two parts, namely:

(a) The shipper's or consignee's signature to an average bond which is usually on the recommended Lloyd's form and approved by underwriters throughout the world.

(b) A cash deposit or the guarantee of the cargo underwriters or a bank. Guarantees must *not* be accepted for a limited period of time.

The receipt given for deposits should be on the special Lloyd's form and must never be issued in duplicate. The deposit is paid into a special joint bank account usually in the names of the shipowner and the Average Adjusters. See Rule xxii.

The shipowner may insure against any disbursements that might be incurred at a port of refuge and such insurance is effected by a provisional cover at and from the port of refuge to a destination for the estimated amount of the disbursements. The premium which is payable at the time of the original declaration is adjusted when the actual amount is known.

Where cargo is discharged at a port of refuge the shipowner retains his responsibility as bailee and it would be considered as wise for an insurance to be taken out by him on behalf of the cargo interests. This is because of the variation from the original intended voyage and as such the risk is regarded neither as shipowners' liability nor double insurance.

A cargo surveyor is engaged to be in attendance to watch the discharge of the cargo, making a careful note of all packages short delivered or damaged by the General Average act. He also makes recommendations as to the disposal of damaged goods, e.g., whether they should be sold, forwarded, reconditioned or accepted with allowances.

When a General Average adjustment is being prepared by the adjusters many supporting documents have to be submitted. These include the manifest of all cargo on board at the time of the incident, an example of the type of bill of lading issued, the signed average bonds and guarantees or deposit receipt counterfoils together with log books, surveyors' reports, accounts for repairs and any other relevant papers.

16 The carriage of dangerous goods

The shipment of all dangerous goods by sea from the United Kingdom, including roll on/roll off ferry services, is governed by The Merchant Shipping (Dangerous Goods) Regulations 1981, which are enforceable by law. They refer to detailed requirements in two publications, the International Maritime Dangerous Goods (IMDG) Code and minimum ancillary or alternative recommendations for the Carriage of Dangerous Goods in Ships; Report of the Standing Advisory Committee 1978 – The *Blue Book*.

The rules lay down that the shipment of dangerous goods must comply with the legal requirements in respect of description, classification, packing, marking and labelling of all such cargo sent forward for shipment by sea. The Blue Book is obtainable from HMSO and the IMDG Code from the International Maritime Organization (IMO). Comprehensive information is also provided by national and international organizations in official publications which contain the regulations and recommendations according to the mode of transport listed below, and it is important that exporters ensure that they have complied with all these requirements to avoid penalties for non-compliance.

16.1. Transport by road

This is governed by the European Agreement for the International Carriage of Dangerous Goods by Road (ADR). The international transport of dangerous goods by road in Europe is subject to these provisions. In addition to the United Kingdom, the contracting countries include Austria, Belgium, Denmark, Finland, France, Federal German Republic, German Democratic Republic, Hungary, Italy, Luxembourg, the Netherlands, Norway, Poland, Portugal, Spain, Sweden, Switzerland and Yugoslavia. The Republic of Ireland is not a contracting party to the ADR convention. The ADR agreement is obtainable from HMSO.

16.2. Transport by rail

This is governed by Annex 1 (RID) to the International Convention concerning the Carriage of Goods by Rail (CIM). The international carriage of dangerous goods by rail is subject to the provisions of RID which has been signed by 33 and ratified by 24 countries in Europe, the Middle East and North Africa. RID can also be obtained from HMSO.

16.3. Air

The Air Navigation Order 1976, Article 41, enacts the requirements of IATA in the United Kingdom legislation. The body has not yet adopted the United Nations recommendations and, therefore, the Dangerous Goods Note is not to be used for dangerous goods sent by air.

Although both road and rail consignment notes make provision for information about dangerous goods, an additional IMO declaration is needed by ferry operators to cover the sea leg of the journey. As the road (CMR) and rail (CIM) notes are usually completed by the carrier or an intermediate freight forwarder, there is the need for a back-up document to substantiate statements about dangerous goods made on behalf of the exporter.

In the UK the SITPRO Dangerous Goods Note (DGN) (Appendix O) which has replaced the Dangerous Goods Declaration combines the documentary functions of the Application for Stowage Space; Dangerous Goods Declaration; Special Stowage Order; Container/Vehicle Packing Certificate; Back-up document for forwarder/haulier equivalent to the FIATA form, STD, the Shippers Declaration for the Transport of Dangerous Goods; and Standard Shipping Note.

16.4. Responsibility for preparation

Under the regulations and recommendations mentioned earlier, the shipper/exporter must provide the carrier with specific information about the goods in a written declaration. Where goods are purchased on Ex-works, Free on Truck, Free on Rail, Free Alongside, Free on Board or Free Carrier terms, the seller and buyer must agree on who is to prepare and sign the DGN as shipper.

16.5. Container/Vehicle Packing Certificate

A Container Packing Certificate which is included in the DGN is a legal requirement under the Merchant Shipping (Dangerous Goods) Regulations 1981, as currently amended, when goods are exported as full container loads. The IMDG Code defines 'freight containers' as including containers loaded on chassis. An amendment to this code recommends the use of Container/Vehicle Packing Certificates for both trailers and rigid vehicles. A separate certificate is required for each container/vehicle, which must be signed by the person responsible for the packing.

16.6. Transport emergency information

The legal requirements for the provision of transport emergency information vary according to the mode of transport and sometimes country of destination. At present, national legislation in, for example, Scandinavian countries and the Netherlands, requires the shipper to provide full emergency instructions. ADR and RID also require written information on action to be taken in the event of an emergency. The Proposals for Dangerous Substances (Conveyance by Road) Regulations, which will rationalize existing United Kingdom domestic transport legislation, will also include a requirement for information in writing. However, exporters regularly dispatching the same goods by the same carriers may, by agreement, not need to provide emergency instructions for each consignment.

Emergency procedures for ships carrying dangerous goods are shortly to be incorporated in the IMDG Code so that it will be possible to establish immediately from the standard classification on the Dangerous Goods Shipping Note the appropriate action to be taken in the event of an incident.

The National Dangerous Goods Shipping Note has been designed to take into account the revised customs procedures laid down in the new export strategy introduced on the 1st October 1981.

16.7. Bulk tank shipments

Where dangerous goods are conveyed in road tank vehicles or tank containers, the operator or owner of the equipment must be in possession of a valid certificate for the tank issued in accordance with the requirements of the competent authority. Detailed information is provided in Annexes 1 and 2 to the *Blue Book* and the IMDG Code, or it can be obtained from the Department of Trade and Industry.

16.8. HM Customs

The DGN is approved by HM Customs for use as a pre-shipment document where the Simplified Clearance Procedure (SCP), effective from 1st October 1981, is used. In these circumstances, one copy of the DGN will be required and retained by Customs at the place of clearance for subsequent forwarding to their statistical office.

For further guidance on this subject, the reader is directed to the SITPRO publication *Dangerous Goods Documentation 1981* from which the above extracts have been taken with their kind permission.

16.9. Classes of dangerous cargo

There are nine classes of dangerous cargo, and a separate declaration must be completed for each class as follows:

16.9.1. *Class 1 – Explosives*

This class is divided into five divisions. British ships loading explosives do so under the *Blue Book* provisions.

16.9.2. *Class 2 – Gases*

16.9.3. *Class 3 – Inflammable liquids*

This class has three subdivisions:

    3.1. Low flash point, F.P. below −18°C.
    3.2. Intermediate flash point, F.P. −18°C up to but not including 23°C.
    3.3. High flash point, F.P. 23°C up to and including 61°C.

16.9.4. *Class 4 – Inflammable solids and substances*

This class has three subdivisions:

    4.1. Inflammable solids.
    4.2. Substances liable to spontaneous combustion.
    4.3. Substances emitting inflammable gases when wet.

16.9.5. Class 5 – Oxidizing substances

This class has two subdivisions:

 5.1. Oxidizing substances (agents).
 5.2. Organic peroxides.

16.9.6. Class 6 – Poisons and infectious substances

This class has two subdivisions:

 6.1. Poisons (toxic substances).
 6.2. Infectious substances.

16.9.7. Class 7 – Radioactive substances

16.9.8. Class 8 – Corrosives

16.9.9. Class 9 – Miscellaneous dangerous substances

16.9.10. Class 10 – Marine pollutants

Classes 1–9 also include marine pollutants, which must be declared whatever class they may be.

The meaning of terms and abbreviations

ABCC	Association of the British Chambers of Commerce.
Act of God	Any accident due to natural causes, without human intervention which could not have been prevented by foresight and care.
Ad valorem	In proportion to the value.
Ad valorem duty	A duty based upon the value of the goods.
Ad valorem freight	Freight chargeable on the value of the goods, and not on weight or measurement.
ADR	European agreement for the international carriage of dangerous goods.
Agent	One who transacts business on behalf of a principal.
AIMS	American Institute of Merchant Shipping.
Arbitration	Process whereby contending parties mutually appoint a person (arbiter) to settle a dispute in order to avoid going to law.
BAF	Bunker Adjustment Factor.
Bailee	A person (or firm) responsible for goods whilst in his care.
Bill of sight	A customs import form used when the importer is unable to make a complete entry. A Customs Officer opens and 'sights' the goods and the information thus provided enables a normal entry to be made.
B/L – Bill of lading (house)	A document of carriage issued by a forwarding agent to his principal or a domestic document between two ocean carriers where they are carrying each other's cargo.
B/L – Bill of lading (ship)	A receipt for goods either received for shipment or shipped on board a named vessel. A document of title and evidence of the contract of carriage.
BIMCO	Baltic and International Maritime Conference.
Blue Book	Government publication covering the rules for carriage of dangerous goods and explosives by sea.
Bonded goods	Imported (dutiable) goods accommodated in a Customs bonded warehouse until the duty on them has been paid.

Break bulk cargo	Cargo consisting of individual packages stowed in a 'conventional ship'.
Broken stowage	Space lost in stowing packages of irregular shape.
Broker	An agent employed as an intermediary to negotiate a business contract, or in the case of insurance to effect a contract of insurance with underwriters.
Brokerage	The reward on a percentage basis paid to a broker for his services.
BS	Bunker Surcharge.
BSC	British Shippers' Council.
BSI	British Standards Institution.
Bulk cargo	Commodity which is carried loose, e.g., grain, oil, ore, coal.
Bulkhead	A transverse underdeck construction of steel plates, capable of withstanding great strain, forming watertight compartments.
Bunker	That part of a ship set aside for the storing of fuel for use on the voyage.
CAACE	Committee of Shipowners' Associations of the European Community. (Comité des Associations d'Armateurs des Communautés Européennes).
CAF	Currency Adjustment Factor.
CAP	Common Agricultural Policy (of the EEC).
Cargo	The general name for goods carried on board a trading vessel.
CBI	Confederation of British Industries.
CCC	Customs Co-operation Council.
CCCN	Customs Co-operation Council Nomenclature (formerly BTN).
CENSA	Council of European and Japanese National Shipowners' Associations.
Certificate of origin	Document certifying the country of origin of goods. Normally signed by a Chamber of Commerce or Embassy.
C & F	Cost and Freight.
Charter-party	A contract made between a shipowner and a charterer for the hire of a ship, or part of her, for a certain specified period of time or voyage at an agreed rate; known as hire money.
C & I	Cost and Insurance.
CIF	Cost, Insurance and Freight.
CIM (Convention Internationale concernant le transport de Marchandises par chemin de fer)	International convention applied by 19 European railways setting out conditions for the international carriage of goods by railway.
Claused bill of lading	An endorsement to the effect that the goods or part thereof are not in good order, i.e., damaged, indadequately packed etc.

Clearance	Goods –	Satisfying HM Customs formalities.
	Ships –	Before a vessel can load outward cargo she must be 'cleared inward' by Customs who, after rummaging the holds etc., issue a certificate known as a Jerque Note which also shows the quantity of dutiable goods left on board under official seal.
CMI		Comité Maritime International.
CMR (Convention relative au contrat de transport international des Marchandises par vois de Route)		International convention for the international carriage of goods by road.
Combined transport bill of lading		A document issued by a Combined Transport Operator (CTO) for the carriage of goods by at least two modes of transport.
Conference system		A conference is an association of liner shipowners operating in the same trade who agree to abide by a set of regulations, and to quote the same rates of freight, to the mutual benefit of shippers and themselves.
Consign		To forward goods from one place to another.
Consignment		Goods in transit to a named destination.
Consignment note		Document used to consign goods.
Consignee		The person to whom goods are sent; the Receiver.
Consignor		The sender of goods; the shipper or his agent.
Consul		A Government Commercial representative appointed to reside in a foreign country to facilitate and protect the commercial relation with his own country.
Contraband		The import or export of prohibited or dutiable goods.
Contract		Involves an offer and an acceptance. Contracts are normally but not necessarily confirmed in writing.
Conventional cargo		Cargo not carried in containers, flats, etc., but stowed in normal packages.
Cooperage		The repairing of casks or the services of a cooper in repairing damaged cargo. Also the opening of cargo for Customs examination and repacking.
CPT		Customs New Import Entry Processing System.
CRN		Customs Registered Number. A system to assist HM Government in the publication of accurate trade statistics. It replaced the Customs Assigned Number (CAN) in October 1981).
CTO		Combined Transport Operator.

Customs entry		Document rendered to obtain Customs clearance on imported goods or to satisfy Customs requirements on exported goods.
Deadfreight		Space booked by a shipper or charterer but not used.
Deck cargo		Cargo shipped on the open deck.
Delivery order		The written authority to deliver goods etc., to a named party in exchange for the bill of lading.
Depot charges	Exports –	An amount for receiving cargo and stowing into a groupage unit.
	Imports –	An amount for receiving a loaded groupage unit and subsequent delivery to motor vehicle for transport to final destination.
Demurrage		Compensation payable for delay to ships, motor vehicles, wagons, containers, etc., beyond a stipulated free period.
Despatch		Reward payable to the shipper or charterer for time saved; the opposite of demurrage.
DGN		Dangerous goods note.
Dock dues		A toll charged on vessels and goods entering or leaving a dock. Raised as revenue to pay for dock maintenance etc.
Dock receipt		Receipt for cargo delivered for shipment.
DoE		Department of the Environment.
DTI		Department of Trade and Industry.
Drawback		Repayment of duty by HM Customs upon the re-export of certain goods which paid duty on import.
Dunnage		Material, usually planking and mats etc., to facilitate the stowage of cargo.
Duty deferment		EEC system permitting the deferred payment of Customs duties for an agreed period, against acceptable guarantees.
ECE		Economic Commission for Europe (UN).
ECGD		Export Credits Guarantee Department.
EDI		Electronic Data Interchange.
EEC		European Economic Community.
Eur Form		An EEC document used by the twelve member countries as a movement certificate to countries who have a Free Trade Association Agreement with the EEC.
Excise		Tax levied by Customs on certain classes of goods produced in this country, e.g., whisky.
Export licence		Document issued by the Government giving permission to export certain controlled goods.

Ex-quay	Selling price includes all charges up to goods being landed on the quay for sellers account. The buyer is responsible for charges after delivery on quay.
Ex-ship	Selling price includes all charges up to port of discharge. All landing and other costs are charged to the account of the purchaser.
Ex-works	Selling price includes all charges up to the manufacturers' collection point. Does not include insurance, freight or transport charges.
FAK	A system whereby freight is not charged in accordance with a commodity tariff, i.e., a flat rate system (freight all kinds).
FAS	Free alongside.
FBL	Freight forwarders combined transport bill of lading.
FCL	Full container load. A container loaded to capacity by one shipper and for his account.
FCL/LCL	Container movement whereby the packing is charged to the account of the merchant and the stripping is to the carrier.
FCR	Freight Forwarders Certificate of Receipt. The forwarding agent's own through document for goods.
Feeder vessel	A container ship used in short sea trades to serve ports at which the ocean vessel does not call.
FIATA	The International Federation of Forwarding Agents Associations.
FIO	Free in and out. The charterer, shipper or consignee pays for the cost of loading and discharge of the cargo.
FIOS	Free in and out and stowed. The charterer, shipper or consignee pays for the cost of loading, discharge and stowage of the cargo.
Flotsam	When cargo is jettisoned, that which floats is termed flotsam.
FOB	Free on board. The shipper/exporter pays all charges excluding freight and insurance which is paid by the consignee. On the continent it is customary for some additional charges to be paid by the consignee.
Freightliner	The name first employed by British Rail for their container hauling operation. This expression is now used by railways generally to denote fast overland container movement.
Freight tonne (F/T)	The weight or measurement of cargo on which the freight is calculated. A weight

	tonne equals 1000 kilo and a measurement tonne equals one cubic metre (M3).
FRT (Freight)	The amount due or paid for the carriage of cargo.
Full and down	A ship is said to 'full and down' when she is cubically full, and down to her plimsoll mark, i.e., her cargo is a perfect combination of weight and measurement.
GATT	General Agreement of Tariffs and Trade.
G/A (General Average)	There is a general average act when any extraordinary sacrifice or expenditure is voluntarily or reasonably made or incurred in time of peril for the purpose of preserving the property imperilled, e.g., if a ship goes aground and is in danger of sinking and the cargo has to be thrown overboard to refloat her, the expenditure and loss incurred is a general average sacrifice, to which both the ship and all the cargo owners contribute.
GCBS	General Council of British Shipping.
Gold Clause Agreement	An agreement drawn up by the British Maritime Law Association in 1950 between shipowners and insurance interests whereby the shipowners' liability of £100 per package/unit in the Hague Rules was increased to £200 due to the depreciation in the value of currency. The time limit for claims was also increased. By an amended agreement, the amount increased to £400 per package/unit for contracts subject to the Hague and Hague-Visby Rules dated on or after 1st July 1977. Now considered redundant.
Groupage	Assembly of different consignments for forwarding together as one unit.
GRT (gross registered tons/ tonnage	The total internal space of a ship measured in units of 100 cubic feet.
IAPH	International Association of Ports and Harbours.
IATA	International Air Transport Association.
ICB	International Container Bureau.
ICC	International Chamber of Commerce.
ICD	Inland Clearance Depot.
ICHCA	International Cargo Handling Co-ordination Association.
ICS	International Chamber of Shipping.
ICWP	Inter-Conference Working Party.
IFF	Institute of Freight Forwarders.
IMO	International Maritime Organization.

IMDG	International Maritime Dangerous Goods Code.
Incoterms	A list of standard trade terms for use in foreign trade and compiled in 1953 by the International Chamber of Commerce (ICC). Revised March 1980.
Indemnity	A document usually countersigned by a bank indemnifying the shipowner/carrier against all consequences arising from certain acts, e.g., the issue of a duplicate set of bills of lading or the release of cargo without the production of bills of lading.
Inherent vice	Inherent inability of cargo to withstand the ordinary incidents of a voyage, i.e., a defect caused by the nature of the commodity. In cargo the shipowner is not responsible.
INSA	International Shipowners Association – Gdynia.
Inward charges	Pilotage and other expenses incurred in entering a port.
IPG	Inter-Governmental Preparatory Group on a Convention for International Multimodal transport.
IRU	International Road Transport Union.
ISF	International Shipping Federation.
ISO	International Standards Organization.
ITI convention	Convention of International Transit of Goods.
JCCC	Joint Customs Consultative Committee.
Jerque note	A certificate issued by a Customs officer stating that all cargo reported has been discharged.
Jetsam	Cargo which, after being jettisoned, is eventually washed ashore.
Jettison	The voluntary throwing overboard of goods or ship's stores in time of peril in order to save the vessel.
kg/kilo	Kilogramme. Unit of weight in the metric system equal to 2.2046 lb.
Lay days	A chartering term meaning the number of days agreed for loading and discharging.
Land bridge	Part of a container routeing involving several modes of transport including an overland movement from port to port.
L/C	Letter of Credit. The basis of international trade by means of which payment is made against surrender of specified documents.
LCL	Less than a full container load. A container holding several different consignments from various shippers.
LCL/FCL	Container movement whereby the

	packing is charged to the account of the carrier and stripping to the account of the goods.
LCL/LCL	Container movement where the packing and stripping is charged to the account of the carrier.
Letter of Indemnity	A document usually countersigned by a bank indemnifying the shipowners against all consequences arising from the issue of a duplicate set of bills of lading, or the release of cargo without the production of bills of lading.
Lien	The right to detain cargo against the satisfaction of a claim, usually for unpaid freight or other charges.
Light dues	Dues paid to Trinity House for the purpose of maintaining lighthouses, lightships and buoys.
Lighterage	Charges made for the use of lighters (barges).
Liner	A vessel belonging to a recognized 'Line' of owners, in a regular trade sailing on advertised dates.
Liner terms	Essential point is that the freight rate includes the cost of loading or discharging the vessel.
Lloyds Register of Shipping	A ship classification society whose function is to maintain standards of construction and maintenance in merchant vessels. They publish an annual 'Register' containing detailed technical information on the world's merchant fleet.
Lump sum freight	A single payment to cover the hire of a vessel or part thereof irrespective of the amount of cargo loaded.
Manifest	A list of cargo loaded on board a ship which gives details of shipper, consignee, marks, numbers, description of packages, etc., and sometimes freight and other charges either paid or collectable.
Movement certificate	A document issued by the exporting country certifying the origin and status of the goods for Customs purposes.
M/R (mate's receipt)	Document signed by the Chief Officer acknowledging the receipt of cargo on board ship, later exchanged for a bill of lading.
Multi-stop	A container movement where more than one packing/stripping place is involved.
m.v.	Motor vessel.
Note of protest	Declaration made by the Master of a vessel before a Notary Public when the vessel has experienced bad weather and

	the Master fears damage from the perils of the sea.
Not negotiable	Cannot be transferred to any other person with the same rights as held by the original owner.
NPC	National Ports Council.
NRT	Nett Registered Tons/Tonnage. The measurement of the enclosed spaces of a ship, except those allocated for navigation, machinery, crew, stores, etc. Measured in units of 100 cubic feet.
NSSN	National Standard Shipping Note. Document in six parts which accompanies cargo to the docks. (See Shipping Note.)
NVOCC	Non-vessel owning common carrier. Usually a forwarding agent issuing a 'house' bill of lading.
OCN	Out of Charge Note. Indicates that goods are clear of Customs.
OCTI	Central Office for International Railway Transport.
OECD	Organization for Economic Co-operation and Development.
Particular Average	Partial loss or damage to cargo caused by an insured risk.
P & I (Protection & Indemnity Association	Known as P and I Clubs and collections of shipowners who come together to share amongst themselves and create their own insurance against what may be described in summary as their third party liabilities.
Pilotage	The act of employing a pilot and the cost of his services.
Port dues	Dues levied by a Port Authority on all vessels entering or leaving the port, usually based on the ship's Gross Register Tonnage.
Prepaid	Paid in advance, e.g., before a service is given or before goods are handed over.
Pratique	Permission to enter a port given by the Port Health Authorities when a vessel has been cleared of quarantine restrictions.
QED	Quicker Export Documentation. A term used by Customs.
Quotation	An offer to perform a service at stated rates.
Rebate	Deduction or discount made from a basic charge.
Report (ship's inward)	Customs document which must be completed and lodged with the Customs for each vessel by the owner or agent before discharge can begin. Normally lists cargo on board, details of vessel, voyage, crew, passengers, etc.

RHA	Road Haulage Association.
RID (réglement International Concernant Le Transport Des Merchandises Dangereuses (Par Chemin De Fer))	International Regulation concerning the transport of dangerous goods (by rail).
RKT	The official German Road Transport Tariff, Reichskraftverkehrstrif.
ROB	Remaining on Board.
RO/RO (roll on roll off)	A vessel having facility for shipping lorries, trailers, etc., without need for cranes.
SCP	Simplified (Customs) Clearance Procedure. All exports after 1st October 1981 are subject to pre-shipment documentation, i.e., Standard Shipping Note or Dangerous Goods Note. Dutiable or restricted goods must still be pre-entered on the appropriate Customs form.
SDR	Special Drawing Rights. Is a unit of account as defined by the International Monetary Fund and is the mean of a selection of currencies designed to 'iron out' currency exchange fluctuations in international currency valuations.
Shipping note	A six part document which accompanies cargo to the docks, one copy of which is used as evidence that the goods have been loaded on board.
Ship's papers	Collective term covering documentation including certificate of registry, clearance certificate, bills of lading, etc., in order to comply with Statutory (International) Regulations.
Short shipment	Goods shut-out of a vessel usually through lack of space or late arrival, are said to be short-shipped.
Shut out	Goods which arrive too late for a vessel or are not loaded because the vessel has a full cargo.
SITC	Standard International Trade Classification.
SITPRO Board	Simplification of International Trade Procedures Board.
SOL	Shipowner's liability.
Sous palan ou sous vergues	A French expression meaning that discharge will be made 'under ship's derrick'; 'under ship's tackle'; 'under ship's slings'; 'over ship's side'; 'at ship's rail'.
Stevedore	The labour engaged to stow cargo on board ship.
Stowage factor	The cubic space occupied by one tonne (1000 kg) of cargo.

Stowage plan	A plan of the vessel showing where all the cargo is stowed.
Stuffing	Packing container units.
Surcharge	A temporary addition to a normal tariff charge, e.g., currency, bunker or port congestion surcharge.
Tally	A record taken of the number of packages delivered to or from a vessel, vehicle, warehouse or unit.
T form	EEC document used by the twelve member countries as a movement certificate certifying the origin and status of goods for Customs purposes and/or a transit document covering the movement of goods over one or more national boundaries.
Tariff	A list of rates and conditions for services, taxes, etc., e.g., freight, stevedoring and HM Customs.
TIR	Transport International Routier.
Total loss	(1) Actual total loss occurs where the subject matter is totally destroyed or so damaged as to cease to be a thing of the kind insured, or where the assured is irretrievably deprived thereof.
	(2) A constructive total loss occurs where the subject matter could not be preserved from being totally lost without an expenditure which would exceed its value when the expenditure had been incurred.
Tramp	A tramp vessel is one used to carry cargo from one port to another, seeking such wherever it is available, in contrast to a Liner which usually traverses a definite route, sailing on specified dates.
Transhipment	Cargo passing out from an import vessel to an export vessel.
TREMCARD	Transport Road Emergency Card (Dangerous Goods).
UIC (Union Internationale des Chemins de Fer)	International Union of Railways.
UNCTAD	United Nations Conference on Trade and Development.
UNCITRAL	United Nations Commission on International Trade Law.
Ullage	The difference between the total capacity and the actual content of a cask or package. In a tank container it is the free space allowed for expansion of a liquid; usually about 5% of the total capacity.
VDR	Verbank Deutscher Reeder (German Shipowners' Association).
Waybill (sea)	A non-negotiable document used as an

alternative to a negotiable bill of lading when all the facilities of a bill of lading are not required and when the owner of the goods does not wish to retain title to them. Waybills are made out to a named consignee and cannot be drawn to 'order'.

WHO   World Health Organization.

Appendix A The *Carriage of Goods by Sea Act 1924*

The Hague Rules

Rules relating to bills of lading

Article I.

Definitions.

In these Rules the following expressions have the meanings hereby assigned to them respectively, that is to say –

- (*a*) 'Carrier' includes the owner or the charterer who enters into a contract of carriage with a shipper:
- (*b*) 'Contract of carriage' applies only to contracts of carriage covered by a bill of lading or any similar document of title, in so far as such a document relates to the carriage of goods by sea, including any bill of lading or any similar document as aforesaid issued under or pursuant to a charterparty from the moment at which such bill of lading or similar document of title regulates the relations between a carrier and a holder of the same:
- (*c*) 'Goods' includes goods, wares, merchandises, and articles of every kind whatsoever, except live animals and cargo which by the contract of carriage is stated as being carried on deck and is so carried:
- (*d*) 'Ship' means any vessel used for the carriage of goods by sea:
- (*e*) 'Carriage of goods' covers the period from the time when the goods are loaded on to the time when they are discharged from the ship.

Article II.

Risks.

Subject to the provisions of Article VI., under every contract of carriage of goods by sea the carrier, in relation to the loading, handling, stowage, carriage, custody, care, and discharge of such goods, shall be subject to the responsibilities and liabilities, and entitled to the rights and immunities hereinafter set forth.

Article III.

Responsibilities and liabilities.

1. The carrier shall be bound, before and at the beginning of the voyage, to exercise due diligence to –

- (*a*) Make the ship seaworthy:
- (*b*) Properly man, equip, and supply the ship:
- (*c*) Make the holds, refrigerating and cool chambers, and all other parts of the ship in which goods are carried, fit and safe for their reception, carriage and preservation.

2. Subject to the provisions of Article IV., the carrier shall properly and carefully load, handle, stow, carry, keep, care for and discharge the goods carried.

3. After receiving the goods into his charge, the carrier, or the master or agent of the carrier, shall on demand of the shipper, issue to the shipper a bill of lading showing among other things –

(a) The leading marks necessary for identification of the goods as the same are furnished in writing by the shipper before the loading of such goods starts, provided such marks are stamped or otherwise shown clearly upon the goods if uncovered, or on the cases or coverings in which goods are contained, in such a manner as should ordinarily remain legible until the end of the voyage;

(b) Either the number of packages or pieces, or the quantity, or weight as the case may be, as furnished in writing by the shipper;

(c) The apparent order and condition of the goods:

Provided that no carrier, master or agent of the carrier, shall be bound to state or show in the bill of lading any marks, number, quantity, or weight which he has reasonable ground for suspecting not accurately to represent the goods actually received, or which he has had no reasonable means of checking.

4. Such a bill of lading shall be *prima facie* evidence of the receipt by the carrier of the goods as therein described in accordance with paragraph 3(a), (b) and (c).

5. The shipper shall be deemed to have guaranteed to the carrier the accuracy at the time of shipment of the marks, number, quantity, and weight, as furnished by him, and the shipper shall indemnify the carrier against all loss, damages, and expenses arising or resulting from inaccuracies in such particulars. The right of the carrier to such indemnity shall in no way limit his responsibility and liability under the contract of carriage to any person other than the shipper.

6. Unless notice of loss or damage and the general nature of such damage be given in writing to the carrier or his agent at the port of discharge before or at the time of the removal of the goods into the custody of the person entitled to delivery thereof under the contract of carriage, or, if the loss or damage be not apparent, within three days, such removal shall be *prima facie* evidence of the delivery by the carrier of the goods as described in the bill of lading.

The notice in writing need not be given if the state of the goods has at the time of their receipt been the subject of joint survey or inspection.

In any event the carrier and the ship shall be discharged from all liability in respect of loss or damage unless suit is brought within one year after delivery of the goods or the date when the goods should have been delivered.

In the case of any actual or apprehended loss or damage the carrier and the receiver shall give all reasonable facilities to each other for inspecting and tallying the goods.

7. After the goods are loaded the bill of lading to be issued by the carrier, master or agent of the carrier, to the shipper shall, if the shipper so demands, be a 'shipped' bill of lading, provided that if the shipper shall have previously taken up any document of title to such goods, he shall surrender the same as against the issue of the 'shipped' bill of lading, but at the option of the carrier such document of title may be noted at the port of shipment by the carrier, master, or agent with the name or names of the ship or ships upon which the goods have been shipped and the date or dates of shipment, and when so noted the same shall for the purposes of this Article be deemed to constitute a 'shipped' bill of lading.

8. Any clause, covenant or agreement in a contract of carriage relieving

the carrier or the ship from liability for loss or damage to or in connection with goods arising from negligence, fault or failure in the duties or obligations provided in this Article or lessening such liability otherwise than as provided in these Rules, shall be null and void and of no effect.

A benefit of insurance of similar clause shall be deemed to be a clause relieving the carrier from liability.

Article IV.

Rights and immunities.

1. Neither the carrier nor the ship shall be liable for loss or damage arising or resulting from unseaworthiness unless caused by want of due diligence on the part of the carrier to make the ship seaworthy, and to secure that the ship is properly manned, equipped and supplied, and to make the holds, refrigerating and cool chambers and all other parts of the ship in which goods are carried fit and safe for their reception, carriage and preservation in accordance with the provisions of paragraph 1 of Article III.

Whenever loss or damage has resulted from unseaworthiness, the burden of proving the exercise of due diligence shall be on the carrier or other person claiming exemption under this section.

2. Neither the carrier nor the ship shall be responsible for loss or damage arising or resulting from –

(a) Act, neglect, or default of the master, mariner, pilot, or the servants of the carrier in the navigation or in the management of the ship:

(b) Fire, unless caused by the actual fault or privity of the carrier:

(c) Perils, dangers and accidents of the sea or other navigable waters:

(d) Act of God:

(e) Act of war:

(f) Act of public enemies:

(g) Arrest or restraint of princes, rulers or people, or seizure under legal process:

(h) Quarantine restrictions:

(i) Act or omission of the shipper or owner of the goods, his agent or representative:

(j) Strikes or lock-outs or stoppage or restraint of labour from whatever cause, whether partial or general:

(k) Riots and civil commotions:

(l) Saving or attempting to save life or property at sea:

(m) Wastage in bulk or weight or any other loss or damage, arising from inherent defect, quality, or vice of the goods:

(n) Insufficiency of packing:

(o) Insufficiency or inadequacy of marks:

(p) Latent defects not discoverable by due diligence:

(q) Any other cause arising without the actual fault or privity of the carrier, or without the fault or neglect of the agents or servants of the carrier, but the burden of proof shall be on the person claiming the benefit of this exception to show that neither the actual fault or privity of the carrier nor the fault or neglect of the agents or servants of the carrier contributed to the loss or damage.

3. The shipper shall not be responsible for loss or damage sustained by the carrier or the ship arising or resulting from any cause without the act, fault or neglect of the shipper, his agents or his servants.

4. Any deviation in saving or attempting to save life or property at sea, or any reasonable deviation shall not be deemed to be an infringement or

breach of these Rules or of the contract of carriage, and the carrier shall not be liable for any loss or damage resulting therefrom.

5. Neither the carrier nor the ship shall in any event be or become liable for any loss or damage to or in connection with goods in an amount exceeding £100 per package or unit, or the equivalent of that sum in other currency, unless the nature and value of such goods have been declared by the shipper before shipment and inserted in the bill of lading.

This declaration if embodied in the bill of lading shall be *prima facie* evidence, but shall not be binding or conclusive on the carrier.

By agreement between the carrier, master or agent of the carrier and the shipper another maximum amount than that mentioned in this paragraph may be fixed, provided that such maximum shall not be less than the figure above named.

Neither the carrier nor the ship shall be responsible in any event for loss or damage to or in connection with goods if the nature or value thereof has been knowingly mis-stated by the shipper in the bill of lading.

6. Goods of an inflammable, explosive or dangerous nature to the shipment whereof the carrier, master or agent of the carrier, has not consented, with knowledge of their nature and character, may at any time before discharge be landed at any place or destroyed or rendered innocuous by the carrier without compensation, and the shipper of such goods shall be liable for all damages and expenses directly or indirectly arising out of or resulting from such shipment.

If any such goods shipped with such knowledge and consent shall become a danger to the ship or cargo, they may in like manner be landed at any place or destroyed or rendered innocuous by the carrier without liability on the part of the carrier except to general average, if any.

Article V.

Surrender of rights and immunities, and increase of responsibilities and liabilities.

A carrier shall be at liberty to surrender in whole or in part all or any of his rights and immunities or to increase any of his responsibilities and liabilities under the Rules contained in any of these Articles, provided such surrender or increase shall be embodied in the bill of lading issued to the shipper.

The provisions of these Rules shall not be applicable to charter-parties, but if bills of lading are issued in the case of a ship under a charter-party they shall comply with the terms of these Rules. Nothing in these Rules shall be held to prevent the insertion in a bill of lading of any lawful provision regarding general average.

Article VI.

Special conditions.

Notwithstanding the provisions of the preceding Articles, a carrier, master or agent of the carrier, and a shipper shall in regard to any particular goods be at liberty to enter into any agreement in any terms as to the responsibility and liability of the carrier for such goods, and as to the rights and immunities of the carrier in respect of such goods, or his obligation as to seaworthiness, so far as this stipulation is not contrary to public policy, or the care or diligence of his servants or agents in regard to the loading, handling, stowage, carriage, custody, care, and discharge of the goods carried by sea, provided that in this case no bill of lading has been or shall be issued and that the terms agreed shall be embodied in a receipt which shall be a non-negotiable document and shall be marked as such.

Any agreement so entered into shall have full legal effect:

Provided that this Article shall not apply to ordinary commercial shipments made in the ordinary course of trade, but only to other shipments where the character or condition of the property to be carried or the circumstances, terms and conditions under which the carriage is to be performed, are such as reasonably to justify a special agreement.

Article VII.

Limitations on the Application of the Rules.

Nothing herein contained shall prevent a carrier or a shipper from entering into any agreement, stipulation, condition, reservation or exemption as to the responsibility and liability of the carrier or the ship for the loss or damage to or in connection with the custody and care and handling of goods prior to the loading on and subsequent to the discharge from the ship on which the goods are carried by sea.

Article VIII.

Limitations of liability.

The provisions of these Rules shall not affect the rights and obligations of the carrier under any statute for the time being in force relating to the limitation of owners of sea-going vessels.

Article IX.

The monetary units mentioned in these Rules are to be taken to be gold value.

Appendix B *Carriage of Goods by Sea Act 1971*

(as amended by Merchant Shipping Act 1981)

The Hague-Visby Rules

Chapter 19

Arrangement of Sections

Section

1. Application of Hague Rules as amended.
2. Contracting States, etc.
3. Absolute warranty of seaworthiness not to be implied in contracts to which Rules apply.
4. Application of Act to British possessions, etc.
5. Extension of application of Rules to carriage from ports in British possessions, etc.
6. Supplemental.
   Schedule – The Hague Rules as amended by the Brussels Protocol 1968.

An Act to amend the law with respect to the carriage of goods by sea.

(8th April 1971)

Application of Hague Rules as amended.

1. – (1) In this Act, 'the Rules' means the International Convention for the unification of certain rules of law relating to bills of lading signed at Brussels on 25th August 1924, as amended by the Protocol signed at Brussels on 23rd February 1968 and by the Protocol signed at Brussels on 21st December 1979.

(2) The provisions of the Rules, as set out in the Schedule to this Act, shall have the force of law.

Substitution of special drawing rights in limitation provisions of Carriage of Goods by Sea Act 1971. (C.10) (15th April 1981)

(3) Without prejudice to subsection (2) above, the said provisions shall have effect (and have the force of law) in relation to and in connection with the carriage of goods by sea in ships where the port of shipment is a port in the United Kingdom, whether or not the carriage is between ports in two different States within the meaning of Article X of the Rules.

(4) Subject to subsection (6) below, nothing in this section shall be taken as applying anything in the Rules to any contract for the carriage of goods by sea, unless the contract expressly or by implication provides for the issue of a bill of lading or any similar document of title.

Section 1(5) repealed taking effect on 4th February 1984. (Commencement No. 2) Order 1983 No. 1906 (C.52)

(5) The Secretary of State may from time to time by order made by statutory instrument specify the respective amounts which for the purposes of paragraph 5 of Article IV of the Rules and of Article IV bis of the Rules are to be taken as equivalent to the sums expressed in francs which are mentioned in sub-paragraph (*a*) of that paragraph.

(6) Without prejudice to Article X(*c*) of the Rules, the Rules shall have the force of law in relation to –

(*a*) any bill of lading if the contract contained in or evidenced by it expressly provides that the Rules shall govern the contract, and

(*b*) any receipt which is a non-negotiable document marked as such if the contract contained in or evidenced by it is a contract for the carriage of goods by sea which expressly provides that the Rules are to govern the contract as if the receipt were a bill of lading.

but subject, where paragraph (*b*) applies, to any necessary modifications and in particular with the omission of Article III of the Rules of the second sentence of paragraph 4 and of paragraph 7.

(7) If and so far as the contract contained in or evidenced by a bill of lading or receipt within paragraph (*a*) or (*b*) of subsection (6) above applies to deck cargo or live animals, the Rules as given the force of law by that subsection shall have effect as if Article I(*c*) did not exclude deck cargo and live animals.

In this subsection 'deck cargo' means cargo which by the contract of carriage is stated as being carried on deck and is so carried.

2. – (1) If Her Majesty by Order in Council certifies to the following effect, that is to say, that for the purposes of the Rules – *[Contracting States, etc.]*

(*a*) a State specified in the Order is a contracting State, or is a contracting State in respect of any place or territory so specified; or

(*b*) any place or territory specified in the Order forms part of a State so specified (whether a contracting State or not),

the Order shall, except so far as it has been superseded by a subsequent Order, be conclusive evidence of the matters so certified.

(2) An Order in Council under this section may be varied or revoked by a subsequent Order in Council.

3. There shall not be implied in any contract for the carriage of goods by sea to which the Rules apply by virtue of this Act any absolute undertaking by the carrier of the goods to provide a seaworthy ship. *[Absolute warranty of seaworthiness not to be implied in contracts to which Rules apply.]*

4. – (1) Her Majesty may by Order in Council direct that this Act shall extend, subject to such exceptions, adaptations and modifications as may be specified in the Order, to all or any of the following territories, that is – *[Application of Act to British possessions, etc.]*

(*a*) any colony (not being a colony for whose external relations a country other than the United Kingdom is responsible),

(*b*) any country outside Her Majesty's dominions in which Her Majesty has jurisdiction in right of Her Majesty's Government of the United Kingdom.

(2) An Order in Council under this section may contain such transitional and other consequential and incidental provisions as appear to Her Majesty to be expedient, including provisions amending or repealing any legislation about the carriage of goods by sea forming part of the law of any of the territories mentioned in paragraphs (*a*) and (*b*) above.

(3) An Order in Council under this section may be varied or revoked by a subsequent Order in Council.

5. – (1) Her Majesty may by Order in Council provide that section 1(3) of this Act shall have effect as if the reference therein to the United Kingdom included a reference to all or any of the following territories, that is – *[Extension of application of Rules to carriage from ports in British possessions, etc.]*

(*a*) the Isle of Man;

(*b*) any of the Channel Islands specified in the Order;

(*c*) any colony specified in the Order (not being a colony for whose external relations a country other than the United Kingdom is responsible);

(*d*) any associated state (as defined by section 1(3) of the *West Indies Act 1967*) specified in the Order; *[1967 c. 4.]*

(*e*) any country specified in the Order, being a country outside Her Majesty's dominions in which Her Majesty has jurisdiction in right of Her Majesty's Government of the United Kingdom.

(2) An Order in Council under this section may be varied or revoked by

a subsequent Order in Council.

Supplemental.

6. – (1) This Act may be cited as the *Carriage of Goods by Sea Act* 1971.

(2) It is hereby declared that this act extends to Northern Ireland.

(3) The following enactments shall be repealed, that is –

1924. c. 22.
1965 c. 57.

(*a*) the *Carriage of Goods by Sea Act* 1924,

(*b*) section 12(4)(*a*) of the *Nuclear Installations Act* 1965,

1889 c. 63.
1968 c. 59.

and without prejudice to section 38(1) of the *Interpretation Act* 1889, the reference to the said Act of 1924 in section 1(1)(*i*)(ii) of the *Hovercraft Act* 1968 shall include a reference to this Act.

(4) It is hereby declared that for the purposes of Article VIII of the Rules [section 18 of the *Merchant Shipping Act* 1979] (which entirely exempts shipowners and others in certain circumstances from liability for loss of, or damage to, goods) is a provision relating to limitation of liability.

(5) This Act shall come into force on such day as Her Majesty may by Order in Council appoint, and, for the purposes of the transition from the law in force immediately before the day appointed under this subsection to the provisions of this Act, the Order appointing the day may provide that those provisions shall have effect subject to such transitional provisions as may be contained in the Order.

Amendment

The words in square brackets in subsection (4) were substituted by the *Merchant Shipping Act* 1979 (c.39), S.19, Sched. 5(5).

Schedule

The Hague Rules as amended by the Brussels Protocol 1968

Article I

In these Rules the following words are employed, with the meanings set out below: –

(*a*) 'Carrier includes the owner or the charterer who enters into a contract of carriage with a shipper

(*b*) 'Contract of carriage' applies only to contracts of carriage covered by a bill of lading or any similar document of title, in so far as such document relates to the carriage of goods by sea, including any bill of lading or any similar document as aforesaid issued under or pursuant to a charter-party from the moment at which such bill of lading or similar document of title regulates the relations between a carrier and a holder of the same.

(*c*) 'Goods' includes goods, wares, merchandise, and articles of every kind whatsoever, except live animals and cargo which by the contract of carriage is stated as being carried on deck and is so carried.

(*d*) 'Ship' means any vessel used for the carriage of goods by sea.

(*e*) 'Carriage of goods' covers the period from the time when the goods are loaded on to the time when they are discharged from the ship.

Article II

Subject to the provisions of Article VI, under every contract of carriage of goods by sea the carrier, in relation to the loading, handling, stowage, carriage, custody, care, and discharge of such goods, shall be subject to the responsibilities and liabilities, and entitled to the rights and immunities hereinafter set forth.

Article III

1. The carrier shall be bound, before and at the beginning of the voyage, to exercise due diligence to –

(a) Make the ship seaworthy.
(b) Properly man, equip, and supply the ship.
(c) Make the holds, refrigerating and cool chambers, and all other parts of the ship in which goods are carried, fit and safe for their reception, carriage and preservation.

2. Subject to the provisions of Article IV, the carrier shall properly and carefully load, handle, stow, carry, keep, care for and discharge the goods carried.

3. After receiving the goods into his charge, the carrier, or the master or agent of the carrier, shall on demand of the shipper, issue to the shipper a bill of lading showing among other things –

Sch.

(a) The leading marks necessary for identification of the goods as the same are furnished in writing by the shipper before the loading of such goods starts, provided such marks are stamped or otherwise shown clearly upon the goods if uncovered, or on the cases or coverings in which goods are contained, in such a manner as should ordinarily remain legible until the end of the voyage.
(b) Either the number of packages or pieces, or the quantity, or weight, as the case may be, as furnished in writing by the shipper.
(c) The apparent order and condition of the goods.

Provided that no carrier, master or agent of the carrier shall be bound to state or show in the bill of lading any marks, number, quantity, or weight which he has reasonable ground for suspecting not accurately to represent the goods actually received, or which he has had no reasonable means of checking.

4. Such a bill of lading shall be *prima facie* evidence of the receipt by the carrier of the goods as therein described in accordance with paragraph 3(a), (b) and (c). However, proof to the contrary shall not be admissible when the bill of lading has been transferred to a third party acting in good faith.

5. The shipper shall be deemed to have guaranteed to the carrier the accuracy at the time of shipment of the marks, number, quantity, and weight, as furnished by him, and the shipper shall indemnify the carrier against all loss, damages, and expenses arising or resulting from inaccuracies in such particulars. The right of the carrier to such indemnity shall in no way limit his responsibility and liability under the contract of carriage to any person other than the shipper.

6. Unless notice of loss or damage and the general nature of such damage be given in writing to the carrier or his agent at the port of discharge before or at the time of the removal of the goods into the custody of the person entitled to delivery thereof under the contract of carriage, or, if the loss or damage be not apparent, within three days, such removal shall be *prima facie* evidence of the delivery by the carrier of the goods as described in the bill of lading.

The notice in writing need not be given if the state of the goods has, at the time of their receipt, been the subject of joint survey or inspection.

Subject to paragraph 6*bis* the carrier and the ship shall in any event be discharged from all liability whatsoever in respect of the goods, unless suit is brought within one year of their delivery or of the date when they should have been delivered. This period may, however, be extended if the parties so agree after the cause of action has arisen.

In the case of any actual or apprehended loss or damage the carrier and the receiver shall give all reasonable facilities to each other for inspecting and tallying the goods.

6bis. An action for indemnity against a third person may be brought even after the expiration of the year provided for in the preceding paragraph if brought within the time allowed by the law of the Court seized of the case. However, the time allowed shall not be less than three months, commencing from the day when the person bringing such action for indemnity has settled the claim or has been served with process in the action against himself.

7. After the goods are loaded the bill of lading to be issued by the carrier, master or agent of the carrier, to the shipper shall, if the shipper so demands, be a 'shipped' bill of lading, provided that if the shipper shall have previously taken up any document of title to such goods, he shall surrender the same as against the issue of the 'shipped' bill of lading, but at the option of the carrier such document of title may be noted at the port of shipment by the carrier, master, or agent with the name or names of the ship or ships upon which the goods have been shipped and the date or dates of shipment, and when so noted, if it shows the particulars mentioned in paragraph 3 of Article III, shall for the purpose of this Article be deemed to constitute a 'shipped' bill of lading.

8. Any clause, covenant, or agreement in a contract of carriage relieving the carrier or the ship from liability for loss or damage to, or in connection with, goods arising from negligence, fault, or failure in the duties and obligations provided in this article or lessening such liability otherwise than as provided in these Rules, shall be null and void and of no effect. A benefit of insurance in favour of the carrier or similar clause shall be deemed to be a clause relieving the carrier from liability.

Article IV

1. Neither the carrier nor the ship shall be liable for loss or damage arising or resulting from unseaworthiness unless caused by want of due diligence on the part of the carrier to make the ship seaworthy, and to secure that the ship is properly manned, equipped and supplied, and to make the holds, refrigerating and cool chambers and all other parts of the ship in which goods are carried fit and safe for their reception, carriage and preservation in accordance with the provisions of paragraph 1 of Article III. Whenever loss or damage has resulted from unseaworthiness the burden of proving the exercise of due diligence shall be on the carrier or other person claiming exemption under this article.

2. Neither the carrier nor the ship shall be responsible for loss or damage arising or resulting from –

(a) Act, neglect, or default of the master, mariner, pilot, or the servants of the carrier in the navigation or in the management of the ship.
(b) Fire, unless caused by the actual fault or privity of the carrier.
(c) Perils, dangers and accidents of the sea or other navigable waters.
(d) Act of God.
(e) Act of war.
(f) Act of public enemies.
(g) Arrest or restraint of princes, rulers or people, or seizure under legal process.
(h) Quarantine restrictions.
(i) Act or omission of the shipper or owner of the goods, his agent or representative.

(*j*) Strikes or lockouts or stoppage or restraint of labour from whatever cause, whether partial or general.

(*k*) Riots and civil commotions.

(*l*) Saving or attempting to save life or property at sea.

(*m*) Wastage in bulk or weight or any other loss or damage, arising from inherent defect, quality, or vice of the goods.

(*n*) Insufficiency of packing.

(*o*) Insufficiency or inadequacy of marks.

(*p*) Latent defects not discoverable by due diligence.

(*q*) Any other cause arising without the actual fault or privity of the carrier, or without the fault or neglect of the agents or servants of the carrier, but the burden of proof shall be on the person claiming the benefit of this exception to show that neither the actual fault or privity of the carrier nor the fault or neglect of the agents or servants of the carrier contributed to the loss or damage.

3. The shipper shall not be responsible for loss or damage sustained by the carrier or the ship arising or resulting from any cause without the act, fault or neglect of the shipper, his agents or his servants.

4. Any deviation in saving or attempting to save life or property at sea or any reasonable deviation shall not be deemed to be an infringement or breach of these Rules or of the contract of carriage, and the carrier shall not be liable for any loss or damage resulting therefrom.

5. (*a*) Unless the nature and value of such goods have been declared by the shipper before shipment and inserted in the bill of lading, neither the carrier nor the ship shall in any event be or become liable for any loss or damage to or in connection with the goods in an amount exceeding the equivalent of 666.67 units of account per package or unit or 2 units of account per kilogramme of gross weight of the goods lost or damaged, whichever is the higher.

Conversion of special drawing rights into sterling. (Commencement No. 2). Order 1983 – 1983 No. 1906 (C. 52)

(*b*) The total amount recoverable shall be calculated by reference to the value of such goods at the place and time at which the goods are discharged from the ship in accordance with the contract or should have been so discharged.

The value of the goods shall be fixed according to the commodity exchange price, or, if there be no such price, according to the current market price, or, if there be no commodity exchange price or current market price, by reference to the normal value of goods of the same kind and quality.

(*c*) Where a container, pallet or similar article of transport is used to consolidate the goods, the number of packages or units enumerated in the bill of lading as packed in such article of transport shall be deemed the number of packages or units for the purpose of this paragraph as far as these packages or units are concerned. Except as aforesaid such article of transport shall be considered the package or unit.

Sch.

(*d*) The unit of account mentioned in this Article is the special drawing right as defined by the International Monetary Fund. The amounts mentioned in sub-paragraph (*a*) of this paragraph shall be converted into national currency on the basis of the value of that currency on a date to be determined by the law of the Court seized of the case.

Note: In its application by virtue of the said Act of 1971 paragraph 5(*d*) of the said Article IV shall have effect as if the date there mentioned were the date of the judgment in question.

(*e*) Neither the carrier nor the ship shall be entitled to the benefit of the limitation of liability provided for in this paragraph if it is proved that the damage resulted from an act or omission of the carrier done with intent to cause damage, or recklessly and with knowledge that damage would probably result.

(*f*) The declaration mentioned in sub-paragraph (*a*) of this paragraph, if embodied in the bill of lading shall be *prima facie* evidence, but shall not be binding or conclusive on the carrier.

(*g*) By agreement between the carrier, master or agent of the carrier and the shipper other maximum amounts than those mentioned in sub-paragraph (*a*) of this paragraph may be fixed, provided that no maximum amount so fixed shall be less than the appropriate maximum mentioned in that sub-paragraph.

(*h*) Neither the carrier nor the ship shall be responsible in any event for loss or damage to, or in connection with, goods if the nature or value thereof has been knowingly mis-stated by the shipper in the bill of lading.

6. Goods of an inflammable, explosive or dangerous nature to the shipment whereof the carrier, master or agent of the carrier has not consented with knowledge of their nature and character, may at any time before discharge be landed at any place, or destroyed or rendered innocuous by the carrier without compensation and the shipper of such goods shall be liable for all damages and expenses directly or indirectly arising out of or resulting from such shipment. If any such goods shipped with such knowledge and consent shall become a danger to the ship or cargo, they may in like manner be landed at any place, or destroyed or rendered innocuous by the carrier without liability on the part of the carrier except to general average, if any.

Article IVbis

1. The defences and limits of liability provided for in these Rules shall apply in any action against the carrier in respect of loss or damage to goods covered by a contract of carriage whether the action be founded in contract or in tort.

2. If such an action is brought against a servant or agent of the carrier (such servant or agent not being an independent contractor), such servant or agent shall be entitled to avail himself of the defences and limits of liability which the carrier is entitled to invoke under these Rules.

3. The aggregate of the amounts recoverable from the carrier, and such servants and agents, shall in no case exceed the limit provided for in these Rules.

4. Nevertheless, a servant or agent of the carrier shall not be entitled to avail himself of the provisions of this article, if it is proved that the damage resulted from an act or omission of the servant or agent done with intent to cause damage or recklessly and with knowledge that damage would probably result.

Article V

A carrier shall be at liberty to surrender in whole or in part all or any of his rights and immunities or to increase any of his responsibilities and obligations under these Rules, provided such surrender or increase shall be embodied in the bill of lading issued to the shipper. The provisions of these Rules shall not be applicable to charter-parties, but if bills of lading are issued in the case of a ship under a charter-party they shall comply with the terms of these Rules. Nothing in these Rules shall be held to prevent the insertion in a bill of lading of any lawful provision regarding general average.

Sch.

Article VI

Notwithstanding the provisions of the preceding articles, a carrier, master or agent of the carrier and a shipper shall in regard to any particular goods be at liberty to enter into any agreement in any terms as to the responsibility and liability of the carrier for such goods, and as to the rights and immunities of the carrier in respect of such goods, or his obligation as to seaworthiness, so far as this stipulation is not contrary to public policy, or the care or diligence of his servants or agents in regard to the loading, handling, stowage, carriage, custody, care and discharge of the goods carried by sea, provided that in this case no bill of lading has been or shall be issued and that the terms agreed shall be embodied in a receipt which shall be a non-negotiable document and shall be marked as such.

Any agreement so entered into shall have full legal effect.

Provided that this article shall not apply to ordinary commercial shipments made in the ordinary course of trade, but only to other shipments where the character or condition of the property to be carried or the circumstances, terms and conditions under which the carriage is to be performed are such as reasonably to justify a special agreement.

Article VII

Sch.

Nothing herein contained shall prevent a carrier or a shipper from entering into any agreement, stipulation, condition, reservation or exemption as to the responsibility and liability of the carrier or the ship for the loss or damage to, or in connection with, the custody and care and handling of goods prior to the loading on, and subsequent to the discharge from, the ship on which the goods are carried by sea.

Article VIII

The provisions of these Rules shall not affect the rights and obligations of the carrier under any statute for the time being in force relating to the limitation of the liability of owners of sea-going vessels.

Article IX

These Rules shall not affect the provisions of any international Convention or national law governing liability for nuclear damage.

Article X

The provisions of these Rules shall apply to every bill of lading relating to the carriage of goods between ports in two different States if:

(*a*) the bill of lading is issued in a contracting State, or
(*b*) the carriage is from a port in a contracting State, or
(*c*) the contract contained in or evidenced by the bill of lading provides that these Rules or legislation of any State giving effect to them are to govern the contract.

whatever may be the nationality of the ship, the carrier, the shipper, the consignee, or any other interested person.

(The last two paragraphs of this article are not reproduced. They require contracting States to apply the Rules to bills of lading mentioned in the article and authorise them to apply the Rules to other bills of lading.)

(Articles 11 to 16 of the International Convention for the unification of certain rules of law relating to bills of lading signed at Brussels on 25th August 1924 are

not reproduced. They deal with the coming into force of the Convention, procedure for ratification, accession and denunciation, and the right to call for a fresh conference to consider amendments to the Rules contained in the Convention).

NOTE:

In its application by virtue of the said Act of 1971 Article X of the Rules set out in the Schedule to that Act shall have effect as if reference to a contracting State included references to a State that is a contracting State in respect of the Rules without amendments made by the said Protocol of 1979 as well as to one that is a contracting State in respect of the Rules as so amended, and section 2 of that Act (certification of contracting States) shall have effect accordingly.

Conversion of Special Drawing Rights into Sterling 1971 (C.19)

The value on a particular day of one special drawing right shall be treated as equal to such a sum in sterling as the International Monetary Fund have fixed as being the equivalent of one special drawing right:–

(*a*) for that day; or

(*b*) if no sum has been so fixed for that day, for the last day before that day for which a sum has been so fixed.

Appendix C The *Pomerene Bills of Lading Act* 1916

(of the United States of America)

U.S.C., title 49 ss 81–124 Public No. 239 – 64th Congress- Approved 29 August, 1916

CHAP.415. – *An Act Relating to bills of lading in interstate and foreign commerce.*

Be it enacted by the Senate and House of Representatives of the United States of America in Congress assembled, That bills of lading issued by any common carrier for the transportation of goods in any Territory of the United States, or the District of Columbia, or from a place in a State to a place in a foreign country, or from a place in one State to a place in another State, or from a place in one State to a place in the same State through another State or foreign country, shall be governed by this Act.

SEC. 2. That a bill in which it is stated that the goods are consigned or destined to a specified person is a straight bill.

SEC. 3. That a bill in which it is stated that the goods are consigned or destined to the order of any person named in such bill is an order bill. Any provision in such a bill or in any notice, contract, rule, regulation, or tariff that it is nonnegotiable shall be null and void and shall not affect its negotiability within the meaning of this Act unless upon its face and in writing agreed to by the shipper.

SEC. 4. That order bills issued in a State for the transportation of goods to any place in the United States on the Continent of North America, except Alaska and Panama, shall not be issued in parts or sets. If so issued, the carrier issuing them shall be liable for failure to deliver the goods described therein to anyone who purchases a part for value in good faith, even though the purchase be after the delivery of the goods by the carrier to a holder of one of the other parts: *Provided, however,* That nothing contained in this section shall be interpreted or construed to forbid the issuing of order bills in parts or sets for such transportation of goods to Alaska, Panama, Porto Rico, the Philippines, Hawaii, or foreign countries, or to impose the liabilities set forth in this section for so doing.

SEC. 5. That when more than one order bill is issued in a State for the same goods to be transported to any place in the United States on the Continent of North America, except Alaska and Panama, the word "duplicate," or some other word or words indicating that the document is not an original bill, shall be placed plainly upon the face of every such bill except the one first issued. A carrier shall be liable for the damage caused by his failure so to do to anyone who has purchased the bill for value in good faith as an original, even though the purchase be after the delivery of the goods by the carrier to the holder of the original bill: *Provided, however,* That nothing contained in this section shall in such case for such transportation of goods to Alaska, Panama, Porto Rico, the Philippines, Hawaii, or foreign countries be interpreted or construed so as to require the placing of the word "duplicate" thereon, or to impose the liabilities set forth in this section for failure so to do.

SEC. 6. That a straight bill shall have placed plainly upon its face by the carrier issuing it "nonnegotiable" or "not negotiable."

This section shall not apply, however, to memoranda or acknowledgments of any informal character.

SEC. 7. That the insertion of an order bill of the name of a person to be notified of the arrival of the goods shall not limit the negotiability of the bill or constitute notice to a purchaser thereof of any rights or equities of such person in the goods.

SEC. 8. That a carrier, in the absence of some lawful excuse, is bound to deliver goods upon a demand made either by the consignee named in the bill for the goods or, if the bill is an order bill, by the holder thereof, if such a demand is accompanied by -

(a) An offer in good faith to satisfy the carrier's lawful lien upon the goods;

(b) Possession of the bill of lading and an offer in good faith to surrender, properly indorsed, the bill which was issued for the goods, if the bill is an order bill; and

(c) A readiness and willingness to sign, when the goods are delivered, an acknowledgment that they have been delivered, if such signature is requested by the carrier.

In case the carrier refuses or fails to deliver the goods, in compliance with a demand by the consignee or holder so accompanied, the burden shall be upon the carrier to establish the existence of a lawful excuse for such refusal or failure.

SEC. 9. That a carrier is justified, subject to the provisions of the three following sections, in delivering goods to one who is -

(a) A person lawfully entitled to the possession of the goods, or

(b) The consignee named in a straight bill for the goods, or

(c) A person in possession of an order bill for the goods, by the terms of which the goods are deliverable to his order; or which has been indorsed to him, or in blank by the consignee, or by the mediate or immediate indorsee of the consignee.

SEC. 10. That where a carrier delivers goods to one who is not lawfully entitled to the possession of them, the carrier shall be liable to anyone having a right of property or possession in the goods if he delivered the goods otherwise than as authorized by subdivisions (b) and (c) of the preceding section; and, though he delivered the goods as authorized by either of said subdivisions, he shall be so liable if prior to such delivery he -

(a) Had been requested, by or on behalf of a person having a right of property or possession in the goods, not to make such delivery, or

(b) Had information at the time of the delivery that it was to a person not lawfully entitled to the possession of the goods.

Such request or information, to be effective within the meaning of this section, must be given to an officer or agent of the carrier, the actual or apparent scope of whose duties includes action upon such a request or information, and must be given in time to enable the officer or agent to whom it is given, acting with reasonable diligence, to stop delivery of the goods.

SEC. 11. That except as provided in section twenty-six, and except when compelled by legal process, if a carrier delivers goods for which an order bill had been issued, the negotiation of which would transfer the right to the possession of the goods, and fails to take up and cancel the bill, such carrier shall be liable for failure to deliver the goods to anyone who for value in a good faith purchases such bill, whether such purchaser acquired title to the bill before or after the delivery of the goods by the carrier and notwithstanding delivery was made to the person entitled thereto.

SEC. 12. That except as provided in section twenty-six, and except when compelled by legal process, if a carrier delivers part of the goods for which an order bill had been issued and fails either –

(a) To take up and cancel the bill, or

(b) To place plainly upon it a statement that a portion of the goods has been delivered with a description which may be in general terms either of the goods or packages that have been so delivered or of the goods or packages which still remain in the carrier's possession, he shall be liable for failure to deliver all the goods specified in the bill to anyone who for value and in good faith purchases it, whether such purchaser acquired title to it before or after the delivery of any portion of the goods by the carrier, and notwithstanding such delivery was made to the person entitled thereto.

SEC. 13. That any alteration, addition, or erasure in a bill after its issue without authority from the carrier issuing the same, either in writing or noted on the bill, shall be void, whatever be the nature and purpose of the change, and the bill shall be enforceable according to its original tenor.

SEC. 14. That where an order bill has been lost, stolen, or destroyed a court of competent jurisdiction may order the delivery of the goods upon satisfactory proof of such loss, theft, or destruction and upon the giving of a bond, with sufficient surety, to be approved by the court, to protect the carrier or any person injured by such delivery from any liability or loss incurred by reason of the original bill remaining outstanding. The court may also in its discretion order the payment of the carrier's reasonable costs and counsel fees: *Provided*, a voluntary indemnifying bond without order of court shall be binding on the parties thereto.

The delivery of the goods under an order of the court, as provided in this section, shall not relieve the carrier from liability to a person to whom the order bill has been or shall be negotiated for value without notice of the proceedings or of the delivery of the goods.

SEC. 15. That a bill, upon the face of which the word "duplicate" or some other word or words indicating that the document is not an original bill is placed, plainly shall impose upon the carrier issuing the same the liability of one who represents and warrants that such bill is an accurate copy of an original bill properly issued, but no other liability.

SEC. 16. That no title to goods or right to their possession asserted by a carrier for his own benefit shall excuse him from liability for refusing to deliver the goods according to the terms of a bill issued for them, unless such title or right is derived directly or indirectly from a transfer made by the consignor or consignee after the shipment, or from the carrier's lien.

SEC. 17. That if more than one person claim the title or possession of goods, the carrier may require all known claimants to interplead, either as a defense to an action brought against him for nondelivery of the goods or as an original suit, whichever is appropriate.

SEC. 18. That if some one other than the consignee or the person in possession of the bill has a claim to the title or possession of the goods, and the carrier has information of such claim, the carrier shall be excused from liability for refusing to deliver the goods, either to the consignee or person in possession of the bill or to the adverse claimant, until the carrier has had a reasonable time to ascertain the validity of the adverse claim or to bring legal proceedings to compel all claimants to interplead.

SEC. 19. That except as provided in the two preceding sections and in section nine, no right or title of the third person, unless enforced by legal process, shall be a defense to an action brought by the consignee of a straight bill or by the holder of an order bill against the carrier for failure to deliver the goods on demand.

SEC. 20. That when goods are loaded by a carrier such carrier shall count the packages of goods, if package freight, and ascertain the kind and quantity if bulk freight, and such carrier shall not, in such cases, insert in the bill of lading or in any notice, receipt, contract, rule, regulation, or tariff, "Shipper's weight, load, and count," or other words of like purport, indicating that the goods were loaded by the shipper and the description of them made by him or in case of bulk freight and freight not concealed by packages the description made by him. If so inserted, contrary to the provisions of this section, said words shall be treated as null and void and as if not inserted therein.

SEC. 21. That when package freight or bulk freight is loaded by a shipper and the goods are described in a bill of lading merely by a statement of marks or labels upon them or upon packages containing them, or by a statement that the goods are said to be goods of a certain kind or quantity, or in a certain condition, or it is stated in the bill of lading that packages are said to contain goods of a certain kind or quantity or in a certain condition, or that the contents or condition of the contents of packages are unknown, or words of like purport are contained in the bill of lading, such statements, if true, shall not make liable the carrier issuing the bill of lading, although the goods are not of the kind or quantity or in the condition which the marks or labels upon them indicate, or of the kind or quantity or in the condition they were said to be by the consignor. The carrier may also by inserting in the bill of lading the words "Shipper's weight, load, and count," or other words of like purport indicate that the goods were loaded by the shipper and the description of them made by him; and if such statement be true, the carrier shall not be liable for damages caused by the improper loading or by the nonreceipt or by the misdescription of the goods described in the bill of lading: *Provided, however,* Where the shipper of bulk freight installs and maintains adequate facilities of weighing such freight, and the same are available to the carrier, then the carrier, upon written request of such shipper and when given a reasonable opportunity so to do, shall ascertain the kind and quantity of bulk freight within a reasonable time after such written request, and the carriers shall not in such cases insert in the bill of lading the words "Shipper's weight," or other words of like purport, and if so inserted contrary to the provisions of this section, said words shall be treated as null and void and as if not inserted therein.

SEC. 22. That if a bill of lading has been issued by a carrier or on his behalf by an agent or employee the scope of whose actual or apparent authority includes the receiving of goods and issuing bills of lading therefor for transportation in commerce among the several States and with foreign nations, the carrier shall be liable to (a) the owner of goods covered by a straight bill subject to existing right of stoppage in transitu or (b) the holder of an order bill, who has given value in good faith, relying upon the description therein of the goods for damages caused by the nonreceipt by the carrier of all or part of the goods or their failure to correspond with the description thereof in the bill at the time of its issue.

SEC. 23. That if goods are delivered to a carrier by the owner or by a person whose act in conveying the title to them to a purchaser for value in good faith would bind the owner, and an order bill is issued for them, they can not thereafter, while in possession of the carrier, be attached by garnishment or otherwise or be levied upon under an execution unless the bill be first surrendered to the carrier or its negotiation enjoined. The carrier shall in no such case be compelled to deliver the actual possession of the goods until the bill is surrendered to him or impounded by the court.

SEC. 24. That a creditor whose debtor is the owner of an order bill shall be entitled to such aid from courts of appropriate jurisdiction by injunction and otherwise in attaching such bill or in satisfying the claim by means thereof as is allowed at law or in equity in regard to property which can not readily by attached or levied upon by ordinary legal process.

SEC. 25. That if an order bill is issued the carrier shall have a lien on the goods therein mentioned for all charges on those goods for freight, storage, demurrage and terminal charges, and expenses necessary for the preservation of the goods or incident to their transportation subsequent to the date of the bill and all other charges incurred in transportation and delivery, unless the bill expressly enumerates other charges for which a lien is claimed. In such case there shall also be a lien for the charges enumerated so far as they are allowed by law and the contract between the consignor and the carrier.

SEC. 26. That after goods have been lawfully sold to satisfy a carrier's lien, or because they have not been claimed, or because they are perishable or hazardous, the carrier shall not thereafter be liable for failure to deliver the goods themselves to the consignee or owner of the goods, or to a holder of the bill given for the goods when they were shipped, even if such bill be an order bill.

SEC. 27. That an order bill may be negotiated by delivery where, by the terms of the bill, the carrier undertakes to deliver the goods to the order of a specified person, and such person or subsequent indorsee of the bill has indorsed it in blank.

SEC. 28. That an order bill may be negotiated by the indorsement of the person to whose order the goods are deliverable by the tenor of the bill. Such indorsement may be in blank or to a specified person. If indorsed to a specified person, it may be negotiated again by the indorsement of such person in blank or to another specified person. Subsequent negotiation may be made in like manner.

SEC. 29. That a bill may be transferred by the holder by delivery, accompanied with an agreement, express or implied, to transfer the title to the bill or to the goods represented thereby. A straight bill can not be negotiated free from existing equities, and the indorsement of such a bill gives the transferee no additional right.

SEC. 30. That an order bill may be negotiated by any person in possession of the same, however such possession may have been acquired, if by the terms of the bill the carrier undertakes to deliver the goods to the order of such person, or if at the time of negotiation the bill is in such form that it may be negotiated by delivery.

SEC. 31. That a person to whom an order bill has been duly negotiated acquires thereby –

(a) Such title to the goods as the person negotiating the bill to him had or had ability to convey to a purchaser in good faith for value, and also such title to the goods as the consignee and consignor had or had power to convey to a purchaser in good faith for value; and

(b) The direct obligation of the carrier to hold possession of the goods for him according to the terms of the bill as fully as if the carrier had contracted directly with him.

SEC. 32. That a person to whom a bill has been transferred, but not negotiated, acquires thereby as against the transferor the title to the goods, subject to the terms of any agreement with the transferor. If the bill is a straight bill such person also acquires the right to notify the carrier of the transfer to him of such bill and thereby to become the direct obligee of whatever obligations the carrier owed to the transferor of the bill immediately before the notification.

Prior to the notification of the carrier by the transferor or transferee of a straight bill the title of the transferee to the goods and the right to acquire the obligation of the carrier may be defeated by garnishment or by attachment or execution upon the goods by a creditor of the transferor, or by a notification to the carrier by the transferor or a subsequent purchaser from the transferor of a subsequent sale of the goods by the transferor.

A carrier has not received notification within the meaning of this section unless an officer or agent of the carrier, the actual or apparent scope of whose duties includes action upon such a notification, has been notified; and no notification shall be effective until the officer or agent to whom it is given has had time, with the exercise of reasonable diligence, to communicate with the agent or agents having actual possession or control of the goods.

SEC. 33. That where an order bill is transferred for value by delivery, the indorsement of the transferor is essential for negotiation, the transferee acquires a right against the transferor to compel him to indorse the bill, unless a contrary intention appears. The negotiation shall take effect as of the time when the indorsement is actually made. This obligation may be specifically enforced.

SEC. 34. That a person who negotiates or transfers for value a bill by indorsement or delivery, unless a contrary intention appears, warrants –

(a) That the bill is genuine;
(b) That he has a legal right to transfer it;
(c) That he has knowledge of no fact which would impair the validity or worth of the bill;
(d) That he has a right to transfer the title to the goods, and that the goods are merchantable or fit for a particular purpose whenever such warranties would have been implied if the contract of the parties had been to transfer without a bill the goods represented thereby.

SEC. 35. That the indorsement of a bill shall not make the indorser liable for any failure on the part of the carrier or previous indorsers of the bill to fulfill their respective obligations.

SEC. 36. That a mortgagee or pledgee or other holder of a bill for security who in good faith demands or receives payment of the debt for which such bill is security, whether from a party to a draft drawn for such debt or from any other person, shall not be deemed by so doing to represent or warrant the genuineness of such bill or the quantity or quality of the goods therein described.

SEC. 37. That the validity of the negotiation of a bill is not impaired by the fact that such negotiation was a breach of duty on the part of the person making the negotiation, or by the fact that the owner of the bill was deprived of the possession of the same by fraud, accident, mistake, duress, loss, theft, or conversion, if the person to whom the bill was negotiated, or a person to whom the bill was subsequently negotiated, gave value therefor in good faith, without notice of the breach of duty, or fraud, accident, mistake, duress, loss, theft, or conversion.

SEC. 38. That where a person, having sold, mortgaged, or pledged goods which are in a carrier's possession and for which an order bill has been issued, or having sold, mortgaged, or pledged the order bill representing such goods, continues in possession of the order bill, the subsequent negotiation thereof by that person under any sale, pledge, or other disposition thereof to any person receiving the same in good faith, for value and without notice of the previous sale, shall have the same effect as if the first purchaser of the goods or bill had expressly authorized the subsequent negotiation.

SEC. 39. That where an order bill has been issued for goods no seller's lien or right of stoppage in transitu shall defeat the rights of any purchaser for value in good faith to whom such bill has been negotiated, whether such negotiation be prior or subsequent to the notification to the carrier who issued such bill of the seller's claim to a lien or right of stoppage in transitu. Nor shall the carrier be obliged to deliver or justified in delivering the goods to an unpaid seller unless such bill is first surrendered for cancellation.

SEC. 40. That, except as provided in section thirty-nine, nothing in this Act shall limit the rights and remedies of a mortgagee or lien holder whose mortgage or lien on goods would be valid, apart from this Act, as against one who for value and in good faith purchased from the owner, immediately prior to the time of their delivery to the carrier, the goods which are subject to the mortgage or lien and obtained possession of them.

SEC. 41. That any person who, knowingly or with intent to defraud, falsely makes, alters, forges, counterfeits, prints or photographs any bill of lading purporting to represent goods received for shipment among the several States or with foreign nations, or with like intent utters or publishes as true and genuine any such falsely altered, forged, counterfeited, falsely printed or photographed bill of lading, knowing it to be falsely altered, forged, counterfeited, falsely printed or photographed, or aids in making, altering, forging, counterfeiting, printing or photographing, or uttering or publishing the same, or issues or aids in issuing or procuring the issue of, or negotiates or transfers for value a bill which contains a false statement as to the receipt of the goods, or as to any other matter, or who, with intent to defraud, violates, or fails to comply with, or aids in any violation of, or failure to comply with any provision of this Act, shall be guilty of a misdemeanor, and, upon conviction, shall be punished for each offense by imprisonment not exceeding five years, or by a fine not exceeding $5,000, or both.

SEC. 42. First. That in this Act, unless the context of subject matter otherwise requires –

"Action" includes counterclaim, set-off, and suit in equity.

"Bill" means bill of lading governed by this Act.

"Consignee" means the person named in the bill as the person to whom delivery of the goods is to be made.

"Consignor" means the person named in the bill as the person from whom the goods have been received for shipment.

"Goods" means merchandise or chattels in course of transportation or which have been or are about to be transported.

"Holder" of a bill means a person who has both actual possession of such bill and a right of property therein.

"Order" means an order by indorsement on the bill.

"Person" includes a corporation or partnership, or two or more persons having a joint or common interest.

To "purchase" includes to take as mortgagee and to take as pledgee.

"State" includes any Territory, District, insular possession, or isthmian possession.

SEC. 43. That the provisions of this Act do not apply to bills made and delivered prior to the taking effect thereof.

SEC. 44. That the provisions and each part thereof and the sections and each part thereof of this Act are independent and severable, and the declaring of any provision or part thereof, or provisions or part thereof, or section or part thereof, or sections or part thereof, unconstitutional shall not impair or render unconstitutional any other provision or part thereof or section or part thereof.

SEC. 45. That this Act shall take effect and be in force on and after the first day of January next after its passage.

Approved, August 29, 1916.

Appendix D The United States *Carriage of Goods by Sea Act* 1936

This Act applies to both inward and outward bills of lading. Under section 13 however *outward* bills of lading must contain a statement that they are subject to the provisions of this Act. The statement is known as the 'US Clause Paramount'. The Harter Act still applies to goods before and after discharge. It also governs contracts for the carriage of goods between ports in the United States unless the parties have expressly agreed to be bound by the 1936 Act.

74th Congress, Chapter 229 (Public - No.521) 16th April 1936.
AN ACT
Relating to the carriage of goods by sea.

Be it enacted by the Senate and House of Representatives of the United States of America in Congress assembled, That every bill of lading or similar document of title which is evidence of a contract for the carriage of goods by sea to or from ports of the United States, in foreign trade, shall have effect subject to the provisions of this Act.

TITLE I

SECTION 1. When used in this Act –

(a) The term "carrier" includes the owner or the charterer who enters into a contract of carriage with a shipper.

(b) The term "contract of carriage" applies only to contracts of carriage covered by a bill of lading or any similar document of title, insofar as such document relates to the carriage of goods by sea, including any bill of lading or any similar document as aforesaid issued under or pursuant to a charter party from the moment at which such bill of lading or similar document of title regulates the relations between a carrier and a holder of the same.

(c) The term "goods" includes goods, wares, merchandise, and articles of every kind whatsoever, except live animals and cargo which by the contract of carriage is stated as being carried on deck and is so carried.

(d) The term "ship" means any vessel used for the carriage of goods by sea.

(e) The term "carriage of goods" covers the period from the time when the goods are loaded on to the time when they are discharged from the ship.

RISKS

SEC. 2. Subject to the provisions of section 6, under every contract of carriage of goods by sea, the carrier in relation to the loading, handling, stowage, carriage, custody, care, and discharge of such goods, shall be subject to the responsibilities and liabilities and entitled to the rights and immunities hereinafter set forth.

RESPONSIBILITIES AND LIABILITIES

SEC. 3. (1) The carrier shall be bound, before and at the beginning of the voyage, to exercise due diligence to –

(a) Make the ship seaworthy;

(b) Properly man, equip, and supply the ship;

(c) Make the holds, refrigerating and cooling chambers, and all other parts of the ship in which goods are carried, fit and safe for their reception, carriage, and preservation.

(2) The carrier shall properly and carefully load, handle, stow, carry, keep, care for, and discharge the goods carried.

(3) After receiving the goods into his charge the carrier, or the master or agent of the carrier, shall, on demand of the shipper, issue to the shipper a bill of lading showing among other things –

(a) The leading marks necessary for identification of the goods as the same are furnished in writing by the shipper before the loading of such goods starts, provided such marks are stamped or otherwise shown clearly upon the goods if uncovered, or on the cases or coverings in which such goods are contained, in such a manner as should ordinarily remain legible until the end of the voyage.

(b) Either the number of packages or pieces, or the quantity or weight, as the case may be, as furnished in writing by the shipper.

(c) The apparent order and condition of the goods: *Provided*, That no carrier, master, or agent of the carrier, shall be bound to state or show in the bill of lading any marks, number, quantity, or weight which he has reasonable ground for suspecting not accurately to represent the goods actually received, or which he has had no reasonable means of checking.

(4) Such a bill of lading shall be prima facie evidence of the receipt by the carrier of the goods as therein described in accordance with paragraphs (3) (a), (b), and (c), of this section: *Provided*, That nothing in this Act shall be construed as repealing or limiting the application of any part of the Act, as amended, entitled "An Act relating to bills of lading in interstate and foreign transportation" approved August 29, 1916 (U.S.C., title 49, secs. 81-124), commonly known as the "Pomerene Bills of Lading Act."

1981 Amendment "Transportation for Commerce".

(5) The shipper shall be deemed to have guaranteed to the carrier the accuracy at the time of shipment of the marks, number, quantity, and weight, as furnished by him; and the shipper shall indemnify the carrier against all loss, damages, and expenses arising or resulting from inaccuracies in such particulars. The right of the carrier to such indemnity shall in no way limit his responsibility and liability under the contract of carriage to any person other than the shipper.

(6) Unless notice of loss or damage and the general nature of such loss or damage be given in writing to the carrier or his agent at the port of discharge before or at the time of the removal of the goods into the custody of the person entitled to delivery thereof under the contract of carriage, such removal shall be prima facie evidence of the delivery by the carrier of the goods as described in the bill of lading. If the loss or damage is not apparent, the notice must be given within three days of the delivery.

Said notice of loss or damage may be endorsed upon the receipt for the goods given by the person taking delivery thereof.

The notice in writing need not be given if the state of the goods has at the time of their receipt been the subject of joint survey or inspection.

In any event the carrier and the ship shall be discharged from all liability in respect of loss or damage unless suit is brought within one year after delivery of the goods or the date when the goods should have been delivered: *Provided*, That if a notice of loss or damage, either apparent or concealed, is not given as provided for in this section, that fact shall not affect or prejudice the right of the shipper to bring suit within one year after the delivery of the goods or the date when the goods should have been delivered.

In the case of any actual or apprehended loss or damage the carrier and the receiver shall give all reasonable facilities to each other for inspecting and tallying the goods.

(7) After the goods are loaded the bill of lading to be issued by the carrier, master, or agent of the carrier to the shipper shall, if the shipper so demands, be a "shipped" bill of lading: *Provided,* That if the shipper shall have previously taken up any document of title to such goods, he shall surrender the same as against the issue of the "shipped" bill of lading, but at the option of the carrier such document of title may be noted at the port of shipment by the carrier, master, or agent with the name or names of the ship or ships upon which the goods have been shipped and the date or dates of shipment, and when so noted the same shall for the purpose of this section be deemed to constitute a "shipped" bill of lading.

(8) Any clause, covenant, or agreement in a contract of carriage relieving the carrier or the ship from liability for loss or damage to or in connection with the goods, arising from negligence, fault, or failure in the duties and obligations provided in this section, or lessening such liability otherwise than as provided in this Act, shall be null and void and of no effect. A benefit of insurance in favor of the carrier, or similar clause, shall be deemed to be a clause relieving the carrier from liability.

RIGHTS AND IMMUNITIES

SEC. 4. (1) Neither the carrier nor the ship shall be liable for loss or damage arising or resulting from unseaworthiness unless caused by want of due diligence on the part of the carrier to make the ship seaworthy, and to secure that the ship is properly manned, equipped, and supplied, and to make the holds, refrigerating and cool chambers, and all other parts of the ship in which goods are carried fit and safe for their reception, carriage, and preservation in accordance with the provisions of paragraph (1) of section 3. Whenever loss or damage has resulted from unseaworthiness, the burden of proving the exercise of due diligence shall be on the carrier or other persons claiming exemption under this section.

(2) Neither the carrier nor the ship shall be responsible for loss or damage arising or resulting from -

(a) Act, neglect, or default of the master, mariner, pilot, or the servants of the carrier in the navigation or in the management of the ship;

(b) Fire, unless caused by the actual fault or privity of the carrier;

(c) Perils, dangers, and accidents of the sea or other navigable waters;

(d) Act of God;

(e) Act of war;

(f) Act of public enemies;

(g) Arrest or restraint of princes, rulers, or people, or seizure under legal process;

(h) Quarantine restrictions;

(i) Act or omission of the shipper or owner of the goods, his agent or representative;

(j) Strikes or lockouts or stoppage or restraint of labor from whatever cause, whether partial or general: *Provided,* that nothing herein contained shall be construed to relieve a carrier from responsibility for the carrier's own acts;

(k) Riots and civil commotions;

(l) Saving or attempting to save life or property at sea;

(m) Wastage in bulk or weight or any other loss or damage arising from inherent defect, quality, or vice of the goods;

(n) Insufficiency of packing;

(o) Insufficiency or inadequacy of marks;

(p) Latent defects not discoverable by due diligence; and

(q) Any other cause arising without the actual fault and privity of the carrier and without the fault or neglect of the agents or servants of the carrier, but the burden of proof shall be on the person claiming the benefit of this exception to show that neither the actual fault or privity of the carrier nor the fault or neglect of the agents or servants of the carrier contributed to the loss or damage.

(3) The shipper shall not be responsible for loss or damage sustained by the carrier or the ship arising or resulting from any cause without the act, fault, or neglect of the shipper, his agents, or his servants.

(4) Any deviation in saving or attempting to save life or property at sea, or any reasonable deviation shall not be deemed to be an infringement or breach of this Act or of the contract of carriage, and the carrier shall not be liable for any loss or damage resulting therefrom: *Provided, however,* That if the deviation is for the purpose of loading or unloading cargo or passengers it shall, prima facie, be regarded as unreasonable.

(5) Neither the carrier nor the ship shall in any event be or become liable for any loss or damage to or in connection with the transportation of goods in an amount exceeding $500 per package lawful money of the United States, or in case of goods not shipped in packages, per customary freight unit, or the equivalent of that sum in other currency, unless the nature and value of such goods have been declared by the shipper before shipment and inserted in the bill of lading. This declaration, if embodied in the bill of lading, shall be prima facie evidence, but shall not be conclusive on the carrier.

By agreement between the carrier, master, or agent of the carrier, and the shipper another maximum amount than that mentioned in this paragraph may be fixed: *Provided,* That such maximum shall not be less than the figure above named. In no event shall the carrier be liable for more than the amount of damage actually sustained.

Neither the carrier nor the ship shall be responsible in any event for loss or damage to or in connection with the transportation of the goods if the nature or value thereof has been knowingly and fraudulently misstated by the shipper in the bill of lading.

(6) Goods of an inflammable, explosive, or dangerous nature to the shipment whereof the carrier, master or agent of the carrier, has not consented with knowledge of their nature and character, may at any time before discharge be landed at any place or destroyed or rendered innocuous by the carrier without compensation, and the shipper of such goods shall be liable for all damages and expenses directly or indirectly arising out of or resulting from such shipment. If any such goods shipped with such knowledge and consent shall become a danger to the ship or cargo, they may in like manner be landed at any place, or destroyed or rendered innocuous by the carrier without liability on the part of the carrier except to general average, if any.

SURRENDER OF RIGHTS AND IMMUNITIES AND INCREASE OF RESPONSIBILITIES AND LIABILITIES

SEC. 5. A carrier shall be at liberty to surrender in whole or in part all or any of his rights and immunities or to increase any of his responsibilities and liabilities under this Act, provided such surrender or increase shall be embodied in the bill of lading issued to the shipper.

The provisions of this Act shall not be applicable to charter parties; but if bills of lading are issued in the case of a ship under a charter party, they shall comply with the terms of this Act. Nothing in this Act shall be held to prevent the insertion in a bill of lading of any lawful provision regarding general average.

SPECIAL CONDITIONS

SEC. 6. Notwithstanding the provisions of the preceding sections, a carrier, master or agent of the carrier, and a shipper shall, in regard to any particular goods be at liberty to enter into any agreement in any terms as to the responsibility and liability of the carrier for such goods, and as to the rights and immunities of the carrier in respect of such goods, or his obligation as to seaworthiness (so far as the stipulation regarding seaworthiness is not contrary to public policy), or the care or diligence of his servants or agents in regard to the loading, handling, stowage, carriage, custody, care, and discharge of the goods carried by sea: *Provided*, That in this case no bill of lading has been or shall be issued and that the terms agreed shall be embodied in a receipt which shall be a nonnegotiable document and shall be marked as such.

Any agreement so entered into shall have full legal effect: *Provided*, That this section shall not apply to ordinary commercial shipments made in the ordinary course of trade but only to other shipments where the character or condition of the property to be carried or the circumstances, terms, and conditions under which the carriage is to be performed are such as reasonably to justify a special agreement.

SEC. 7. Nothing contained in this Act shall prevent a carrier or a shipper from entering into any agreement, stipulation, condition, reservation, or exemption as to the responsibility and liability of the carrier or the ship for the loss or damage to or in connection with the custody and care and handling of goods prior to the loading on and subsequent to the discharge from the ship on which the goods are carried by sea.

SEC. 8. The provisions of this Act shall not affect the rights and obligations of the carrier under the provisions of the Shipping Act, 1916, or under the provisions of sections 4281 to 4289, inclusive, of the Revised Statutes of the United States, or of any amendments thereto; or under the provisions of any other enactment for the time being in force relating to the limitation of the liability of the owners of seagoing vessels.

TITLE II

SECTION 9. Nothing contained in this Act shall be construed as permitting a common carrier by water to discriminate between competing shippers similarly placed in time and circumstances, either (a) with respect to their right to demand and receive bills of lading subject to the provisions of this Act; or (b) when issuing such bills of lading, either in the surrender of any of the carrier's rights and immunities or in the increase of any of the carrier's responsibilities and liabilities pursuant to section 5, title I, of this Act; or (c) in any other way prohibited by the Shipping Act, 1916, as amended.

SEC. 10. (Repealed by the Transportation Act 1940.)

SEC. 11. Where under the customs of any trade the weight of any bulk cargo inserted in the bill of lading is a weight ascertained or accepted by a third party other than the carrier or the shipper, and the fact that the weight is so ascertained or accepted is stated in the bill of lading, then, notwithstanding anything in this Act, the bill of lading shall not be deemed to be prima facie evidence against the carrier of the receipt of goods of the weight so inserted in the bill of lading, and the accuracy therefore at the time of shipment shall not be deemed to have been guaranteed by the shipper.

SEC. 12. Nothing in this Act shall be construed as superseding any part of the Act entitled "An Act relating to navigation of vessels, bills of lading, and to certain obligations, duties, and rights in connection with the carriage of property", approved February 13, 1893, or of any other law which would be applicable in the absence of this Act, insofar as they relate to the duties, responsibilities, and liabilities of the ship or carrier prior to the time when the goods are loaded on or after the time they are discharged from the ship.

SEC. 13. This Act shall apply to all contracts for carriage of goods by sea to or from ports of the United States in foreign trade. As used in this Act the term "United States" includes its districts, territories, and possessions: *Provided, however*, That the Philippine Legislature may by law exclude its application to transportation to or from ports of the Philippine Islands. The term "foreign trade" means the transportation of goods between the ports of the United States and ports of foreign countries. Nothing in this Act shall be held to apply to contracts for carriage of goods by sea between any port of the United States or its possessions, and any other port of the United States or its possessions: *Provided, however*, That any bill of lading or similar document of title which is evidence of a contract for the carriage of goods by sea between such ports, containing an express statement that it shall be subject to the provisions of this Act, shall be subjected hereto as fully as if subject hereto by the express provisions of this Act: *Provided further*, That every bill of lading or similar document of title which is evidence of a contract for the carriage of goods by sea from ports of the United States, in foreign trade, shall contain a statement that it shall have effect subject to the provisions of this Act.

SEC. 14. Upon the certification of the Secretary of Commerce that the foreign commerce of the United States in its competition with that of foreign nations is prejudiced by the provisions, or any of them, of title I of this Act, or by the laws of any foreign country or countries relating to the carriage of goods by sea, the President of the United States may, from time to time, by proclamation, suspend any or all provisions of title I of this Act for such periods of time or indefinitely as may be designated in the proclamation. The President may at any time rescind such suspension of title I hereof, and any provisions thereof which may have been suspended shall thereby be reinstated and again apply to contracts thereafter made for the carriage of goods by sea. Any proclamation of suspension or rescission of any such suspension shall take effect on a date named therein, which date shall be not less than ten days from the issue of the proclamation.

Any contract for the carriage of goods by sea, subject to the provisions of this Act, effective during any period when title I hereof, or any part thereof, is suspended, shall be subject to all provisions of law now or hereafter applicable to that part of title I which may have thus been suspended.

SEC. 15. This Act shall take effect ninety days after the date of its approval; but nothing in this Act shall apply during a period not to exceed one year following its approval to any contract for the carriage of goods by sea, made before the date on which this Act is approved, nor to any bill of lading or similar document of title issued, whether before or after such date of approval in pursuance of any such contract as aforesaid.

SEC. 16. This act may be cited as the "Carriage of Goods by Sea Act."

Approved, April 16, 1936.

Appendix E The Hamburg Rules

Annex I. United Nations Convention on the Carriage of Goods by Sea, 1978

Preamble

The states parties to this convention, having recognized the desirability of determining by agreement certain rules relating to the carriage of goods by sea, have decided to conclude a Convention for this purpose and have thereto agreed as follow:

Part I. General Provisions

Article 1.

Definitions
In this Convention:
  1. 'Carrier' means any person by whom or in whose name a contract of carriage of goods by sea has been concluded with a shipper.
  2. 'Actual carrier' means any person to whom the performance of the carriage of the goods, or of part of the carriage, has been entrusted by the carrier, and includes any other person to whom such performance has been entrusted.
  3. 'Shipper' means any person by whom or in whose name or on whose behalf a contract of carriage of goods by sea has been concluded with a carrier, or any person by whom or in whose name or on whose behalf the goods are actually delivered to the carrier in relation to the contract of carriage by sea.
  4. 'Consignee' means the person entitled to take delivery of the goods.
  5. 'Goods' includes live animals; where the goods are consolidated in a container, pallet or similar article of transport or where they are packed, 'goods' includes such article of transport or packaging if supplied by the shipper.
  6. 'Contract of carriage by sea' means any contract whereby the carrier undertakes against payment of freight to carry goods by sea from one port to another; however, a contract which involves carriage by sea and also carriage by some other means is deemed to be a contract of carriage by sea for the purposes of this Convention only in so far as it relates to the carriage by sea.
  7. 'Bill of lading' means a document which evidences a contract of carriage by sea and the taking over or loading of the goods by the carrier, and by which the carrier undertakes to deliver the goods against surrender of the document. A provision in the document that the goods are to be delivered to the order of a named person, or to order, or to bearer, constitutes such an undertaking.
  8. 'Writing' includes, *inter alia*, telegram and telex.

Article 2.

Scope of application

1. The provisions of this Convention are applicable to all contracts of carriage by sea between two different States, if:

(a) the port of loading as provided for in the contract of carriage by sea is located in a Contracting State, or

(b) the port of discharge as provided for in the contract of carriage by sea is located in a Contracting State, or

(c) one of the optional ports of discharge provided for in the contract of carriage by sea is the actual port of discharge and such port is located in a Contract State, or

(d) the bill of lading or other document evidencing the contract of carriage by sea is issued in a Contracting State, or

(e) the bill of lading or other document evidencing the contract of carriage by sea provides that the provisions of this Convention or the legislation of any State giving effect to them are to govern the contract.

2. The provisions of the Convention are applicable without regard to the nationality of the ship, the carrier, the actual carrier, the shipper, the consignee or any other interested person.

3. The provisions of this Convention are not applicable to charter-parties. However, where a bill of lading is issued pursuant to a charter-party, the provisions of the Convention apply to such a bill of lading if it governs the relation between the carrier and the holder of the bill of lading, not being the charterer.

4. If a contract provides for future carriage of goods in a series of shipments during an agreed period, the provisions of this Convention apply to each shipment. However, where a shipment is made under a charter-party, the provisions of paragraph 3 of this article apply.

Article 3.

Interpretation of the Convention

In the interpretation and application of the provisions of this Convention regard shall be had to its international character and to the need to promote uniformity.

Part II. Liability of the carrier

Article 4.

Period of responsibility

1. The responsibility of the carrier for the goods under this Convention covers the period during which the carrier is in charge of the goods at the port of loading, during the carriage and at the port of discharge.

2. For the purpose of paragraph 1 of this article, the carrier is deemed to be in charge of the goods

(a) from the time he has taken over the goods from:
  (i) the shipper, or a person acting on his behalf; or
  (ii) an authority or other third party to whom, pursuant to law or regulations applicable at the port of loading, the goods must be handed over for shipment;

(b) until the time he has delivered the goods:

(i) by handing over the goods to the consignee; or

(ii) in cases where the consignee does not receive the goods from the carrier, by placing them at the disposal of the consignee in accordance with the contract or with the law or with the usage of the particular trade, applicable at the port of discharge; or

(iii) by handing over the goods to an authority or other third party to whom, pursuant to law or regulations applicable at the port of discharge, the goods must be handed over.

3. In paragraphs 1 and 2 of this article, reference to the carrier or to the consignee means, in addition to the carrier or the consignee, the servants or agents, respectively, of the carrier or the consignee.

Article 5.

Basis of liability

1. The carrier is liable for loss resulting from loss of or damage to the goods, as well as from delay in delivery, if the occurrence which caused the loss, damage or delay took place while the goods were in his charge as defined in Article 4, unless the carrier proves that he, his servants or agents took all measures that could reasonably be required to avoid the occurrence and its consequences.

2. Delay in delivery occurs when the goods have not been delivered at the port of discharge provided for in the contract of carriage by sea within the time expressly agreed upon or, in the absence of such agreement, within the time which it would be reasonable to require of a diligent carrier, having regard to the circumstances of the case.

3. The person entitled to make a claim for the loss of goods may treat the goods as lost if they have not been delivered as required by Article 4 within 60 consecutive days following the expiry of the time for delivery according to paragraph 2 of this article.

4. (*a*) The carrier is liable

(i) for loss of or damage to the goods or delay in delivery caused by fire, if the claimant proves that the fire arose from fault or neglect on the part of the carrier, his servants or agents;

(ii) for such loss, damage or delay in delivery which is proved by the claimant to have resulted from the fault or neglect of the carrier, his servants or agents, in taking all measures that could reasonably be required to put out the fire and avoid or mitigate its consequences.

(*b*) In case of fire on board the ship affecting the goods, if the claimant or the carrier so desires, a survey in accordance with shipping practices must be held into the cause and circumstances of the fire, and a copy of the surveyor's report shall be made available on demand to the carrier and the claimant.

5. With respect to live animals, the carrier is not liable for loss, damage or delay in delivery resulting from any special risks inherent in that kind of carriage. If the carrier proves that he has complied with any special instructions given to him by the shipper respecting the animals and that, in the circumstances of the case, the loss, damage or delay in delivery could be attributed to such risks, it is presumed that the loss, damage or delay in delivery was so caused, unless there is proof that all or a part of the loss, damage or delay in delivery resulted from fault or neglect on the part of the carrier, his servants or agents.

6. The carrier is not liable, except in general average, where loss, damage

or delay in delivery resulted from measures to save life or from reasonable measures to save property at sea.

7. Where fault or neglect on the part of the carrier, his servants or agents combines with another cause to produce loss, damage or delay in delivery the carrier is liable only to the extent that the loss, damage or delay in delivery is attributable to such fault or neglect, provided that the carrier proves the amount of the loss, damage or delay in delivery not attributable thereto.

Article 6.

Limits of liability

1. (*a*) The liability of the carrier for loss resulting from loss of or damage to goods according to the provisions of Article 5 is limited to an amount equivalent to 835 units of account per package or other shipping unit or 2.5 units of account per kilogramme of gross weight of the goods lost or damaged, whichever is the higher.

(*b*) The liability of the carrier for delay in delivery according to the provisions of Article 5 is limited to an amount equivalent to two and a half times the freight payable for the goods delayed, but not exceeding the total freight payable under the contract of carriage of goods by sea.

(*c*) In no case shall the aggregate liability of the carrier, under both sub-paragraphs (*a*) and (*b*) of this paragraph, exceed the limitation which would be established under sub-paragraph (*a*) of this paragraph for total loss of the goods with respect to which such liability was incurred.

2. For the purpose of calculating which amount is the higher in accordance with paragraph 1(*a*) of this article, the following rules apply:

(*a*) Where a container, pallet or similar article of transport is used to consolidate goods, the package or other shipping units enumerated in the bill of lading, if issued, or otherwise in any other document evidencing the contract of carriage by sea, as packed in such article of transport are deemed packages or shipping units. Except as aforesaid the goods in such article of transport are deemed one shipping unit.

(*b*) In cases where the article of transport itself has been lost or damaged, that article of transport, if not owned or otherwise supplied by the carrier, is considered one separate shipping unit.

3. Unit of account means the unit of account mentioned in Article 26.

4. By agreement between the carrier and the shipper, limits of liability exceeding those provided for in paragraph 1 may be fixed.

Article 7.

Application to non-contractual claims

1. The defences and limits of liability provided for in this Convention apply in any action against the carrier in respect of loss or damage to the goods covered by the contract of carriage by sea, as well as of delay in delivery whether the action is founded in contract, in tort or otherwise.

2. If such an action is brought against a servant or agent of the carrier, such servant or agent, if he proves that he acted within the scope of his employment, is entitled to avail himself of the defences and limits of liability which the carrier is entitled to invoke under this Convention.

3. Except as provided in Article 8, the aggregate of the amounts recoverable from the carrier and from any persons referred to in paragraph 2 of this article shall not exceed the limits of liability provided for in this Convention.

Article 8.

Loss of right to limit responsibility

1. The carrier is not entitled to the benefit of the limitation of liability provided for in Article 6 if it is proved that the loss, damage or delay in delivery resulted from an act or omission of the carrier done with the intent to cause such loss, damage or delay, or recklessly and with knowledge that such loss, damage or delay would probably result.

2. Notwithstanding the provisions of paragraph 2 of Article 7, a servant or agent of the carrier is not entitled to the benefit of the limitation of liability provided for in Article 6 if it is proved that the loss, damage or delay in delivery resulted from an act of omission of such servant or agent, done with the intent to cause such loss, damage or delay, or recklessly and with knowledge that such loss, damage or delay would probably result.

Article 9.

Deck cargo

1. The carrier is entitled to carry the goods on deck only if such carriage is in accordance with an agreement with the shipper or with the usage of the particular trade or is required by statutory rules or regulations.

2. If the carrier and the shipper have agreed that the goods shall or may be carried on deck, the carrier must insert in the bill of lading or other document evidencing the contract of carriage by sea a statement to that effect. In the absence of such a statement the carrier has the burden of proving that an agreement for carriage on deck has been entered into; however, the carrier is not entitled to invoke such an agreement against a third party, including a consignee, who has acquired the bill of lading in good faith.

3. Where the goods have been carried on deck contrary to the provisions of paragraph 1 of this article or where the carrier may not under paragraph 2 of this article invoke an agreement for carriage on deck, the carrier, notwithstanding the provisions of paragraph 1 of Article 5, is liable for loss of or damage to the goods, as well as for delay in delivery, resulting solely from the carriage on deck, and the extent of his liability is to be determined in accordance with the provisions of Article 6 or Article 8 of this Convention, as the case may be.

4. Carriage of goods on deck contrary to express agreement for carriage under deck is deemed to be an act or omission of the carrier within the meaning of Article 8.

Article 10.

Liability of the carrier and actual carrier

1. Where the performance of the carriage or part thereof has been entrusted to an actual carrier, whether or not in pursuance of a liberty under the contract of carriage by sea to do so, the carrier nevertheless remains responsible for the entire carriage according to the provisions of this Convention. The carrier is responsible, in relation to the carriage performed by the actual carrier, for the acts and omissions of the actual carrier and of his servants and agents acting within the scope of their employment.

2. All the provisions of this Convention governing the responsibility of the carrier also apply to the responsibility of the actual carrier for the carriage performed by him. The provisions of paragraphs 2 and 3 of Article 7 and of paragraph 2 of Article 8 apply if an action is brought against a servant or agent of the actual carrier.

3. Any special agreement under which the carrier assumes obligations not imposed by this Convention or waives rights conferred by this Convention affects the actual carrier only if agreed to by him expressly and in writing. Whether or not the actual carrier has so agreed, the carrier nevertheless remains bound by the obligations or waivers resulting from such special agreement.

4. Where and to the extent that both the carrier and the actual carrier are liable, their liability is joint and several.

5. The aggregate of the amounts recoverable from the carrier, the actual carrier and their servants and agents shall not exceed the limits of liability provided for in this Convention.

6. Nothing in this Article shall prejudice any right of recourse as between the carrier and the actual carrier.

Article 11.

Through carriage

1. Notwithstanding the provisions of paragraph 1 of Article 10, where a contract of carriage by sea provides explicitly that a specified part of the carriage covered by the said contract is to be performed by a named person other than the carrier, the contract may also provide that the carrier is not liable for loss, damage or delay in delivery caused by an occurrence which takes place while the goods are in the charge of the actual carrier during such part of the carriage. Nevertheless, any stipulation limiting or excluding such liability is without effect if no judicial proceedings can be instituted against the actual carrier in a court competent under paragraph 1 or 2 of Article 21. The burden of proving that any loss, damage or delay in delivery has been caused by such an occurrence rests upon the carrier.

2. The actual carrier is responsible in accordance with the provisions of paragraph 2 of Article 10 for loss, damage or delay in delivery caused by an occurrence which takes place while the goods are in his charge.

Part III. Liability of the shipper

Article 12.

General rule

The shipper is not liable for loss sustained by the carrier or the actual carrier, or for damage sustained by the ship, unless such loss or damage was caused by the fault or neglect of the shipper, his servants or agents. Nor is any servant or agent of the shipper liable for such loss or damage unless the loss or damage was caused by fault or neglect on his part.

Article 13.

Special rules on dangerous goods

1. The shipper must mark or label in a suitable manner dangerous goods as dangerous.

2. Where the shipper hands over dangerous goods to the carrier or an actual carrier, as the case may be, the shipper must inform him of the dangerous character of the goods and, if necessary, of the precautions to be taken. If the shipper fails to do so and such carrier or actual carrier does not otherwise have knowledge of their dangerous character:

(a) the shipper is liable to the carrier and any actual carrier for the loss resulting from the shipment of such goods, and

(b) the goods may at any time be unloaded, destroyed or rendered innocuous, as the circumstances may require, without payment of compensation.

3. The provisions of paragraph 2 of this Article may not be invoked by any person if during the carriage he has taken the goods in his charge with knowledge of their dangerous character.

4. If, in cases where the provisions of paragraph 2, sub-paragraph (b), of this article do not apply or may not be invoked, dangerous goods become an actual danger to life or property, they may be unloaded, destroyed or rendered innocuous, as the circumstances may require, without payment of compensation except where there is an obligation to contribute in general average or where the carrier is liable in accordance with the provisions of Article 5.

Part IV. Transport Documents

Article 14.

Issue of bill of lading

1. When the carrier or the actual carrier takes the goods in his charge, the carrier must, on demand of the shipper, issue to the shipper a bill of lading.

2. The bill of lading may be signed by a person having authority from the carrier. A bill of lading signed by the master of the ship carrying the goods is deemed to have been signed on behalf of the carrier.

3. The signature on the bill of lading may be in handwriting, printed in facsimile, perforated, stamped, in symbols, or made by any other mechanical or electronic means, if not inconsistent with the law of the country where the bill of lading is issued.

Article 15.

Contents of bill of lading

1. The bill of lading must include, *inter alia*, the following particulars:

(a) the general nature of the goods, the leading marks necessary for identification of the goods, an express statement, if applicable, as to the dangerous character of the goods, the number of packages or pieces, and the weight of the goods or their quantity otherwise expressed, all such particulars as furnished by the shipper;

(b) the apparent condition of the goods;

(c) the name and principal place of business of the carrier;

(d) the name of the shipper;

(e) the consignee if named by the shipper;

(f) the port of loading under the contract of carriage by sea and the date on which the goods were taken over by the carrier at the port of loading;

(g) the port of discharge under the contract of carriage by sea;

(h) the number of originals of the bill of lading, if more than one;

(i) the place of issuance of the bill of lading;

(j) the signature of the carrier or a person acting on his behalf;

(k) the freight to the extent payable by the consignee or other indication that freight is payable by him;

(l) the statement referred to in paragraph 3 of Article 23;

(m) the statement, if applicable, that the goods shall or may be carried on deck;

(n) the date or the period of delivery of the goods at the port of discharge if expressly agreed upon between the parties; and

(o) any increased limit or limits of liability where agreed in accordance with paragraph 4 of Article 6.

2. After the goods have been loaded on board, if the shipper so demands, the carrier must issue to the shipper a 'shipped' bill of lading which, in addition to the particulars required under paragraph 1 of this article, must state that the goods are on board a named ship or ships, and the date or dates of loading. If the carrier has previously issued to the shipper a bill of lading or other document of title with respect to any of such goods, on request of the carrier, the shipper must surrender such document in exchange for a 'shipped' bill of lading. The carrier may amend any previously issued document in order to meet the shipper's demand for a 'shipped' bill of lading if, as amended, such document includes all the information required to be contained in a 'shipped' bill of lading.

3. The absence in the bill of lading of one or more particulars referred to in this article does not affect the legal character of the document as a bill of lading provided that it nevertheless meets the requirements set out in paragraph 7 of Article 1.

Article 16.

Bills of lading, reservations and evidentiary effect

1. If the bill of lading contains particulars concerning the general nature, leading marks, number of packages or pieces, weight or quantity of the goods which the carrier or other person issuing the bill of lading on his behalf knows or has reasonable grounds to suspect do not accurately represent the goods actually taken over or, where a 'shipped' bill of lading is issued, loaded, or if he had no reasonable means of checking such particulars, the carrier or such other person must insert in the bill of lading a reservation specifying these inaccuracies, grounds of suspicion or the absence of reasonable means of checking.

2. If the carrier or other person issuing the bill of lading on his behalf fails to note on the bill of lading the apparent condition of the goods, he is deemed to have noted on the bill of lading that the goods were in apparent good condition.

3. Except for particulars in respect of which and to the extent to which a reservation permitted under paragraph 1 of the Article has been entered:

(a) the bill of lading is *prima facie* evidence of the taking over or, where a 'shipped' bill of lading is issued, loading, by the carrier of the goods as described in the bill of lading; and

(b) proof to the contrary by the carrier is not admissible if the bill of lading has been transferred to a third party, including a consignee, who in good faith has acted in reliance on the description of the goods therein.

4. A bill of lading which does not, as provided in paragraph 1, subparagraph (k) of Article 15, set forth the freight or otherwise indicate that freight is payable by the consignee or does not set forth demurrage incurred at the port of loading payable by the consignee, is *prima facie* evidence that no freight or such demurrage is payable by him. However, proof to the contrary by the carrier is not admissible when the bill of lading has been transferred to a third party, including a consignee, who in good faith has acted in reliance on the absence in the bill of lading of any such indication.

Article 17.

Guarantees by the shipper

1. The shipper is deemed to have guaranteed to the carrier the accuracy of particulars relating to the general nature of the goods, their marks, number, weight and quantity as furnished by him for insertion in the bill of lading. The shipper must indemnify the carrier against the loss resulting from inaccuracies in such particulars. The shipper remains liable even if the bill of lading has been transferred by him. The right of the carrier to such indemnity in no way limits his liability under the contract of carriage by sea to any person other than the shipper.

2. Any letter of guarantee or agreement by which the shipper undertakes to indemnify the carrier against loss resulting from the issuance of the bill of lading by the carrier, or by a person acting on his behalf, without entering a reservation relating to particulars furnished by the shipper for insertion in the bill of lading, or to the apparent condition of the goods, is void and of no effect as against any third party, including a consignee, to whom the bill of lading has been transferred.

3. Such letter of guarantee or agreement is valid as against the shipper unless the carrier or the person acting on his behalf, by omitting the reservation referred to in paragraph 2 of this Article, intends to defraud a third party, including a consignee, who acts in reliance on the description of the goods in the bill of lading. In the latter case, if the reservation omitted relates to particulars furnished by the shipper for insertion in the bill of lading, the carrier has no right of indemnity from the shipper pursuant to paragraph 1 of this Article.

4. In the case of intended fraud referred to in paragraph 3 of this Article the carrier is liable, without the benefit of the limitation of liability provided for in this Convention, for the loss incurred by a third party, including a consignee, because he has acted in reliance on the description of the goods in the bill of lading.

Article 18.

Documents other than bills of lading

Where a carrier issues a document other than a bill of lading to evidence the receipt of the goods to be carried, such a document is *prima facie* evidence of the conclusion of the contract of carriage by sea and the taking over by the carrier of the goods therein described.

Part V. Claims and actions

Article 19.

Notice of loss, damage or delay

1. Unless notice of loss or damage, specifying the general nature of such loss or damage, is given in writing by the consignee to the carrier not later than the working day after the day when the goods were handed over to the consignee, such handing over is *prima facie* evidence of the delivery by the carrier of the goods as described in the document of transport or, if no such document has been issued, in good condition.

2. Where the loss or damage is not apparent, the provisions of paragraph 1 of this Article apply correspondingly if notice in writing is not given within 15 consecutive days after the day when the goods were handed over to the consignee.

3. If the state of the goods at the time they were handed over to the consignee has been the subject of a joint survey or inspection by the parties, notice in writing need not be given of loss or damage ascertained during such survey or inspection.

4. In the case of any actual or apprehended loss or damage the carrier and the consignee must give all reasonable facilities to each other for inspecting and tallying the goods.

5. No compensation shall be payable for loss resulting from delay in delivery unless a notice has been given in writing to the carrier within 60 consecutive days after the day when the goods were handed over to the consignee.

6. If the goods have been delivered by an actual carrier, any notice given under this article to him shall have the same effect as if it had been given to the carrier, and any notice given to the carrier shall have effect as if given to such actual carrier.

7. Unless notice of loss or damage, specifying the general nature of the loss or damage, is given in writing by the carrier or actual carrier to the shipper not later than 90 consecutive days after the occurrence of such loss or damage or after the delivery of the goods in accordance with paragraph 2 of Article 4, whichever is later, the failure to give such notice is *prima facie* evidence that the carrier or the actual carrier has sustained no loss or damage due to the fault or neglect of the shipper, his servants or agents.

8. For the purpose of this article, notice given to a person acting on the carrier's or the actual carrier's behalf, including the master or the officer in charge of the ship, or to a person acting on the shipper's behalf is deemed to have been given to the carrier, to the actual carrier or to the shipper, respectively.

Article 20.

Limitation of actions

1. Any action relating to carriage of goods under this Convention is time-barred if judicial or arbitral proceedings have not been instituted within a period of two years.

2. The limitation period commences on the day on which the carrier has delivered the goods or part thereof or, in cases where no goods have been delivered, on the last day on which the goods should have been delivered.

3. The day on which the limitation period commences is not included in the period.

4. The person against whom a claim is made may at any time during the running of the limitation period extend that period by a declaration in writing to the claimant. This period may be further extended by another declaration or declarations.

5. An action for indemnity by a person held liable may be instituted even after the expiration of the limitation period provided for in the preceding paragraphs if instituted within the time allowed by the law of the State where proceedings are instituted. However, the time allowed shall not be less than 90 days commencing from the day when the person instituting such action for indemnity has settled the claim or has been served with process in the action against himself.

Article 21.

Jurisdiction

1. In judicial proceedings relating to carriage of goods under this

Convention the plaintiff, at his option, may institute an action in a court which, according to the law of the State where the court is situated, is competent and within the jurisdiction of which is situated one of the following places:

(a) the principal place of business or, in the absence thereof, the habitual residence of the defendant; or

(b) the place where the contract was made provided that the defendant has there a place of business, branch or agency through which the contract was made; or

(c) the port of loading or the port of discharge; or

(d) any additional place designated for that purpose in the contract of carriage by sea.

2. (a) Notwithstanding the preceding provisions of this article, an action may be instituted in the courts of any port or place in a Contracting State at which the carrying vessel or any other vessel of the same ownership may have been arrested in accordance with applicable rules of the law of that State and of international law. However, in such a case, at the petition of the defendant, the claimant must remove the action, at his choice, to one of the jurisdictions referred to in paragraph 1 of this Article for the determination of the claim, but before such removal the defendant must furnish security sufficient to ensure payment of any judgment that may subsequently be awarded to the claimant in the action.

(b) All questions relating to the sufficiency or otherwise of the security shall be determined by the court of the port or place of the arrest.

3. No judicial proceedings relating to carriage of goods under this Convention may be instituted in a place not specified in paragraph 1 or 2 of this Article. The provisions of this paragraph do not constitute an obstacle to the jurisdiction of the Contracting States for provisional or protective measures.

4. (a) Where an action has been instituted in a court competent under paragraph 1 or 2 of this article or where judgment has been delivered by such a court, no new action may be started between the same parties on the same grounds unless the judgment of the court before which the first action was instituted is not enforceable in the country in which the new proceedings are instituted;

(b) for the purpose of this article the institution of measures with a view to obtaining enforcement of a judgment is not to be considered as the starting of a new action;

(c) for the purpose of this article, the removal of an action to a different court within the same country, or to a court in another country, in accordance with paragraph 2 (a) of this article, is not to be considered as the starting of a new action.

5. Notwithstanding the provisions of the preceding paragraphs, an agreement made by the parties, after a claim under the contract of carriage by sea has arisen, which designates the place where the claimant may institute an action, is effective.

Article 22.

Arbitration

1. Subject to the provisions of this article, parties may provide by agreement evidenced in writing that any dispute that may arise relating to carriage of goods under this Convention shall be referred to arbitration.

2. Where a charter-party contains a provision that disputes arising

thereunder shall be referred to arbitration and a bill of lading issued pursuant to the charter-party does not contain a special annotation providing that such provision shall be binding upon the holder of the bill of lading, the carrier may not invoke such provision as against a holder having acquired the bill of lading in good faith.

3. The arbitration proceedings shall, at the option of the claimant, be instituted at one of the following places:

(a) a place in a State within whose territory is situated:
    (i) the principal place of business of the defendant or, in the absence thereof, the habitual residence of the defendant; or
    (ii) the place where the contract was made, provided that the defendant has there a place of business, branch or agency through which the contract was made; or
    (iii) the port of loading or the port of discharge; or
(b) any place designated for that purpose in the arbitration clause or agreement.

4. The arbitrator or arbitration tribunal shall apply the rules of this Convention.

5. The provisions of paragraphs 3 and 4 of this Article are deemed to be part of every arbitration clause or agreement, and any term of such clause or agreement which is inconsistent therewith is null and void.

6. Nothing in this article affects the validity of an agreement relating to arbitration made by the parties after the claim under the contract of carriage by sea has arisen.

Part VI. Supplementary provisions

Article 23.

Contractual stipulations

1. Any stipulation in a contract of carriage by sea, in a bill of lading, or in any other document evidencing the contract of carriage by sea is null and void to the extent that it derogates, directly or indirectly, from the provisions of this Convention. The nullity of such a stipulation does not affect the validity of the other provisions of the contract or document of which it forms a part. A clause assigning benefit of insurance of the goods in favour of the carrier, or any similar clause, is null and void.

2. Notwithstanding the provisions of paragraph 1 of this Article, a carrier may increase his responsibilities and obligations under this Convention.

3. Where a bill of lading or any other document evidencing the contract of carriage by sea is issued, it must contain a statement that the carriage is subject to the provisions of this Convention which nullify any stipulation derogating therefrom to the detriment of the shipper or the consignee.

4. Where the claimant in respect of the goods has incurred loss as a result of a stipulation which is null and void by virtue of the present Article, or as a result of the omission of the statement referred to in paragraph 3 of this Article, the carrier must pay compensation to the extent required in order to give the claimant compensation in accordance with the provisions of this Convention for any loss of or damage to the goods as well as for delay in delivery. The carrier must, in addition, pay compensation for costs incurred by the claimant for the purpose of exercising his right, provided that costs incurred in the action where the foregoing provision is invoked are to be determined in accordance with the law of the State where proceedings are instituted.

Article 24.

General average

1. Nothing in this Convention shall prevent the application of provisions in the contract of carriage by sea or national law regarding the adjustment of general average.

2. With the exception of Article 20, the provisions of this Convention relating to the liability of the carrier for loss of or damage to the goods also determine whether the consignee may refuse contribution in general average and the liability of the carrier to indemnify the consignee in respect of any such contribution made or any salvage paid.

Article 25.

Other conventions

1. This Convention does not modify the rights or duties of the carrier, the actual carrier and their servants and agents, provided for in international conventions or national law relating to the limitation of liability of owners of seagoing ships.

2. The provisions of Articles 21 and 22 of this Convention do not prevent the application of the mandatory provisions of any other multilateral convention already in force at the date of this Convention relating to matters dealt with in the said articles, provided that the dispute arises exclusively between parties having their principal place of business in States members of such other convention. However, this paragraph does not affect the application of paragraph 4 of Article 22 of this Convention.

3. No liability shall arise under the provisions of this Convention for damage caused by a nuclear incident if the operator of a nuclear installation is liable for such damage.

(*a*) under either the Paris Convention of 29 July 1960 on Third Party Liability in the Field of Nuclear Energy as amended by the Additional Protocol of 28 January 1964 or the Vienna Convention of 21 May 1963 on Civil Liability for Nuclear Damage, or

(*b*) by virtue of national law governing the liability for such damage, provided that such law is in all respects as favourable to persons who may suffer damage as either the Paris or Vienna Conventions.

4. No liability shall arise under the provisions of this Convention for any loss of or damage to or delay in delivery of luggage for which the carrier is responsible under any international convention or national law relating to the carriage of passengers and their luggage by sea.

5. Nothing contained in this Convention prevents a Contracting State from applying any other international convention which is already in force at the date of this Convention and which applies mandatorily to contracts of carriage of goods primarily by a mode of transport other than transport by sea. This provision also applies to any subsequent revision or amendment of such international convention.

Article 26.

Unit of account

1. The unit of account referred to in Article 6 of this Convention is the Special Drawing Right as defined by the International Monetary Fund. The amounts mentioned in Article 6 are to be converted into the national currency of a State according to the value of such currency at the date of

judgment or the date agreed upon by the parties. The value of a national currency, in terms of the Special Drawing Right, of a Contracting State which is a member of the International Monetary Fund is to be calculated in accordance with the method of valuation applied by the International Monetary Fund in effect at the date in question for its operations and transactions. The value of a national currency in terms of the Special Drawing Right of a Contracting State which is not a member of the International Monetary Fund is to be calculated in a manner determined by that State.

2. Nevertheless, those States which are not members of the International Monetary Fund and whose law does not permit the application of the provisions of paragraph 1 or this Article may, at the time of signature, or at the time of ratification, acceptance, approval or accession or at any time thereafter, declare that the limits of liability provided for in this Convention to be applied in their territories shall be fixed as: 12500 monetary units per package or other shipping unit or 37.5 monetary units per kilogramme of gross weight of the goods.

3. The monetary unit referred to in paragraph 2 of this Article corresponds to sixty-five and a half milligrammes of gold of millesimal fineness 900. The conversion of the amounts referred to in paragraph 2 into the national currency is to be made according to the law of the State concerned.

4. The calculation mentioned in the last sentence of paragraph 1 and the conversion mentioned in paragraph 3 of this Article is to be made in such a manner as to the express in the national currency of the Contracting State as far as possible the same real value for the amounts in Article 6 as is expressed there in units of account. Contracting States must communicate to the depositary the manner of calculation pursuant to paragraph 1 of this Article, or the result of the conversion mentioned in paragraph 3 of this Article, as the case may be, at the time of signature or when depositing their instruments of ratification, acceptance, approval or accession, or when availing themselves of the option provided for in paragraph 2 of this Article and whenever there is a change in the manner of such calculation or in the result of such conversion.

Part VII. Final clauses

Article 27.

Depositary

The Secretary-General of the United Nations is hereby designated as the depositary of this Convention.

Article 28.

Signature, ratification, acceptance, approval, accession

1. This Convention is open for signature by all States until 30 April 1979 at the Headquarters of the United Nations, New York.

2. This Convention is subject to ratification, acceptance or approval by the signatory States.

3. After 30 April 1979, this Convention will be open for accession by all States which are not signatory States.

4. Instruments of ratification, acceptance, approval and accession are to be deposited with the Secretary-General of the United Nations.

Article 29.

Reservations

No reservations may be made to this Convention.

Article 30.

Entry into force

1. This Convention enters into force on the first day of the month following the expiration of one year from the date of deposit of the 20th instrument of ratification, acceptance, approval or accession.

2. For each State which becomes a Contracting State to this Convention after the date of the deposit of the 20th instrument of ratification, acceptance, approval or accession, this Convention enters into force on the first day of the month following the expiration of one year after the deposit of the appropriate instrument on behalf of that State.

3. Each Contracting State shall apply the provisions of this Convention to contracts of carriage by sea concluded on or after the date of the entry into force of this Convention in respect of that State.

Article 31.

Denunciation of other conventions

1. Upon becoming a Contracting State to this Convention, any State party to the International Convention for the Unification of Certain Rules relating to Bills of Lading signed at Brussels on 25 August 1924 (1924 Convention) must notify the Government of Belgium as the depositary of the 1924 Convention of its denunciation of the said Convention with a declaration that the denunciation is to take effect as from the date when this Convention enters into force in respect of that State.

2. Upon the entry into force of this Convention under paragraph 1 of Article 30, the depositary of this Convention must notify the Government of Belgium as the depositary of the 1924 Convention of the date of such entry into force, and of the names of the Contracting States in respect of which the Convention has entered into force.

3. The provisions of paragraphs 1 and 2 of this Article apply correspondingly in respect of States parties to the Protocol signed on 23 February 1968 to amend the International Convention for the Unification of Certain Rules relating to Bills of Lading signed at Brussels on 25 August 1924.

4. Notwithstanding Article 2 of this Convention, for the purposes of paragraph 1 of this Article, a Contracting State may, if it deems it desirable, defer the denunciation of the 1924 Convention and of the 1924 Convention as modified by the 1968 Protocol for a maximum period of five years from the entry into force of this Convention. It will then notify the Government of Belgium of its intention. During this transitory period, it must apply to the Contracting States this Convention to the exclusion of any other one.

Article 32.

Revision and amendment

1. At the request of not less than one-third of the Contracting States to this Convention, the depositary shall convene a conference of the Contracting States for revising or amending it.

2. Any instrument of ratification, acceptance, approval or accession

deposited after the entry into force of an amendment to this Convention, is deemed to apply to the Convention as amended.

Article 33.

Revision of the limitation amounts and unit of account or monetary unit

1. Notwithstanding the provisions of Article 32, a conference only for the purpose of altering the amount specified in Article 6 and paragraph 2 of Article 26, or of substituting either or both of the units defined in paragraphs 1 and 3 of Article 26 by other units is to be convened by the depositary in accordance with paragraph 2 of this article. An alteration of the amounts shall be made only because of a significant change in their real value.

2. A revision conference is to be convened by the depositary when not less than one-fourth of the Contracting States so request.

3. Any decision by the conference must be taken by a two-thirds majority of the participating States. The amendment is communicated by the depositary to all the Contracting States for acceptance and to all the States signatories of the Convention for information.

4. Any amendment adopted enters into force on the first day of the month following one year after its acceptance by two-thirds of the Contracting States. Acceptance is to be effected by the deposit of a formal instrument to that effect, with the depositary.

5. After entry into force of an amendment a Contracting State which has accepted the amendment is entitled to apply the Convention as amended in its relations with Contracting States which have not within six months after the adoption of the amendment notified the depositary that they are not bound by the amendment.

6. Any instrument of ratification, acceptance, approval or accession deposited after the entry into force of an amendment to this Convention, is deemed to apply to the Convention as amended.

Article 34.

Denunciation

1. A Contracting State may denounce this Convention at any time by means of a notification in writing addressed to the depositary.

2. The denunciation takes effect on the first day of the month following the expiration of one year after the notification is received by the depositary. Where a longer period is specified in the notification, the denunciation takes effect upon the expiration of such longer period after the notification is received by the depositary.

DONE at Hamburg, this thirty-first day of March one thousand nine hundred and seventy-eight, in a single original, of which the Arabic, Chinese, English, French, Russian and Spanish texts are equally authentic.

IN WITNESS WHEREOF the undersigned plenipotentiaries, being duly authorized by their respective Governments, have signed the present Convention.

Annex II

Common understanding adopted by the United Nations Conference on the Carriage of Goods by Sea

It is the common understanding that the liability of the carrier under this Convention is based on the principle of presumed fault or neglect. This means that, as a rule, the burden of proof rests on the carrier but, with respect to certain cases, the provisions of the Convention modify this rule.

Annex III

Resolution adopted by the United Nations Conference on the Carriage of Goods by Sea

"The United Nations Conference on the Carriage of Goods by Sea,

"*Noting* with appreciation the kind invitation of the Federal Republic of Germany to hold the Conference in Hamburg,

"*Being aware* that the facilities placed at the disposal of the Conference and the generous hospitality bestowed on the participants by the Government of the Federal Republic of Germany and by the Free and Hanseatic City of Hamburg, have in no small measure contributed to the success of the Conference,

"*Expresses* its gratitude to the Government and people of the Federal Republic of Germany, and

"*Having adopted* the Convention on the Carriage of Goods by Sea on the basis of a draft Convention prepared by the United Nations Commission on International Trade Law at the request of the United Nations Conference on Trade and Development,

"*Expresses* its gratitude to the United Nations Commission on International Trade Law and to the United Nations Conference on Trade and Development for their outstanding contribution to the simplification and harmonization of the law of the carriage of goods by sea, and

"*Decides* to designate the Convention adopted by the Conference as the: 'UNITED NATIONS CONVENTION ON THE CARRIAGE OF GOODS BY SEA, 1978', and

"*Recommends* that the rules embodied therein be known as the 'HAMBURG RULES'."

Appendix F *The York-Antwerp Rules 1974*

Rule of Interpretation

In the adjustment of general average the following lettered and numbered Rules shall apply to the exclusion of any Law and Practice inconsistent therewith.

Except as provided by the numbered Rules, general average shall be adjusted according to the lettered Rules.

Rule A

There is a general average act when, and only when, any extraordinary sacrifice or expenditure is intentionally and reasonably made or incurred for the common safety for the purpose of preserving from peril the property involved in a common maritime adventure.

Rule B

General average sacrifices and expenses shall be borne by the different contributing interests on the basis hereinafter provided.

Rule C

Only such losses, damages or expenses which are the direct consequence of the general average act shall be allowed as general average.

Loss or damage sustained by the ship or cargo through delay, whether on the voyage or subsequently, such as demurrage, and any indirect loss whatsoever, such as loss of market, shall not be admitted as general average.

Rule D

Rights to contribution in general average shall not be affected, though the event which gave rise to the sacrifice or expenditure may have been due to the fault of one of the parties to the adventure, but this shall not prejudice any remedies or defences which may be open against or to that party in respect of such fault.

Rule E

The onus of proof is upon the party claiming in general average to show that the loss or expense claimed is properly allowable as general average.

Rule F

Any extra expense incurred in place of another expense which would have been allowable as general average shall be deemed to be general average and so allowed without regard to the saving, if any, to other interests, but only up to the amount of the general average expense avoided.

Rule G

General average shall be adjusted as regards both loss and contribution upon the basis of values at the time and place when and where the adventure ends.

This rule shall not affect the determination of the place at which the average statement is to be made up.

Rule I. Jettison of Cargo

No jettison of cargo shall be made good as general average, unless such cargo is carried in accordance with the recognized custom of the trade.

Rule II. Damage by Jettison and Sacrifice for the Common Safety

Damage done to a ship and cargo, or either of them, by or in consequence of a sacrifice made for the common safety, and by water which goes down a ship's hatches opened or other opening made for the purpose of making a jettison for the common safety, shall be made good as general average.

Rule III. Extinguishing Fire on Shipboard

Damage done to a ship and cargo, or either of them, by water or otherwise, including damage by beaching or scuttling a burning ship, in extinguishing a fire on board the ship, shall be made good as general average; except that no compensation shall be made for damage by smoke or heat however caused.

Rule IV. Cutting away Wreck

Loss or damage sustained by cutting away wreck or parts of the ship which have been previously carried away or are effectively lost by accident shall not be made good as general average.

Rule V. Voluntary Stranding

When a ship is intentionally run on shore for the common safety, whether or not she might have been driven on shore, the consequent loss or damage shall be allowed in general average.

Rule VI. Salvage remuneration

Expenditure incurred by the parties to the adventure on account of salvage, whether under contract or otherwise, shall be allowed in general average to the extent that the salvage operations were undertaken for the purpose of preserving from peril the property involved in the common maritime adventure.

Rule VII. Damage to Machinery and Boilers

Damage caused to any machinery and boilers of a ship which is ashore and in a position of peril, in endeavouring to refloat, shall be allowed in general average when shown to have arisen from an actual intention to float the ship for the common safety at the risk of such damage; but where a ship is afloat no loss or damage caused by working the propelling machinery and boilers shall in any circumstances be made good as general average.

Rule VIII. Expenses lightening a Ship when Ashore, and Consequent Damage

When a ship is ashore and cargo and ship's fuel and stores or any of them are discharged as a general average act, the extra cost of lightening, lighter hire and reshipping (if incurred), and the loss or damage sustained thereby, shall be admitted as general average.

Rule IX. Ship's Materials and Stores Burnt for Fuel

Ships' materials and stores, or any of them, necessarily burnt for fuel for the common safety at a time of peril, shall be admitted as general average, when and only when an ample supply of fuel had been provided; but the estimated quantity of fuel that would have been consumed, calculated at the price current at the ship's last port of departure at the date of her leaving, shall be credited to the general average.

Rule X. Expenses at Port of Refuge, etc.

(a) When a ship shall have entered a port or place of refuge, or shall have returned to her port or place of loading in consequence of accident, sacrifice or other extraordinary circumstances, which render that necessary for the common safety, the expenses of entering such port or place shall be admitted as general average; and when she shall have sailed thence with her original cargo, 'or a part of it, the corresponding expenses of leaving such port or place consequent upon such entry or return shall likewise be admitted as general average.

When a ship is at any port or place of refuge and is necessarily removed to another port or place because repairs cannot be carried out in the first port or place, the provisions of this Rule shall be applied to the second port or place as if it were a port or place of refuge and the cost of such removal including temporary repairs and towage shall be admitted as general average. The provisions of Rule XI shall be applied to the prolongation of the voyage occasioned by such removal.

(b) The cost of handling on board or discharging cargo, fuel or stores whether at a port or place of loading, call or refuge, shall be admitted as general average, when the handling or discharge was necessary for the common safety or to enable damage to the ship caused by sacrifice or accident to be repaired, if the repairs were necessary for the safe prosecution of the voyage, except in cases where the damage to the ship is discovered at a port or place of loading or call without any accident or other extraordinary circumstances connected with such damage having taken place during the voyage.

The cost of handling on board or discharging cargo, fuel or stores shall not be admissible as general average when incurred solely for the purpose of restowage due to shifting during the voyage, unless such restowage is necessary for the common safety.

(c) Whenever the cost of handling or discharging cargo, fuel or stores is admissible as general average, the costs of storage, including insurance if reasonably incurred, reloading and stowing of such cargo, fuel or stores shall likewise be admitted as general average.

But when the ship is condemned or does not proceed on her original voyage, storage expenses shall be admitted as general average only up to the date of the ship's condemnation of or the abandonment of the voyage or up to the date of completion of discharge of cargo if the condemnation or abandonment takes place before that date.

Rule XI. Wages and Maintenance of Crew and other Expenses bearing up for and in a Port of Refuge, etc.

(a) Wages and maintenance of master, officers and crew reasonably incurred and fuel and stores consumed during the prolongation of the voyage occasioned by a ship entering a port or place of refuge or returning to her port or place of loading shall be admitted as general average when the expenses of entering such port or place are allowable in general average in accordance with Rule X(a).

(b) When a ship shall have entered or been detained in any port or place in consequence of accident, sacrifice or other extraordinary circumstances which render that necessary for the common safety, or to enable damage to the ship caused by sacrifice or accident to be repaired, if the repairs were necessary for the safe prosecution of the voyage, the wages and maintenance of the master, officers and crew reasonably incurred during the extra period of detention in such port or place until the ship shall or should have been made ready to proceed upon her voyage, shall be admitted in general average.

Provided that when damage to the ship is discovered at a port or place of loading or call without any accident or other extraordinary circumstance connected with such damage having taken place during the voyage, then the wages and maintenance of master, officers and crew and fuel and stores consumed during the extra detention for repairs to damages so discovered shall not be admissible as general average, even if the repairs are necessary for the safe prosecution of the voyage.

When the ship is condemned or does not proceed on her original voyage, wages and maintenance of the master, officers and crew and fuel and stores consumed shall be admitted as general average only up to the date of the ship's condemnation or of the abandonment of the voyage or up to the date of completion of discharge of cargo if the condemnation or abandonment takes place before that date.

Fuel and stores consumed during the extra period of detention shall be admitted as general average, except such fuel and stores as are consumed in effecting repairs not allowable in general average.

Port charges incurred during the extra period of detention shall likewise be admitted as general average except such charges as are incurred solely by reason of repairs not allowable in general average.

(c) For the purpose of this and the other Rules wages shall include all payments made to or for the benefit of the master, officers and crew, whether such payments be imposed by law upon the shipowners or be made under the terms or articles of employment.

(d) When overtime is paid to the master, officers or crew for maintenance of the ship or repairs, the cost of which is not allowable in general average, such overtime shall be allowed in general average only up to the saving in expense which would have been incurred and admitted as general average, had such overtime not been incurred.

Rule XII. Damage to Cargo in Discharging, etc.

Damage to or loss of cargo, fuel or stores caused in the act of handling, discharging, storing, reloading and stowing shall be made good as general average, when and only when the cost of those measures respectively is admitted as general average.

Rule XIII. Deductions from Cost of Repairs

Repairs to be allowed in general average shall not be subject to deductions in respect of "new for old" where old material or parts are replaced by new unless the ship is over fifteen years old in which case there shall be a deduction of one third. The deductions shall be regulated by the age of the ship from the 31st December of the year of completion of construction to the date of the general average act, except for insulation, life and similar boats, communications and navigational apparatus and equipment, machinery and boilers for which the deductions shall be regulated by the age of the particular parts to which they apply.

The deductions shall be made only from the cost of the new material or parts when finished and ready to be installed in the ship.

No deduction shall be made in respect of provisions, stores, anchors and chain cables.

Drydock and slipway dues and costs of shifting the ship shall be allowed in full.

The costs of cleaning, painting or coating of bottom shall not be allowed in general average unless the bottom has been painted or coated within the twelve months preceding the date of the general average act in which case one half of such costs shall be allowed.

Rule XIV. Temporary Repairs

Where temporary repairs are effected to a ship at a port of loading, call or refuge, for the common safety, or of damage caused by general average sacrifice, the cost of such repairs shall be admitted as general average.

Where temporary repairs of accidental damage are effected in order to enable the adventure to be completed, the cost of such repairs shall be admitted as general average without regard to the saving, if any, to other interests, but only up to the saving in expense which would have been incurred and allowed in general average if such repairs had not been effected there.

No deductions "new for old" shall be made from the cost of temporary repairs allowable as general average.

Rule XV. Loss of Freight

Loss of freight arising from damage to or loss of cargo shall be made good as general average, either when caused by a general average act, or when the damage to or loss of cargo is so made good.

Deduction shall be made from the amount of gross freight lost, of the charges which the owner thereof would have incurred to earn such freight, but has, in consequence of the sacrifice, not incurred.

Rule XVI. Amount to be made good for Cargo Lost or Damaged by Sacrifice

The amount to be made good as general average for damage to or loss of cargo sacrificed shall be the loss which has been sustained thereby, based on the value at the time of discharge, ascertained from the commercial invoice rendered to the receiver or if there is no such invoice from the shipped value. The value at the time of discharge shall include the cost of insurance and freight except insofar as such freight is at the risk of interests other than the cargo.

When cargo so damaged is sold and the amount of the damage has not been otherwise agreed, the loss to be made good in general average shall be the difference between the net proceeds of sale and the net sound value as computed in the first paragraph of this Rule.

Rule XVII. Contributory Values

The contribution to a general average shall be made upon the actual net values of the property at the termination of the adventure except that the value of cargo shall be the value at the time of discharge, ascertained from the commercial invoice rendered to the receiver or if there is no such invoice from the shipped value. The value of the cargo shall include the cost of insurance and freight unless and insofar as such freight is at the risk of interests other than the cargo, deducting therefrom any loss or damage suffered by the cargo prior to or at the time of discharge. The value of the ship shall be assessed without taking into account the beneficial or detrimental effect of any demise or time charter-party to which the ship may be committed.

To these values shall be added the amount made good as general average for property sacrificed, if not already included, deduction being made from the freight and passage money at risk of such charges and crew's wages as would not have been incurred in earning the freight had the ship and cargo been totally lost at the date of the general average act and have not been allowed as general average; deduction being also made from the value of the property of all extra charges incurred in respect thereof subsequently to the general average act, except such charges as are allowed in general average.

Where cargo is sold short of destination, however, it shall contribute upon the actual net proceeds of sale, with the addition of any amount made good as general average.

Passengers' luggage and personal effects not shipped under bill of lading shall not contribute in general average.

Rule XVIII. Damage to Ship

The amount to be allowed as general average for damage or loss to the ship, her machinery and/or gear caused by the general average act shall be as follows:

(a) When repaired or replaced.

The actual reasonable cost of repairing or replacing such damage or loss, subject to deductions in accordance with Rule XIII;

(b) When not repaired or replaced.

The reasonable depreciation arising from such damage or loss, but not exceeding the estimated cost of repairs. But where the ship is an actual total loss or when the cost of repairs of the damage would exceed the value of the ship when repaired, the amount to be allowed as general average shall be the difference between the estimated sound value of the ship after deducting therefrom the estimated cost of repairing damage which is not general average and the value of the ship in her damaged state which may be measured by the net proceeds of sale, if any.

Rule XIX. Undeclared or Wrongfully Declared Cargo

Damage or loss caused to goods loaded without the knowledge of the shipowner or his agent or to goods wilfully misdescribed at time of shipment shall not be allowed as general average, but such goods shall remain liable to contribute, if saved.

Damage or loss caused to goods which have been wrongfully declared on shipment at a value which is lower than their real value shall be contributed for at the declared value, but such goods shall contribute upon their actual value.

Rule XX. Provision of Funds

A commission of 2 per cent, on general average disbursements, other than the wages and maintenance of master, officers and crew and fuel and stores not replaced during the voyage, shall be allowed in general average, but when the funds are not provided by any of the contributing interests, the necessary cost of obtaining the funds required by means of a bottomry bond or otherwise, or the loss sustained by owners of goods sold for the purpose, shall be allowed in general average.

The cost of insuring money advanced to pay for general average disbursements shall also be allowed in general average.

Rule XXI. Interest on Losses made good in General Average

Interest shall be allowed on expenditure, sacrifices and allowances charged to general average at the rate of 7 per cent, per annum, until the date of the general average statement, due allowance being made for any interim reimbursement from the contributory interests or from the general average deposit fund.

Rule XXII. Treatment of Cash Deposits

Where cash deposits have been collected in respect of cargo's liability for general average, salvage or special charges, such deposits shall be paid without any delay into a special account in the joint names of a representative nominated on behalf of the shipowner and a representative nominated on behalf of the depositors in a bank to be approved by both. The sum so deposited together with accrued interest, if any, shall be held as security for payment to the parties entitled thereto of the general average, salvage or special charges payable by cargo in respect to which the deposits have been collected. Payments on account or refund of deposits may be made if certified to in writing by the average adjuster. Such deposits and payments or refunds shall be without prejudice to the ultimate liability of the parties.

Appendix G An example of through bill of lading conditions.

DEFINITION OF GOODS. "Goods" means the cargo accepted from the Shipper and includes any container, transportable tank, flat or pallet not supplied by or on behalf of the Carrier.

1. CLAUSE PARAMOUNT. IT IS MUTUALLY AGREED that this Bill of Lading shall have effect subject to the provisions of the International Convention relating to Bills of Lading dated Brussels 25th August 1924 (hereinafter called the Hague Rules), except where legislation giving effect to the Hague Rules as amended by the Protocol signed in Brussels 23rd February 1968 (hereinafter called the Hague Visby Rules) is compulsorily applicable, in which case this Bill of Lading shall have effect subject to the provisions of such legislation. Neither the Hague Rules nor the Hague Visby Rules shall apply where the goods carried hereunder are live animals or cargo which is stated on the face hereof as being carried on deck and is so carried. Provided that nothing contained in this Bill of Lading shall deprive the Carrier of any limitations of or exemptions from liability conferred on the Carrier or the ship by any statute or enactment whatsoever (whether of the United Kingdom or otherwise).

2. RESPONSIBILITY FOR CONVEYANCE, DISCHARGE AND DELIVERY

(a) The Carrier's obligations in respect of the goods shall begin when the goods are accepted at the ocean vessel's rail at the port of loading and shall continue until the goods are discharged at the ocean vessel's rail at the port of discharge. The Carrier shall not in any circumstances whatsoever be liable for any loss or delay of or damage to the goods (whether in his actual or constructive possession or not) howsoever caused occurring before they are accepted at the ocean vessel's rail at the port of loading or after they are discharged at the ocean vessel's rail at the port of discharge.

(b) Notwithstanding anything contained in Sub-Clause (a) above, where by the nature of this Bill of Lading the contract of carriage is in respect of through-transit of containerised or otherwise unitised goods from a place of acceptance to a place of delivery which are expressly stated on the face of this Bill of Lading, the Carrier shall be responsible for loss or damage of whatsoever nature and howsoever arising to the extent following but no further;

(i) with respect to such loss or damage occurring during the carriage by sea or at the sea terminal at the port of loading or the port of discharge to the extent prescribed by the Hague Rules or the Hague Visby Rules, whichever are applicable by Clause 1 above, or

(ii) with respect to such loss or damage not covered by paragraph (i) occurring during the handling, storage or carriage of the goods by a sub-contractor or agent of the Carrier or his agent in which case the liability of the Carrier shall be limited to that amount recoverable by the Carrier or his agent from the sub-contractor or agent in respect of such loss or damage, or

(iii) if it cannot be proved where the goods were when the loss or damage occurred, the loss or damage shall be deemed to have occurred at sea and the Carrier shall be liable to the extent prescribed by the Hague Rules.

The Carrier shall be entitled to sub-contract on any terms the whole or any part of the carriage, loading, unloading, storage, warehousing, handling and all duties whatsoever undertaken by the Carrier in relation to the goods.

3. DISCHARGE AND DELIVERY. The vessel may commence discharging immediately on arrival without notice to the Consignee or any other person and notwithstanding any provision on the face hereof to notify any party which provision (if any) shall impose no obligation whatsoever on the Carrier, and discharge continuously with or without sorting the goods or separating them from other goods (whether or not such other goods are in the same ownership), irrespective of weather, by day and by night, Sundays and holidays included, any custom of the port to the contrary notwithstanding, on to quay, or into shed, warehouse, depot, hulk, lighter, premises, vehicle or any other vessel or craft as the Carrier of his Agents may determine. Delivery overside to Consignee's lighters is at the vessel's option, and, if given, is subject to the Consignee providing sufficient lighters and men to receive the goods as fast as the vessel can deliver, any custom of the port to the contrary notwithstanding. Such discharge shall constitute due delivery of the goods under this Bill of Lading. The Consignee shall bear any charges or expenses incurred by the Consignee or by the Carrier wholly or partially in respect of sorting the goods or separating them from other goods (whether in the same ownership or not) on shore or on board for any purpose whatsoever, including any charges or expenses in connection with storage on shore or afloat pending such sorting or separation; and any apportionment of such charges or expenses by the Carrier among different consignees by any method whatsoever in the discretion of the Carrier shall for the purpose of this clause be final and binding upon the Consignee.

OPTIONAL CARGO. The port of discharge for optional cargo must be declared to the vessel's Agents at the first of the optional ports named in the option not later than 48 hours before the vessel's expected arrival there, or failing such declaration the Carrier may in his absolute discretion discharge the same at the first or any optional port and such discharge shall be deemed a complete fulfilment by the Carrier of the contractual and intended voyage and all the remedies and rights of the Carrier, his servants or agents shall have effect accordingly. Any option must be for the total quantity of goods under this Bill of Lading.

4. ACKNOWLEDGMENT OF WEIGHT, QUALITY, MARKS, ETC. The Carrier, his Agents and servants shall not in any circumstances whatever be under any liability for insufficient packing or inaccuracies, obliteration or absence of marks, numbers, address or description, nor for delivery to drop marks, or quality marks or countermarks or numbers, nor for failure to notify the Consignee of the arrival of the goods, any custom of the port to the contrary notwithstanding. The Carrier is only responsible for leading marks, provided such marks are stamped or otherwise shown clearly upon the goods if uncovered or on the cases or covering in which such goods are contained, in letters at least two inches high and in such manner as should ordinarily remain legible until the end of the voyage. No acknowledgment is made as to the contents of cases, packages, barrels or containers.

5. THE CARRIER'S RIGHTS IF CONSIGNEE NOT READY. If the goods are not taken by the Consignee at the time when the vessel is entitled to call upon him to take possession, or if they are not removed from alongside the vessel without delay, the Carrier shall be at liberty, at the sole risk and expense of the Shipper, Consignee and/or Owner of the goods, to enter and land or remove the goods, or to put them into craft or store.

6. LANDING, LANDING CHARGES. The goods shall in all cases be landed by the vessel, and not by the Consignee, and the landing charges shall be payable by the Consignee against delivery. Lighterage, and expenses of weighing, measuring, valuing and counting cargo if any, at port of discharge to be paid by the Consignee of the goods, any custom or alleged custom of the port to the contrary notwithstanding.

7. VOYAGE. The vessel may at any time whatsoever sail with or without pilots, and/or tugs, adjust compasses, sail at reduced speed, be drydocked at any place, with or without cargo on board, tow or be towed and assist vessels in all situations; proceed by any route whatsoever in the Carrier's or Master's absolute discretion whether or not such route is the nearest or most direct or customary or advertised route between the ports of shipment and discharge; proceed to or stay at any port or place whatsoever and sail before or after advertised sailing dates. These liberties may be exercised at any time whatsoever whether before or after shipment or before or after proceeding towards or calling at the port of discharge, and these liberties may be exercised for any reason whatsoever including the vessel's future engagements. The exercise of any of the above liberties shall be deemed to be part of the contractual voyage.

8. DECK CARGO AND STOWAGE

(a) Notwithstanding anything contained in Sub-Clause (b) hereunder, in the case of live animals and cargo, which in this Bill of Lading is stated to be carried on deck, and is so carried, the Carrier shall be under no liability whatsoever for loss, damage or delay howsoever and whensoever occasioned.

(b) The vessel may carry goods of all kinds, dangerous or otherwise. The Carrier may stow the goods in poop, foc'sle, deckhouse, shelter deck, the passenger space, bunker space or any other covered-in space and in containers, and such goods shall be deemed for all purposes to be stowed under deck. The goods may also be stowed on deck, whether in containers or not, with or without notice to the Shipper, and if they are so carried, the Hague Rules or the Hague Visby Rules whichever are applicable by Clause 1 above, shall apply notwithstanding carriage on or under deck, and the goods and/or container shall contribute to General Average, whether carried on or under deck.

9. CARRIER'S LIBERTIES IN THE EVENT OF BLOCKADE, DELAY, ETC. In case of war, hostilities, strikes, port congestion, lock-outs, civil commotions, quarantine, ice, storms or any other cause whatsoever beyond the Carrier's control (whether any of the foregoing are actual or threatened and whether or not existing or anticipated at the commencement of the voyage) which matters or any of them in the judgment of the Master or Carrier (either of whose decision shall be absolute and binding on all parties) may result in damage to or loss of the vessel or give rise to risk of capture, seizure or detention of vessel or cargo, are likely to prejudice the interest of the vessel including her future engagements and/or her cargo whether by delay or otherwise howsoever or make it unsafe or imprudent for any reason to proceed on or continue the voyage or the Carriage by land or enter or discharge at the port or place of discharge or transhipment, or give rise to delay or difficulty in reaching, discharging at or leaving the port or place of discharge or transhipment, or the place of delivery, the Carrier shall have the following liberties any warranty or rule of law notwithstanding:–

(i) To proceed to such convenient port as the Carrier shall in his absolute discretion select and there discharge the goods.

(ii) To carry the goods back to the country of shipment and discharge them there.

(iii) To retain the goods on board the ship and/or return them to the original port of discharge in the same or substituted ship and there discharge the goods at the sole risk and expense of the Shipper/Consignee and/or Owner of the goods.

(iv) To abandon the carriage of the goods by land at such convenient place as the Carrier shall in his absolute discretion select, and discharge the goods from the container.

When the goods have been abandoned or discharged from the ship or container as herein provided they shall thereafter be at the sole risk and expense of the Consignee, and such discharge shall constitute a full performance of all the Carrier's obligations hereunder, the Carrier, Master or Agents giving immediate notice of such discharge to the Consignee of the goods so far as he is known. Full freight and charges shall be deemed to be earned hereunder, and the Carrier shall be entitled to payment for all extra expense incurred in the performance of any of the foregoing liberties for which (together with freight and charges) he shall have a lien on the goods.

10. CARRIER'S LIBERTIES IN THE EVENT OF WAR, ETC. The ship shall have liberty to comply with any orders, directions or recommendations as to departure, arrival, routes, ports of call, stoppages, destination, delivery or otherwise howsoever given by the Government of the Nation under whose flag the vessel sails or any department thereof, or by any other Government, or any department thereof, or any person acting or purporting to act with the authority of such Government or of any department thereof, or by any committee or person having under the terms of the War Risk Insurance on the ship the right to give such orders, directions or recommendations and if by reason of and in compliance with any such orders, directions or recommendations anything is done or is not done the same shall not be deemed a deviation and delivery in accordance with such orders, directions or recommendations shall be a fulfilment of the contract voyage and the freight shall be payable accordingly.

11. CONTAINERS. (i) The Carrier has no responsibility whatsoever for the functioning of reefer containers or trailers, not owned nor leased by the Carrier.

(ii) SHIPPER PACKED CONTAINERS. If a container has not been filled, packed, stuffed or loaded by the Carrier, the Carrier shall not be liable for loss of or damage to the contents and the Merchant shall indemnify the Carrier against any loss, damage, liability or expense incurred by the Carrier, if such loss, damage, liability or expense has been caused by:–

(a) The manner in which the container has been filled, packed, stuffed or loaded; or

(b) The unsuitability of the contents for carriage in containers; or

(c) The unsuitability or defective conditions of the container arising without any want of due diligence on the part of the Carrier to make the container reasonably fit for the purpose for which it is required; or

(d) The unsuitability or defective condition of the container which would have been apparent upon reasonable inspection by the Merchant at or prior to the time when the container was filled, packed, stuffed or loaded.

(iii) INSPECTION OF GOODS. The Carrier shall be entitled, but under no obligation, to open any container at any time and to inspect the contents. If it thereupon appears that the contents or any part thereof cannot safely or properly be carried or carried further either at all or without incurring any additional expense or taking any measures in relation to the container or its contents or any part thereof, the Carrier may abandon the transportation thereof and/or take any measures and/or incur any reasonable additional expense to carry or to continue the carriage or to store the same ashore or afloat under cover or in the open, at any place, which storage shall be deemed to constitute the delivery under this Bill of Lading. The Merchant shall indemnify the Carrier against any reasonable additional expenses so incurred.

(iv) REPOSITIONING OF CONTAINERS. Where containers owned or leased by the Carrier are unpacked at the Consignees' or Receivers' premises, they are jointly and severally responsible for returning the empty containers with interiors brushed and clean to the port or place of discharge or to the point or place designated by the Carrier, his servants or agents within the time prescribed to them. Should a container not be returned within the prescribed time the Consignee or Receivers shall be liable for any demurrage, loss or expenses which may arise from such non-return.

(v) CONTAINER EQUIPMENT INTERCHANGE CONDITIONS Shipper and Consignee engage with Carrier to indemnify the Owner/Lessee of container (whether the Owner/Lessee of container be the Carrier or not) against all loss of or damage to any such container, and against all loss and damage occasioned by any container or any defect therein to the Owner/Lessee of container or to any third party to whom the Owner/Lessee of container may be liable by reason of such loss or damage, where such loss or damage occurs or is sustained while the container is on the premises or in the custody of the Shipper or Consignee or any Agent therefor, and howsoever such loss or damage may be caused, even if by the breach of contract, fault or negligence of the Carrier and/or the Owner/Lessee of container.

12. PORT, CUSTOMS, CONSULAR AND OTHER REGULATIONS

(a) The Shippers shall furnish all particulars necessary to enable the Bill of Lading to be made out in accordance with the prescriptions and regulations of the Port, Customs and Consular Authorities.

(b) All Consular, Health or other Certificates required to accompany the goods shall be procured by the Shipper and all detention charges or penalties accruing to the Ship or her cargo owing to the want of any such Certificate shall be borne and paid by the Shipper, Consignee and/or Owner of the goods.

(c) The Consignee and/or Owner of the goods shall bear and pay all tonnage dues, shed dues, harbour dues, customs dues and charges, wharfage charges and other dues and charges payable in respect of the goods.

(d) The Shipper, Consignee and/or Owner of the goods shall comply with the regulations and requirements of the Port, Customs and other authorities and shall bear and pay all duties, taxes, fines, imposts, expenses, loss or damage of whatever nature incurred or suffered by reason of the breach thereof or the illegal, incorrect or insufficient marking, numbering or addressing of packages or units or descriptions of their weight or contents, and shall indemnify the Carrier and his Agents and the ship and the Owner of the other cargo on board against all claims, demands, losses and expenses in respect thereof.

(e) In the event of the goods, by reason of their not being marked with the name of the country from which they are exported, or otherwise not complying with the Customs Regulations at the port of discharge, the Carrier shall be at liberty to bring back or to reship such goods to the port of shipment at the sole risk and expense of the Shipper, Consignee and/or Owners of the goods.

(f) The Collector of the port or other duly appointed official is authorised to grant a general order for the discharge of the ship immediately on the ships' arrival.

(g) Should the Carrier desire to discharge beyond usual Customs hours the Consignee shall if so required sign immediately an application for the purpose.

(h) The Carrier or his Agents may in respect of dutiable goods transhipped at the port of discharge give such undertaking as the Customs Authorities at that port require with respect to dealing with the goods at the port where duty is payable, and all charges involved or liabilities incurred shall be borne by the Shipper, Consignee and/or Owner of the goods.

13. DAMAGED PACKAGES, ETC. The Shipper, Consignee and/or Owner of the goods shall bear and pay the cost of all mending, baling and cooperage of and repairs to or replacement of packages, boxes, crates, wrappers, bags, barrels or other containers or coverings resulting from insufficiency of packing or from excepted perils.

14. TRANSHIPMENT CARGO. The Carrier acts only as a forwarding agent in arranging the carriage of the cargo prior to its loading on to and subsequent to its discharge from the ocean vessel.

15. TRANSHIPMENT AND FORWARDING. The Carrier may at any time and for any purpose whatsoever discharge the goods or any part thereof from the vessel whether before or after sailing from the port of loading and/or land to store the same either on shore or afloat, and/or tranship or forward the same by another vessel or other vessels, whether prior or subsequent to the sailing of the vessel and whether sailing from the port of receipt of the goods or from any other port and whether belonging to the Carrier or to any other persons, and/or may forward the same by any mode or method or modes or methods of conveyance whether by water, land or air or otherwise howsoever and whether under one or more bills of lading and/or other contracts of on-carriage. In any such case the responsibility of each carrier acting as such is limited to that part of the transit actually undertaken by him and the Carrier shall not be liable for any loss, damage or delay howsoever caused to the goods arising after discharge from his vessel. In respect of the storage and/or forwarding of the goods after such discharge, the Carrier acts only as forwarding agent, making contracts for such storage and/or forwarding on the terms and subject to the limitation of liability in use by the persons with whom such contracts are made. Unless the value of the goods is declared at the time of shipment and is stated hereon and extra freight as may be agreed upon is paid, the Carrier shall in no event be under any obligation to declare to the oncarrier any valuation of the goods, even though the oncarrier's contract of carriage contains a valuation or limitation of liability less than that contained in this Bill of Lading. If the goods cannot be forwarded immediately to destination, any charges incurred for storage shall be borne by the Owner of the goods. If the goods are forwarded by more than one conveyance the Consignee must take delivery of each portion immediately after arrival.

16. DANGEROUS, INFLAMMABLE, RADIOACTIVE, DAMAGING OR CONTAMINATING GOODS

(i) The Shippers undertake not to tender for transportation any goods which are of a dangerous, inflammable, radioactive or damaging or contaminating nature without previously giving written notice of their nature to the Carrier and marking the goods, and if applicable, the container, flat, trailer, etc., as required by any laws or regulations which may be applicable during the carriage.

(ii) If the requirements of Sub-Clause (i) are not complied with the Shipper shall indemnify the Carrier against all loss, damage or expense arising out of the goods being tendered for transportation or handled or carried by the Carrier.

(iii) Goods which are or at any time become dangerous, inflammable, radioactive or damaging or contaminating may at any time or place be unloaded, jettisoned, destroyed or rendered harmless without compensation and the Shipper, Consignee and/or Owner of such goods shall bear and pay for all charges and expenses incurred in or in consequence of such unloading, destruction, jettisoning or rendering harmless. If the Shipper has not given notice of their nature to the Carrier under Sub-Clause (i) above the Carrier shall be under no liability to make any General Average contribution in respect of such goods.

(iv) In the event of infestation arising from cargo carried under this Bill of Lading, the Shipper and/or Owner of the goods shall indemnify the Carrier against all consequential liabilities, costs and expenses arising therefrom.

17. CLAIMS. Subject to any limits of liability under the Hague Rules or the Hague Visby Rules, whichever are applicable by Clause 1 above, the liability of the Carrier in a case of loss of or damage to or detention of the goods in circumstances involving him in responsibility shall be calculated on, and shall in no case exceed, the shippers' net invoice costs and disbursements less all charges saved. In the case of ad valorem cargo, the Carrier's responsibility shall not exceed the value of the goods declared before the time of shipment and inserted in this Bill of Lading. Where bulk goods or goods without marks, or goods with the same marks are shipped to more than one Consignee the Consignees and/or Owners of the goods shall jointly and severally bear any expense or loss in dividing the goods or parcels into pro rata quantities and any deficiency shall fall upon them in such proportion as the Carrier, his servants or agents shall decide.

The Carrier does not undertake that the goods shall arrive at the port of discharge or place of delivery at any particular time or to meet any particular market or use and the Carrier shall in no circumstances whatsoever be liable for any direct, indirect or consequential loss or damage caused by delay.

18. CALCULATION OF FREIGHT. Freight on the goods shall be deemed earned on shipment, and shall be paid vessel and/or goods lost or not lost. The freight, together with Primage and Charges, shall be due and paid to the Carrier at the port of shipment (unless otherwise agreed) at the time of shipment in the required freely transferable currency at the time of shipment calculated at the mean of the closing rates of exchange in London for the last working day of the week prior to the date when the vessel commences to load. These conditions will also apply where freight is paid at a place other than the port of shipment. The Shipper shall nevertheless remain responsible for the freight until payment is made.

Interest at 2% over the Bank of England minimum lending rate shall be paid on any freight primage and charges remaining unpaid after due date of payment. Full freight is due on damaged or unsound goods and on packages, barrels or containers received part full or empty. The freight payable hereunder has been calculated and based upon the particulars of the goods furnished by the Shipper to the Carrier. The Carrier shall be entitled at any time to open and to re-weigh or re-measure or re-value any goods and if the weight or measurement or value as furnished by the Shipper is found to be incorrect, freight shall be paid by the Shipper, Consignee and/or Owner of the goods on the excess weight or measurement or value so ascertained together with the expenses incident to re-weighing or re-measuring or re-valuing which expenses shall be considered as freight but otherwise such expenses shall be payable by the Carrier. The Shipper shall, if required by the Carrier so to do, furnish forthwith on demand to the Carrier the invoice or a true copy thereof relating to the goods. If the description or (in cases where the value has been stated) the value of the goods has been mis-stated by the Shipper, double the amount of such freight shall, if required by the Carrier, be paid (as liquidated damages) by the Shipper, Consignee and/or Owner of the goods as would have been charged if the goods had been accurately described or valued, and a certificate signed by the Carrier or his Agents shall be conclusive evidence for all purposes of the amount that would have been so charged.

19. LIEN. The Carrier his servants or agents shall have a lien on the goods and a right to sell the goods whether privately or by public auction for all freight (including additional freight payable under Clause 18) primage, dead freight, demurrage, detention charges, Salvage, General Average contributions, and for all other charges and expenses whatsoever, which are for account of the goods or of the Shipper, Consignee and/or Owner of the goods under this Bill of Lading, and for the costs and expenses of exercising such lien and of such sale and also for all previously unsatisfied debts whatsoever due to him by the Shipper, Consignee and/or Owner of the goods. Nothing in this clause shall prevent the Carrier from recovering from the Shipper, Consignee and/or Owner of the goods the difference between the amount due from them or any of them to him and the amount realised by the exercise of the rights given to the Carrier under this Clause.

20. GENERAL AVERAGE, AND SALVAGE

(a) General Average shall be payable according to York-Antwerp Rules 1974 and shall be adjusted at any port or place selected by the Carrier.

(b) In the event of accident, danger, damage or disaster before or after the commencement of the voyage, resulting from any cause whatsoever, whether due to negligence or not, for which, or for the consequence of which, the Carrier is not responsible, by statute, contract or otherwise, the goods, Shippers, Consignees and/or Owner of the goods shall contribute with the Carrier in General Average to the payment of any sacrifices, losses or expenses of a General Average nature that may be made or incurred and shall pay salvage and special charges incurred in respect of the goods.

(c) If a salving vessel is owned or operated by the Carrier, salvage shall be paid for as fully as if the said salving vessel or vessels belonged to strangers. Such deposit as the Carrier or his agents may deem sufficient to cover the estimated contribution of the goods and any salvage and special charges thereon shall, if required, be made by the goods, Shippers, Consignees and/or Owners of the goods to the Carrier before delivery.

21. BOTH TO BLAME COLLISION CLAUSE. If the ship comes into collision with another ship as a result of the negligence of the other ship and any act, neglect or default of the Master, Mariners, pilots or the servants of the Carrier in the navigation or in the management of the ship, the Owners of the goods carried hereunder will indemnify the Carrier against all loss or liability to the other non-carrying ship or her Owners in so far as such loss or liability represent loss of, or damage to, or any claim whatsoever of the Owners of the said goods, paid or payable by the other or non-carrying ship or her Owners to the Owners of the said goods and set off, recouped or recovered by the other or non-carrying ship or her Owners as part of their claim against the carrying ship or Carrier. The foregoing provisions shall also apply where the Owners, Operators or those in charge of any ship or ships or objects other than or in addition to, the colliding ships or objects are at fault in respect to a collision or contact.

22. RIGHTS AND IMMUNITIES OF ALL SERVANTS AND AGENTS OF THE CARRIER

(a) No servant or agent of the Carrier (including every independent contractor from time to time employed by the Carrier) shall in any circumstances whatsoever be under any liability whatsoever to the Shipper, Consignee, Owner of the goods, or Holder of this Bill of Lading for any loss, damage or delay of whatsoever kind arising or resulting directly or indirectly from any act, neglect or default on his part while acting in the course of or in connection with his employment and, but without prejudice to the generality of the foregoing provisions in this Clause, every exemption, limitation, condition and liberty herein contained and every right, exemption from liability, defence and immunity of whatsoever nature applicable to the Carrier or to which the Carrier is entitled hereunder shall also be available and shall extend to protect every such servant or agent of the Carrier acting as aforesaid and for the purpose of all the foregoing provisions of this Clause the Carrier is or shall be deemed to be acting as agent or trustee on behalf of and for the benefit of all persons who are or might be his servants or agents from time to time (including independent contractors as aforesaid) and all such persons shall to this extent be or be deemed to be parties to the contract in or evidenced by this Bill of Lading.

(b) The Carrier shall be entitled to be paid by the Shipper, Consignee, Owner of the goods and/or Holder of this Bill of Lading (who shall be jointly and severally liable to the Carrier therefor) on demand any sum recovered or recoverable by either such Shipper, Consignee, Owner of the goods and/or Holder of this Bill of Lading or any other from such servant or agent of the Carrier for any such loss, damage, delay or otherwise.

23. SURRENDER OF BILL OF LADING. Subject to the Law and/or custom in force at the port or place of discharge, the Bill of Lading duly endorsed must be surrendered in exchange for Delivery Order or the goods.

24. AGENCY CLAUSE. If the ship is not owned by or chartered by demise to the Company or Line by whom this Bill of Lading is issued (as may be the case notwithstanding anything that appears to the contrary) this Bill of Lading shall take effect only as a contract with the Owner or Demise Charterer, as the case may be, as Principal made through the agency of the said Company or Line who act as agents only and shall be under no personal liability whatsoever in respect thereof.

25. JURISDICTION. All claims arising under this Bill of Lading shall be determined according to English Law in England to the exclusion of the jurisdiction of the Courts of any other country unless the contrary is expressly agreed to.

Appendix H A combined transport document. The conditions on the reverse side are also shown.

BILL OF LADING FOR COMBINED TRANSPORT SHIPMENT OR PORT TO PORT SHIPMENT

B/L No.

SHIPPER

BOOKING REF.

BEACON

SHIPPERS REF.

BRITISH SHIPPING LINES JOINT SERVICE BETWEEN
EUROPE AND EAST AFRICA/MAURITIUS

CONSIGNEE

operated by the Lines detailed on the reverse of this Document

CARRIER

NOTIFY PARTY AND ADDRESS If it is agreed that no responsibility shall attach to the Carrier or his Agents for failure to notify the Consignees of the arrival of the goods (see Clause 20 on the reverse).

PLACE OF RECEIPT (Applicable only when this document is used as a Combined Transport Bill of Lading)

VESSEL AND VOY. No.

PLACE OF DELIVERY (Applicable only when this document is used as a Combined Transport Bill of Lading)

PORT OF LOADING

PORT OF DISCHARGE

MARKS AND Nos. CONTAINER Nos.	NUMBER AND KIND OF PACKAGES; DESCRIPTION OF GOODS	GROSS WEIGHT Kg	MEASUREMENT M³

ABOVE PARTICULARS AS DECLARED BY SHIPPER BUT NOT ACKNOWLEDGED BY THE CARRIER (SEE CLAUSE 11)

✱ TOTAL No. OF CONTAINERS/PACKAGES RECEIVED BY THE CARRIER

Received by the Carrier from the Shipper in apparent good order and condition (unless otherwise noted herein) the total number or quantity of Containers or other packages or units indicated in the box opposite entitled "✱ Total No. of Containers/Packages received by the Carrier" for Carriage subject to all the terms and conditions hereof (INCLUDING THE TERMS AND CONDITIONS ON THE REVERSE HEREOF AND THE TERMS AND CONDITIONS OF THE CARRIER'S APPLICABLE TARIFF) from the Place of Receipt or the Port of Loading, whichever is applicable, to the Port of Discharge or the Place of Delivery, whichever is applicable. One original Bill of Lading must be surrendered, duly endorsed, in exchange for the Goods. In accepting this Bill of Lading the Merchant expressly accepts and agrees to all its terms and conditions whether printed, stamped or written, or otherwise incorporated, notwithstanding the non-signing of this Bill of Lading by the Merchant.

MOVEMENT

FREIGHT AND CHARGES (indicate whether prepaid or collect)

Origin Inland Haulage Charge

PLACE AND DATE OF ISSUE

Origin Terminal Handling/LCL Service Charge

IN WITNESS of the contract herein contained the number of originals stated opposite have been issued, one of which being accomplished, the other(s) to be void.

Ocean Freight

NUMBER OF ORIGINAL BILLS OF LADING

Destination Terminal Handling/LCL Service Charge

For the Carrier:

Destination Inland Haulage Charge

ICS
CT B/L
April 78

P & O CONTAINERS LTD., Beagle House, Braham Street, London E1 8EP
ELLERMAN LINES plc., 12-20 Camomile Street, London EC3A 7EX
Thos. & Jas. HARRISON LTD., Mersey Chambers, Liverpool L2 8UF

TERMS AND CONDITIONS

1. DEFINITIONS

"Carrier" means the party named on the face of this document as being the carrier.

"Merchant" includes the Shipper, Holder, Consignee, Receiver of the Goods, any Person owning or entitled to the possession of the Goods or of this Bill of Lading and anyone acting on behalf of any such Person, all of whom shall be jointly and severally liable to the Carrier for the due fulfilment of all obligations undertaken by the Merchant in this Bill of Lading.

"Holder" means any Person for the time being in possession of this Bill of Lading to whom the property in the Goods has passed on or by reason of the consignment of the Goods or the endorsement of this Bill of Lading or otherwise.

"Person" includes an individual, group, company or other entity.

"Sub-Contractor" includes owners and operators of vessels (other than the Carrier), stevedores, terminal and groupage operators, road and rail transport operators and any independent contractor employed by the Carrier in performance of the Carriage.

"Indemnify" includes defend, indemnify and hold harmless.

"Goods" means the whole or any part of the cargo received from the Shipper and includes any equipment or Container not supplied by or on behalf of the Carrier.

"Container" includes any container, trailer, transportable tank, flat or pallet, or any similar article used to consolidate goods and any equipment thereof or connected thereto.

"Carriage" means the whole or any part of the operations and services undertaken by the Carrier in respect of the Goods.

"Combined Transport" arises if the Place of Receipt and/or the Place of Delivery are indicated on the face hereof in the relevant spaces.

"Port to Port Shipment" arises if the Carriage called for by this Bill of Lading is not Combined Transport.

"Freight" includes all charges payable to the Carrier in accordance with the applicable Tariff and this Bill of Lading.

"Hague Rules" means the provisions of the International Convention for the Unification of Certain Rules relating to Bills of Lading signed at Brussels on 25th August, 1924 and includes the amendments by the Protocol signed at Brussels on 23rd February, 1968, but only if such amendments are compulsorily applicable to this Bill of Lading. (It is expressly provided that nothing in this Bill of Lading shall implement Article X(c) of said Rules as amended by said Protocol).

2. CARRIER'S TARIFF

The terms and conditions of the Carrier's applicable Tariff are incorporated herein. Particular attention is drawn to the terms and conditions therein relating to container and vehicle demurrage. Copies of the relevant provisions of the applicable Tariff are obtainable from the Carrier or his agents upon request. In the case of inconsistency between this Bill of Lading and the applicable Tariff, this Bill of Lading shall prevail.

3. WARRANTY

The Merchant warrants that in agreeing to the terms and conditions hereof he is, or has the authority of, the Person owning or entitled to the possession of the Goods and this Bill of Lading.

4. SUB-CONTRACTING AND INDEMNITY

(1) The Carrier shall be entitled to sub-contract the Carriage on any terms whatsoever.

(2) The Merchant undertakes that no claim or allegation shall be made against any Person whomsoever by whom the Carriage is performed or undertaken (including all Sub-Contractors of the Carrier), other than the Carrier, which imposes or attempts to impose upon any such Person, or any vessel owned by any such Person, any liability whatsoever in connection with the Goods or the Carriage of the Goods, whether or not arising out of negligence on the part of such Person and, if any such claim or allegation should nevertheless be made, to indemnify the Carrier against all consequences thereof. Without prejudice to the foregoing every such Person shall have the benefit of every right, defence, limitation and liberty of whatsoever nature herein contained or otherwise available to the Carrier as if such provisions were expressly for his benefit; and in entering into this contract, the Carrier, to the extent of these provisions, does so not only on his own behalf but also as agent and trustee for such Persons.

(3) The provisions of Clause 4 (2) including but not limited to the undertakings of the Merchant contained therein, shall extend to claims or allegations of whatsoever nature against other Persons chartering space on the carrying vessel.

(4) The Merchant further undertakes that no claim or allegation in respect of the Goods shall be made against the Carrier by any Person other than in accordance with the terms and conditions of this Bill of Lading which imposes or attempts to impose upon the Carrier any liability whatsoever in connection with the Goods or the Carriage of the Goods, whether or not arising out of negligence on the part of the Carrier and, if any such claim or allegation should nevertheless be made, to indemnify the Carrier against all consequences thereof.

5. CARRIER'S RESPONSIBILITY
Port-to-Port Shipment

If the Carriage called for by this Bill of Lading is a Port-to-Port Shipment, the liability (if any) of the Carrier for loss of or damage to the Goods occurring from and during loading onto any seagoing vessel up to and during discharge from that vessel or from another seagoing vessel into which the Goods have been transhipped shall be determined in accordance with any national law making the Hague Rules compulsorily applicable to this Bill of Lading, or in any other case in accordance with the Hague Rules, Articles 1-8 inclusive.

Notwithstanding the above, unless and to the extent that any applicable compulsory law provides to the contrary (in which case the Carrier shall have the benefit of every right, defence, limitation and liberty in the Hague Rules as applied by this clause during such additional compulsory period of responsibility, notwithstanding that the loss or damage did not occur at sea), the Carrier shall be under no liability whatsoever for loss of or damage to the Goods, howsoever occurring, if such loss or damage arises prior to loading onto or subsequent to discharge from the vessel.

6. CARRIER'S RESPONSIBILITY
Combined Transport

If the Carriage called for by this Bill of Lading is Combined Transport, the Carrier undertakes to perform and/or in his own name to procure performance of the Carriage from the Place of Receipt or the Port of Loading, whichever is applicable, to the Port of Discharge or the Place of Delivery, whichever is applicable, and, save as is otherwise provided in this Bill of Lading, the Carrier shall be liable for loss or damage occurring during the Carriage only to the extent set out below.

(1) If the stage of the Carriage during which loss or damage occurred is not known

(a) Exclusions

If the stage of the Carriage during which the loss or damage occurred is not known, the Carrier shall be relieved of liability for any loss or damage if such loss or damage was caused by:

- (i) an act or omission of the Merchant,
- (ii) insufficiency of or defective condition of packing or marking,
- (iii) handling, loading, stowage or unloading of the Goods by or on behalf of the Merchant,
- (iv) inherent vice of the Goods,
- (v) strike, lock-out, stoppage or restraint of labour,
- (vi) a nuclear incident,
- (vii) any cause or event which the Carrier could not avoid and the consequences whereof he could not prevent by the exercise of reasonable diligence,
- (viii) compliance with instructions of any Person entitled to give them.

(b) Burden of Proof

The burden of proof that the loss or damage was due to one or more of the causes or events specified in this Clause 6 (1) shall rest upon the Carrier. Save that if the Carrier establishes that, in the circumstances of the case, the loss or damage could be attributed to one or more of the causes or events specified in Clause 6 (1) (a) (ii), (iii) or (iv), it shall be presumed that it was so caused. The Merchant shall, however, be entitled to prove that the loss or damage was not, in fact, caused either wholly or partly by one or more of these causes or events.

(c) Limitation of Liability

Except as provided in Clauses 7(2), 7(3) or 27, if Clause 6(1) operates total compensation shall in no circumstances whatsoever and howsoever arising exceed 2 SDRs per kilo of the gross weight of the Goods lost or damaged. (SDR means Special Drawing Right as defined by the International Monetary Fund).

2. If the stage of the Carriage during which the loss or damage occurred is known

Notwithstanding anything provided for in Clause 6 (1) and subject to Clauses 15 and 16, if it is known during which stage of the Carriage the loss or damage occurred, the liability of the Carrier in respect of such loss or damage shall be determined:

(a) by the provisions contained in any international convention or national law which provisions—

- (i) cannot be departed from by private contract to the detriment of the Merchant; and
- (ii) would have applied if the Merchant had made a separate and direct contract with the Carrier in respect of the particular stage of the Carriage during which the loss or damage occurred and received as evidence thereof any particular document which must be issued in order to make such international convention or national law applicable; or

(b) if no international convention or national law would apply by virtue of Clause 6 (2) (a), by the Hague Rules, Articles 1-8 inclusive if the loss or damage is known to have occurred during waterborne Carriage; or

(c) by the provisions of Clause 6 (1) if the provisions of Clause 6 (2) (a) and (b) above do not apply.

For the purposes of Clause 6 (2), references in the Hague Rules to carriage by sea shall be deemed to include references to all waterborne Carriage and the Hague Rules shall be construed accordingly.

(3) If the Place of Receipt or Place of Delivery is not named on the face hereof

Subject to Clause 5,

(a) if the Place of Receipt is not named on the face hereof, the Carrier shall be under no liability whatsoever for loss of or damage to the Goods, howsoever occurring, if such loss or damage arises prior to loading onto the vessel.

(b) if the Place of Delivery is not named on the face hereof, the Carrier shall be under no liability whatsoever for loss of or damage to the Goods, howsoever occurring, if such loss or damage arises subsequent to discharge from the vessel.

(4) Notice of Loss or Damage

Unless under Clause 6 (2) an international convention or national law applies, which contains alternative provisions relating to notice of loss or damage (in which case such alternative provisions shall apply), the Carrier shall be deemed prima facie to have delivered the Goods as described in this Bill of Lading unless notice of loss of or damage to the Goods, indicating the general nature of such loss or damage, shall have been given in writing to the Carrier or to his representative at the Place of Delivery (or the Port of Discharge if no Place of Delivery is named on the face hereof) before or at the time of removal of the Goods into the custody of the Person entitled to delivery thereof under this Bill of Lading, or, if the loss or damage is not apparent, within three working days thereafter.

(5) Time-bar

Unless under Clause 6 (2) an international convention or national law applies, which contains alternative provisions relating to time-bars (in which case such alternative provisions shall apply), the Carrier shall be discharged of all liability unless suit is brought and notice thereof given to the Carrier within nine months after delivery of the Goods or the date when the Goods should have been delivered.

7. SUNDRY LIABILITY PROVISIONS

(1) Basis of Compensation

Compensation shall be calculated by reference to the value of the Goods at the place and time they are delivered to the Merchant, or at the place and time they should have been delivered. For the purpose of determining the extent of the Carrier's liability for loss of or damage to the Goods, the sound value of the Goods is agreed to be the invoice value plus freight and insurance if paid.

(2) Hague Rules Limitation

If the Hague Rules are applicable otherwise than by national law, in determining the liability of the Carrier the liability shall in no event exceed £100 sterling per package or unit. If the Hague Rules are applicable by national law, the liability of the Carrier shall in no event exceed the limit provided in the applicable national law.

(3) Ad Valorem

The Merchant agrees and acknowledges that the Carrier has no knowledge of the value of the Goods, and that higher compensation than that provided herein may not be claimed unless, with the consent of the Carrier, the value of the Goods declared by the Shipper prior to the commencement of the Carriage is stated on this Bill of Lading and extra Freight paid, if required. in that case, the amount of the declared value shall be substituted for the limits laid down herein. Any partial loss or damage shall be adjusted pro rata on the basis of such declared value.

(4) Delay

The Carrier does not undertake that the Goods shall arrive at the Port of Discharge or Place of Delivery at any particular time or to meet any particular market or use, and the Carrier shall in no circumstances whatsoever and howsoever arising be liable for direct, indirect or consequential loss or damage caused by delay.

(5) Scope of Application

- (a) The terms and conditions of this Bill of Lading shall at all times govern all responsibilities of the Carrier in connection with or arising out of the supply of a Container to the Merchant, not only during the Carriage, but also during the periods prior to and/or subsequent to the Carriage.
- (b) The rights, defences, limitations and liberties of whatsoever nature provided for in this Bill of Lading shall apply in any action against the Carrier for loss or damage or delay, howsoever occurring and whether the action be founded in contract or in tort and even if the loss, damage or delay arose as a result of unseaworthiness, negligence or fundamental breach of contract.
- (c) Save as is otherwise provided herein, the Carrier shall in no circumstances whatsoever and howsoever arising be liable for direct or indirect or consequential loss or damage.

(6) Compulsory Inspection by Authorities

If by order of the authorities at any place, a Container has to be opened for the Goods to be inspected, the Carrier will not be liable for any loss or damage incurred as a result of any opening, unpacking, inspection or repacking. The Carrier shall be entitled to recover the cost of such opening, unpacking, inspection and repacking from the Merchant.

8. SHIPPER-PACKED CONTAINERS

If a Container has not been packed by or on behalf of the Carrier:

(1) The Carrier shall not be liable for loss of or damage to the Goods caused by:

- (a) the manner in which the Container has been packed, or
- (b) the unsuitability of the Goods for carriage in the Container supplied, or
- (c) the unsuitability or defective condition of the Container, provided that, if the Container has been supplied by or on behalf of the Carrier, this unsuitability or defective condition could have been apparent upon inspection by the Merchant at or prior to the time when the Container was packed.

(2) If a Shipper-Packed Container is delivered by the Carrier with its original seal as affixed by the Shipper intact, such delivery shall constitute full and complete performance of the Carrier's obligations hereunder and the Carrier shall not be liable for any loss of or damage to Goods ascertained at delivery.

(3) The Merchant shall indemnify the Carrier against any loss, damage, liability or expense whatsoever and howsoever arising caused by one or more of the matters referred to in Clauses 8 (1) and 8 (2), save that, if the loss, damage, liability or expense was caused by a matter referred to in Clause 8 (1) (c), the Merchant shall not be liable to indemnify the Carrier in respect thereof unless the proviso referred to in that Clause applies.

9. INSPECTION OF GOODS

The Carrier or any Person to whom the Carrier has sub-contracted the Carriage or any Person authorised by the Carrier shall be entitled, but under no obligation, to open any Container or package at any time and to inspect the Goods.

10. CARRIAGE AFFECTED BY CONDITION OF GOODS

If it appears at any time that the Goods cannot safely or properly be carried or carried further, either at all or without incurring any additional expense or taking any measure(s) in relation to the Container or the Goods the Carrier may without notice to the Merchant take any measure(s) and/or incur any additional expense to carry or to continue the Carriage thereof, and/or sell or dispose of the Goods, and/or abandon the Carriage and/or store them ashore or afloat, under cover or in the open, at any place, whichever the Carrier, in his absolute discretion, considers most appropriate, which abandonment, storage, sale or disposal shall be deemed to constitute due delivery under this Bill of Lading. The Merchant shall indemnify the Carrier against any additional expense so incurred.

11. DESCRIPTION OF GOODS

(1) This Bill of Lading shall be prima facie evidence of the receipt by the Carrier from the Shipper in apparent good order and condition, except as otherwise noted, of the total number of Containers or other packages or units indicated in the box on the face hereof entitled "* Total No of Containers/Packages received by the Carrier".

(2) Except as provided in Clause 11 (1), no representation is made by the Carrier as to the weight, contents, measure, quantity, quality, description, condition, marks, numbers or value of the Goods, and the Carrier shall be under no responsibility whatsoever in respect of such description or particulars.

(3) If any particulars of any Letter of Credit and/or Import Licence and/or Sale Contract and/or Invoice or Order number and/or details of any contract to which the Carrier is not a party are shown on the face of this Bill of Lading, such particulars are included solely at the request of the Merchant for his convenience. The Merchant agrees that the inclusion of such particulars shall not be regarded as a declaration of value and in no way affects the Carrier's liability under this Bill of Lading. The Merchant further agrees to indemnify the Carrier against all consequences of including such particulars in this Bill of Lading.

The Merchant acknowledges that, except when the provisions of Clause 7(3) apply, the value of the Goods is unknown to the Carrier.

12. SHIPPER'S/MERCHANT'S RESPONSIBILITY

(1) The Shipper warrants to the Carrier that the particulars relating to the Goods as set out overleaf have been checked by the Shipper on receipt of this Bill of Lading and that such particulars, and any other particulars furnished by or on behalf of the Shipper, are adequate and correct. The Shipper also warrants that the Goods are lawful goods and contain no contraband.

(2) The Merchant shall indemnify the Carrier against all loss, damage, fines and expenses arising or resulting from any breach of any of the warranties in Clause 12(1) hereof or from any other cause in connection with the Goods for which the Carrier is not responsible.

(3) The Merchant shall comply with all regulations or requirements of customs, port and other authorities, and shall bear and pay all duties, taxes, fines, imposts, expenses or losses (including, without prejudice to the generality of the foregoing, the full return Freight for the Goods if returned, or if on-carried, the full Freight from the Port of Discharge or the Place of Delivery nominated herein to the amended Port of Discharge or the amended Place of Delivery) incurred or suffered by reason of any failure to so comply, or by reason of any illegal, incorrect or insufficient marking, numbering or addressing of the Goods, and shall indemnify the Carrier in respect thereof.

(4) If Containers supplied by or on behalf of the Carrier are unpacked at the Merchant's premises, the Merchant is responsible for returning the empty Containers, with interiors brushed and clean, to the point or place designated by the Carrier, his servants or agents, within the time prescribed. Should a Container not be returned within the prescribed time, the Merchant shall be liable for any demurrage, loss or expenses which may arise from such non-return.

13. FREIGHT

(1) Freight shall be deemed fully earned on receipt of the Goods by the Carrier and shall be paid and non-returnable in any event.

(2) The Merchant's attention is drawn to the stipulations concerning currency in which the Freight is to be paid, rate of exchange, devaluation and other contingencies relative to Freight in the applicable Tariff.

(3) Freight has been calculated on the basis of particulars furnished by or on behalf of the Shipper. The Carrier may at any time open any Container or other package or unit in order to identify, weigh, measure or value the contents and, if the particulars furnished by or on behalf of the Shipper are incorrect, it is agreed that a sum equal to double the correct Freight less the Freight charged, shall be payable as liquidated damages to the Carrier.

(4) All Freight shall be paid without any set-off, counter-claim, deduction or stay of execution before delivery of the Goods.

(5) Any Person engaged by the Merchant to perform forwarding services in respect of the Goods shall be considered to be the exclusive agent of the Merchant for all purposes and any payment of Freight to such Person shall not be considered payment to the Carrier in any event. Failure of such Person to pay any part of the Freight to the Carrier shall be considered a default by the Merchant in the payment of Freight.

14. LIEN

The Carrier shall have a lien on the Goods and any documents relating thereto for all sums payable to the Carrier under this contract by any of the Persons defined as Merchant in Clause 1 and for general average contributions, to whomsoever due. The Carrier shall also have a lien against the current Holder on the Goods and any documents relating thereto for all sums due from him to the Carrier under any other contract. In any event any lien shall extend to cover the cost of recovering the sums due, and for that purpose the Carrier shall have the right to sell the Goods by public auction or private treaty, without notice to the Merchant.

15. OPTIONAL STOWAGE AND DECK CARGO

(1) The Goods may be packed by the Carrier in Containers and consolidated with other goods in Containers.

(2) Goods, whether or not packed in Containers, may be carried on deck or under deck without notice to the Merchant. All such Goods whether carried on deck or under deck, shall participate in general average and shall be deemed to be within the definition of goods for the purposes of the Hague Rules and shall be carried subject to these Rules.

(3) Notwithstanding Clause 15 (2), in the case of Goods which are stated on the face hereof as being carried on deck and which are so carried the Hage Rules shall not apply and the Carrier shall be under no liability whatsoever for loss, damage or delay, howsoever arising.

16. LIVE ANIMALS

The Hague Rules shall not apply to the Carriage of live animals, which are carried at the sole risk of the Merchant. The Carrier shall be under no liability whatsoever for any injury, illness, death, delay or destruction howsoever arising. Should the Master in his sole discretion consider that any live animal is likely to be injurious to any other live animal or any person or property on board, or to cause the vessel to be delayed or impeded in the prosecution of the Carriage, such live animal may be destroyed and thrown overboard without any liability attaching to the Carrier. The Merchant shall indemnify the Carrier against all or any extra costs incurred for any reason whatsoever in connection with the Carriage of any live animal.

17. METHODS AND ROUTE OF CARRIAGE

(1) The Carrier may at any time and without notice to the Merchant:

- (a) use any means of carriage whatsoever,
- (b) transfer the Goods from one conveyance to another, including but not limited to transhipping or carrying them on another vessel than that named on the face hereof,
- (c) unpack and remove the Goods which have been packed into a Container and forward them in a Container or otherwise,
- (d) proceed by any route in his discretion (whether or not the nearest or most direct or customary or advertised route), at any speed, and proceed to or stay at any place or port whatsoever, once or more often and in any order,
- (e) load or unload the Goods at any place or port (whether or not such port is named overleaf as the Port of Loading or Port of Discharge) and store the Goods at any such place or port,
- (f) comply with any orders or recommendations given by any government or authority, or any Person acting or purporting to act as or on behalf of such government or authority, or having under the terms of any insurance on any conveyance employed by the Carrier the right to give orders or directions,
- (g) permit the vessel to proceed with or without pilots, to tow or be towed, or to be dry-docked.

(2) The liberties set out in Clause 17 (1) may be invoked by the Carrier for any purpose whatsoever, whether or not connected with the Carriage of the Goods, including loading or unloading other goods, bunkering, undergoing repairs, adjusting instruments, picking up or landing any persons, including but not limited to persons involved with the operation or maintenance of the vessel and assisting vessels in all situations. Anything done in accordance with Clause 17 (1) or any delay arising therefrom shall be deemed to be within the contractual Carriage and shall not be a deviation.

(3) By tendering the Goods for Carriage without any written request for Carriage in a specialised Container, or within a specific temperature range, or subject to any particular attention, or for Carriage otherwise than in a Container, the Merchant accepts that the Carriage may properly be undertaken in a general purpose container in the customary manner.

18. MATTERS AFFECTING PERFORMANCE

If at any time the Carriage is or is likely to be affected by any hindrance, risk, delay, difficulty or disadvantage of any kind (other than the inability of the Goods safely or properly to be carried or carried further) and howsoever arising (even though the circumstances giving rise to such hindrance, risk, delay, difficulty or disadvantage existed at the time this contract was entered into or the Goods were received for Carriage), the Carrier (whether or not the Carriage is commenced) may either:

- (a) Without notice to the Merchant, abandon the Carriage of the Goods and place the Goods at the Merchant's disposal at any place or port which the Carrier may deem safe and convenient, whereupon the responsibility of the Carrier in respect of such Goods shall cease. The Carrier shall nevertheless be entitled to full Freight on the Goods received for Carriage, and the Merchant shall pay any additional costs of the Carriage to, and delivery and storage at, such place or port; or
- (b) Upon notice to the Merchant, suspend the Carriage of the Goods and store them ashore or afloat upon the terms of this Bill of Lading. The Carrier will endeavour to forward the Goods, the Carriage of which has been suspended, as soon as possible after the cause of hindrance, risk, delay, difficulty or disadvantage has been removed, but the Carrier makes no representations as to the maximum period between such removal and the forwarding of the Goods to the Port of Discharge or Place of Delivery, whichever is applicable, named in this Bill of Lading. The Carrier shall be entitled to payment of such additional Freight as the Carrier may determine, including, but not restricted to, charges for storage, handling and any other services to the Goods, and for Freight from the place of suspension to the Port of Discharge or Place of Delivery, whichever is applicable, without giving credit for Freight already paid in respect of the Carriage.

If the Carrier elects to suspend the Carriage under Clause 18 (b) this shall not prejudice his right subsequently to abandon the Carriage under Clause 18 (a).

19. DANGEROUS GOODS

(1) No goods which are or may become dangerous, inflammable or damaging (including radio-active materials), or which are or may become liable to damage any property whatsoever, shall be tendered to the Carrier for Carriage without his express consent in writing, and without the Container or other covering in which the Goods are to be carried as well as the Goods themselves being distinctly marked on the outside so as to indicate the nature and character of any such Goods and so as to comply with any applicable laws, regulations or requirements. If any such Goods are delivered to the Carrier without such written consent and/or marking, or if in the opinion of the Carrier the Goods are or are liable to become of a dangerous, inflammable or damaging nature, they may at any time be destroyed, disposed of, abandoned, or rendered harmless without compensation to the Merchant and without prejudice to the Carrier's right to Freight.

(2) The Merchant undertakes that such Goods are packed in a manner adequate to withstand the risks of Carriage having regard to their nature and in compliance with all laws or regulations which may be applicable during the Carriage.

(3) Whether or not the Merchant was aware of the nature of the Goods, the Merchant shall indemnify the Carrier against all claims, losses, damages or expenses arising in consequence of the Carriage of such Goods.

(4) Nothing contained in this Clause shall deprive the Carrier of any of his rights provided for elsewhere.

20. NOTIFICATION AND DELIVERY

(1) Any mention herein of parties to be notified of the arrival of the Goods is solely for information of the Carrier, and failure to give such notification shall not involve the Carrier in any liability nor relieve the Merchant of any obligation hereunder.

(2) If no Place of Delivery is named on the face hereof, the Carrier shall be at liberty to discharge the Goods at the Port of Discharge, without notice, directly they come to hand at or onto any wharf, craft or place, on any day and at any time, whereupon the liability of the Carrier (if any) in respect of the Goods discharged as aforesaid shall wholly cease, notwithstanding any charges, dues or other expenses that may be or become payable, unless and to the extent that any applicable compulsory law provides to the contrary (in which case the terms and conditions of this Bill of Lading shall continue to operate during such additional compulsory period of responsibility). The Merchant shall take delivery of the Goods upon discharge.

(3) If a Place of Delivery is named on the face hereof, the Merchant shall take delivery of the Goods within the time provided for in the Carrier's applicable Tariff (see Clause 2).

(4) If the delivery of the Goods is not taken by the Merchant at the time and place the Carrier is entitled to call upon the Merchant to take delivery thereof, the Carrier shall be entitled, without notice, to unpack the Goods if packed in Containers and/or to store the Goods ashore, afloat, in the open or under cover, at the sole risk of the Merchant. Such storage shall constitute due delivery hereunder, and thereupon the liability of the Carrier in respect of the Goods stored as aforesaid shall wholly cease, and the costs of such storage (if paid or payable by the Carrier or any agent or Sub-Contractor of the Carrier) shall forthwith upon demand be paid by the Merchant to the Carrier.

(5) If the Merchant fails to take delivery of the Goods within thirty days of delivery becoming due under Clause 20 (2) or (3), or if in the opinion of the Carrier they are likely to deteriorate, decay, become worthless or incur charges whether for storage or otherwise in excess of their value, the Carrier may, without prejudice to any other rights which he may have against the Merchant, without notice and without any responsibility whatsoever attaching to him, sell, destroy or dispose of the Goods and apply any proceeds of sale in reduction of the sums due to the Carrier from the Merchant in respect of this Bill of Lading.

(6) If, at the place where the Carrier is entitled to call upon the Merchant to take delivery of the Goods under Clause 20 (2) or (3), the Carrier is obliged to hand over the Goods into the custody of any customs, port or other authority, such hand-over shall constitute due delivery to the Merchant under this Bill of Lading.

(7) Refusal by the Merchant to take delivery of the Goods in accordance with the terms of this Clause, notwithstanding his having been notified of the availability of the Goods for delivery, shall constitute a waiver by the Merchant to the Carrier of any claim whatsoever relating to the Goods or the Carriage thereof.

(8) Subject to the Carrier agreeing in writing to a request of the Merchant to amend the Place of Delivery stated herein, the terms and conditions of this Bill of Lading shall continue to apply, to the extent provided by the applicable Tariff, until the Goods are delivered by the Carrier to the Merchant at the amended Place of Delivery. If the aplicable Tariff does not explicitly provide for the continued application of the terms and conditions of the Bill of Lading then the Carrier shall act as agent only of the Merchant in arranging for delivery of the Goods to the amended Place of Delivery but shall then be under no personal liability whatsoever for loss, damage or delay to the Goods, howsoever arising.

21. FCL MULTIPLE BILLS OF LADING

(1) Goods will only be delivered in a Container to the Merchant if all Bills of Lading in respect of the contents of the Container have been surrendered authorising delivery to a single Merchant at a single Place of Delivery. In the event that this requirement is not fulfilled the Carrier may unpack the Container and, in respect of Goods for which Bills of Lading have been surrendered, deliver these to the Merchant on an LCL basis. Such delivery shall constitute due delivery hereunder, but will only be effected against payment by the Merchant of LCL Service Charges and any charges appropriate to LCL Goods (as laid down in the Tariff) together with the actual costs incurred for any additional services rendered.

(2) If this is an FCL multiple Bill of Lading (as evidenced by the qualification of the tally acknowledged overleaf to the effect that it is "One of . . . part cargoes in the Container"), then the Goods detailed overleaf are said to comprise part of the contents of the Container indicated. If the Carrier is required to deliver the Goods to more than one Merchant and if all or part of the total Goods within the Container consists of bulk Goods or unappropriated Goods, or is or becomes mixed or unmarked or unidentifiable, the Holders of Bills of Lading relating to Goods within the Container shall take delivery thereof (including any damaged portion) and bear any shortage in such proportions as the Carrier shall in his absolute discretion determine, and such delivery shall constitute due delivery hereunder.

22. GENERAL AVERAGE & SALVAGE

(1) In the event of accident, danger, damage or disaster before or after the commencement of the voyage, resulting from any cause whatsoever, due to negligence or not, for which, or for the consequences of which, the Carrier is not responsible, by statute, contract or otherwise, the Merchant shall contribute with the Carrier in general average to the payment of any sacrifices, losses or expenses of a general average nature that may be made or incurred, and shall pay salvage and special charges incurred in respect of the Goods. All expenses in connection with a general average or salvage act to avoid damage to the environment always to be considered general average expenses.

(2) Any general average on a vessel operated by the Carrier shall be adjusted according to the York/Antwerp Rules of 1974 at any port or place and in any currency at the option of the Carrier. Any general average on a vessel not operated by the Carrier (whether a seagoing or inland waterways vessel) shall be adjusted according to the requirements of the operator of that vessel. In either cases the Merchant shall give such cash deposit or other security as the Carrier may deem sufficient to cover the estimated general average contribution of the Goods before delivery if the Carrier requires, or, if the Carrier does not so require, within three months of the delivery of the Goods, whether or not at the time of delivery the Merchant had notice of the Carrier's lien. The Carrier shall be under no obligation to exercise any lien for general average contribution due to the Merchant.

(3) Conversion into the currency of the adjustment shall be calculated at the rate prevailing on the date of payment for disbursements and on the date of completion of discharge of the vessel for allowances, contributory values etc.

(4) In the event of any general average credit balances due to Merchants still being unclaimed 5 years after the date of issue of the adjustment, these shall be paid to the owner or disponent owner of the vessel, who will hold such credit balances pending application by the Merchants entitled thereto.

(5) If a salving vessel is owned or operated by the Carrier, salvage shall be paid for as fully as if the salving vessel or vessels belonged to strangers.

23. VARIATION OF THE CONTRACT

No servant or agent of the Carrier shall have the power to waive or vary any of the terms of this Bill of Lading, unless such waiver or variation is in writing and is specifically authorised or ratified in writing by the Carrier.

24. LAW AND JURISDICTION

(1) Law of Application

Insofar as anything has not been dealt with by the terms and conditions of this Bill of Lading, English law shall apply. English law shall also be applied in interpreting the terms and conditions hereof.

(2) Jurisdiction

All actions arising under this Bill of Lading shall be brought before the High Court of Justice in London to the exclusion of the jurisdiction of the courts of any other place, unless the Carrier appeals to another jurisdiction or voluntarily submits himself thereto.

25. VALIDITY

In the event that anything herein contained is inconsistent with any applicable international convention or national law which cannot be departed from by private contract the provisions hereof shall to the extent of such inconsistency but no further be null and void.

26. BOTH-TO-BLAME COLLISION

The Both-to-Blame collision clause as published by the Baltic and International Maritime Conference is hereby incorporated into this Bill of Lading.

27. USA CLAUSE PARAMOUNT

(1) If the Carriage covered by this Bill of Lading includes Carriage to, from or through a port or place in the United States of America, this Bill of Lading shall be subject to the United States Carriage of Goods by Sea Act 1936 (US COGSA), the terms of which are incorporated herein and shall be paramount throughout Carriage by sea and the entire time that the Goods are in the actual custody of the Carrier or his sub-contractor at the sea terminal in the United States of America before loading onto the vessel or after discharge therefrom, as the case may be. As thus applies other than at sea, US COGSA is applied to determine the liability of the Carrier who shall be entitled to the benefits of the defences and limitations therein, notwithstanding that loss did not occur at sea.

(2) The Carrier shall not be liable in any capacity whatsoever for loss, damage or delay of or to the Goods while the goods are in the United States of America away from the sea terminal and are not in the actual custody of the Carrier. At these times the Carrier acts as agent only to procure Carriage by Persons (one or more) under the usual terms and conditions of those Persons. If, for any reason, the Carrier is denied the right to act as agent only at these times, his liability for loss, damage or delay to the goods shall be determined in accordance with Clause 6 hereof.

(3) If this Bill of Lading is accepted by a groupage agent acting as a non vessel owning common carrier (NVOCC), who has in turn issued other contracts of carriage to third parties, said NVOCC hereby warrants that all contracts of carriage issued by him in respect of Goods the subject of this Bill of Lading shall incorporate the terms and conditions of this Bill of Lading. Said NVOCC further agrees to indemnify and hold harmless the Carrier, his servants, agents and sub-contractors against all consequences of his failing so to incorporate.

(4) If the US COGSA applies the liability of the Carrier and/or the vessel shall not exceed US$ 500 per package or customary freight unit (in accordance with Section 1304(5) thereof), unless the value of the Goods has been declared on the face hereof, in which case Clause 7(3) shall apply.

(5) Notwithstanding the provisions of Clause 24, if the Place of Receipt, Port of Loading, Port of Discharge or Place of Delivery named herein is in the United States of America, the Merchant shall have the option to refer the claim or dispute to the United States District Courts for the Southern District of New York in accordance with the law of the United States of America.

Appendix I BIMCO liner bill of lading. A full set of clauses can be found on the reverse of this bill which is not shown.

LINER BILL OF LADING

B/L No.

Reference No.

Shipper

Consignee

Notify address

Pre-carriage by*	Place of receipt by pre-carrier*

Vessel	Port of loading

Port of discharge	Place of delivery by on-carrier*

Marks and Nos.	Number and kind of packages; description of goods	Gross weight	Measurement

Particulars furnished by the Merchant

Freight details, charges etc.

SHIPPED on board in apparent good order and condition, weight, measure, marks, numbers, quality, contents and value unknown, for carriage to the Port of Discharge or so near thereunto as the Vessel may safely get and lie always afloat, to be delivered in the like good order and condition at the aforesaid Port unto Consignees or their Assigns, they paying freight as indicated to the left plus other charges incurred in accordance with the provisions contained in this Bill of Lading. In accepting this Bill of Lading the Merchant expressly accepts and agrees to all its stipulations on both pages, whether written, printed, stamped or otherwise incorporated, as fully as if they were all signed by the Merchant.
One original Bill of Lading must be surrendered duly endorsed in exchange for the goods or delivery order.
IN WITNESS whereof the Master of the said Vessel has signed the number of original Bills of Lading stated below, all of this tenor and date, one of which being accomplished, the others to stand void.

Daily demurrage rate (additional Clause A)

* Applicable only when document used as a Through Bill of Lading

Freight payable at	Place and date of issue
Number of original Bs/L	Signature

Printed and Sold by S. STRAKER & SONS LTD.
25 Lime Street, London, E.C.3
By Authority of the Baltic & International Maritime Conference
Copenhagen

Appendix J BIMCO 'COGENBILL' for use with charter-parties. The conditions of carriage on the reverse side are also shown.

CODE NAME: "CONGENBILL" . EDITION 1978

Shipper

BILL OF LADING

TO BE USED WITH CHARTER-PARTIES

B/L No.

Reference No.

Consignee

Notify address

Vessel   **Port of loading**

Port of discharge

Shipper's description of goods   Gross weight

(of which   on deck at Shipper's risk; the Carrier not
being responsible for loss or damage howsoever arising)

Freight payable as per
CHARTER-PARTY dated ....

FREIGHT ADVANCE.
Received on account of freight:

....

Time used for loading .... days .... hours.

S H I P P E D at the Port of Loading in apparent good order and
condition on board the Vessel for carriage to the
Port of Discharge or so near thereto as she may safely get the goods
specified above.

Weight, measure, quality, quantity, condition, contents and value un-known.

IN WITNESS whereof the Master or Agent of the said Vessel has signed
the number of Bills of Lading indicated below all of this tenor and date,
any one of which being accomplished the others shall be void.

FOR CONDITIONS OF CARRIAGE SEE OVERLEAF

Freight payable at	Place and date of issue
Number of original Bs/L	Signature

Printed and Sold by S. Straker & Sons Ltd.
25 Lime Street, London, E.C.3
By Authority of the Baltic & International Maritime Conference
Copenhagen

Conditions of Carriage.

(1) All terms and conditions, liberties and exceptions of the Charter Party, dated as overleaf, are herewith incorporated. The Carrier shall in no case be responsible for loss of or damage to cargo arisen prior to loading and after discharging.

(2) General Paramount Clause.

The Hague Rules contained in the International Convention for the Unification of certain rules relating to Bills of Lading, dated Brussels the 25th August 1924 as enacted in the country of shipment shall apply to this contract. When no such enactment is in force in the country of shipment, the corresponding legislation of the country of destination shall apply, but in respect of shipments to which no such enactments are compulsorily applicable, the terms of the said Convention shall apply.

Trades where Hague-Visby Rules apply.

In trades where the International Brussels Convention 1924 as amended by the Protocol signed at Brussels on February 23rd 1968 – the Hague-Visby Rules – apply compulsorily, the provisions of the respective legislation shall be considered incorporated in this Bill of Lading. The Carrier takes all reservations possible under such applicable legislation, relating to the period before loading and after discharging and while the goods are in the charge of another Carrier, and to deck cargo and live animals.

(3) General Average.

General Average shall be adjusted, stated and settled according to York-Antwerp Rules 1974, in London unless another place is agreed in the Charter.

Cargo's contribution to General Average shall be paid to the Carrier even when such average is the result of a fault, neglect or error of the Master, Pilot or Crew. The Charterers, Shippers and Consignees expressly renounce the Netherlands Commercial Code, Art. 700, and the Belgian Commercial Code, Part II, Art. 148.

(4) New Jason Clause.

In the event of accident, danger, damage or disaster before or after the commencement of the voyage, resulting from any cause whatsoever, whether due to negligence or not, for which, or for the consequence of which, the Carrier is not responsible, by statute, contract or otherwise, the goods, Shippers, Consignees or owners of the goods shall contribute with the Carrier in general average to the payment of any sacrifices, losses or expenses of a general average nature that may be made or incurred and shall pay salvage and special charges incurred in respect of the goods.

If a salving ship is owned or operated by the Carrier, salvage shall be paid for as fully as if the said salving ship or ships belonged to strangers. Such deposit as the Carrier or his agents may deem sufficient to cover the estimated contribution of the goods and any salvage and special charges thereon shall, if required, be made by the goods, Shippers, Consignees or owners of the goods to the Carrier before delivery.

(5) Both-to-Blame Collision Clause.

If the Vessel comes into collision with another ship as a result of the negligence of the other ship and any act, neglect or default of the Master, Mariner, Pilot or the servants of the Carrier in the navigation or in the management of the Vessel, the owners of the cargo carried hereunder will indemnify the Carrier against all loss or liability to the other or non-carrying ship or her Owners in so far as such loss or liability represents loss of, or damage to, or any claim whatsoever of the owners of said cargo, paid or payable by the other or non-carrying ship or her Owners to the owners of said cargo and set-off, recouped or recovered by the other or non-carrying ship or her Owners as part of their claim against the carrying Vessel or Carrier. The foregoing provisions shall also apply where the Owners, operators or those in charge of any ship or ships or objects other than, or in addition to, the colliding ships or objects are at fault in respect of a collision or contact.

Appendix K BIMCO 'blank back' liner bill of lading.

**BIMCO BLANK BACK FORM OF
LINER BILL OF LADING**

B/L No.

Reference No.

Shipper

Consignee

Notify address

Pre-carriage by*	Place of receipt by pre-carrier*
Vessel	Port of loading
Port of discharge	Place of delivery by on-carrier*

Marks and Nos.	Number and kind of packages; description of goods	Gross weight	Measurement

Particulars furnished by the Merchant

Freight details, charges etc.	RECEIVED the goods as specified above according to Shipper's declaration in apparent good order and condition – unless otherwise stated herein – weight, measure, marks, numbers, quality, contents and value unknown.

The contract evidenced by this Bill of Lading is subject to the exceptions, limitations, conditions and liberties (including those relating to pre-carriage and on-carriage) set out in the Carrier's Standard Conditions of Carriage applicable to the voyage covered by this Bill of Lading and operative on its date of issue. If the Carrier does not have Standard Conditions of Carriage, this Bill of Lading is subject to the exceptions, limitations, conditions and liberties set out in the "Conlinebill" Liner Bill of Lading operative on its date of issue.

The "Conlinebill" Liner Bill of Lading and the Carrier's Standard Conditions of Carriage incorporate or are deemed to incorporate the Hague Rules contained in the Brussels Convention dated 25th August 1924 and any compulsorily applicable national enactment of either the Hague Rules as such or as amended by the Hague-Visby Rules contained in the Brussels Protocol dated 23rd February 1968.

A copy of the Carrier's Standard Conditions of Carriage applicable hereto may be inspected or will be supplied on request at the office of the Carrier or the Carrier's Principal agents.

IN WITNESS whereof the number of original Bills of Lading stated below have been signed, all of this tenor and date, one of which being accomplished, the others to be void.

Daily demurrage rate (if agreed)	Freight payable at	Place and date of issue
	Number of original Bs/L	Signature
* Applicable only when document used as a Through Bill of Lading		

Printed and sold by Fr. G. Knudtzon, Ltd., 55, Toldbodgade, Copenhagen, by authority of The Baltic and International Maritime Conference. (BIMCO), Copenhagen.

Appendix L   Common short form bill of lading.

Shipper

**COMMON
SHORT FORM
BILL OF LADING**

UK Customs
Assigned No.   B/L No.

Shipper's Reference

F/Agent's Reference

Consignee (if "Order" state Notify Party and Address)

Name of Carrier

Notify Party and Address (leave blank if stated above)

The contract evidenced by this Short Form Bill of Lading is subject to the exceptions, limitations, conditions and liberties (including those relating to pre-carriage and on-carriage) set out in the Carrier's Standard Conditions applicable to the voyage covered by this Short Form Bill of Lading and operative on its date of issue.
If the carriage is one where the provisions of the Hague Rules contained in the International Convention for unification of certain rules relating to Bills of Lading dated Brussels on 25th August, 1924, as amended by the Protocol signed at Brussels on 23rd February, 1968 (the Hague Visby Rules) are compulsorily applicable under Article X, the said Standard Conditions contain or shall be deemed to contain a Clause giving effect to the Hague Visby Rules. Otherwise, except as provided below, the said Standard Conditions contain or shall be deemed to contain a Clause giving effect to the provisions of the Hague Rules.
The Carrier hereby agrees that to the extent of any inconsistency the said Clause shall prevail over the exceptions, limitations, conditions and liberties set out in the Standard Conditions in respect of any period to which the Hague Rules or the Hague Visby Rules by their terms apply. Unless the Standard Conditions expressly provide otherwise, neither the Hague Rules nor the Hague Visby Rules shall apply to this contract where the goods carried hereunder consist of live animals or cargo which by this contract is stated as being carried on deck and is so carried.
Notwithstanding anything contained in the said Standard Conditions, the term Carrier in this Short Form Bill of Lading shall mean the Carrier named on the front thereof.
A copy of the Carrier's said Standard Conditions applicable hereto may be inspected or will be supplied on request at the office of the Carrier or the Carrier's Principal Agents.

Pre-Carriage by*	Place of Receipt by Pre-Carrier*
Vessel	Port of Loading
Port of Discharge	Place of Delivery by On-Carrier*

Marks and Nos;   Container No.   Number and kind of packages; Description of Goods   Gross Weight   Measurement

*Applicable only when document used as a Through Bill of Lading

Particulars declared by Shipper

Freight Details; Charges etc.

RECEIVED FOR CARRIAGE as above in apparent good order and condition, unless otherwise stated hereon, the goods described in the above particulars.

IN WITNESS whereof the number of original Bills of Lading stated below have been signed, all of this tenor and date, one of which being accomplished the others to stand void.

GCBS
CSF
BL
1979

Ocean Freight Payable at   Place and Date of Issue

Number of Original Bs/L   Signature for Carrier; Carrier's Principal Place of Business

710

Printed by P. C. Richardson & Co. Ltd., 6 Whittington Avenue EC3V 1JY   01-626 3118
Authorised and Licensed by the
General Council of British Shipping © 1979

Appendix M Non-negotiable sea waybill.

Shipper

SEA WAYBILL

NON-NEGOTIABLE

SWB No.

Reference No.

Consignee

Name of Carrier

Notify address

RECEIVED in apparent good order and condition and, as far as ascertained by reasonable means of checking, as specified below unless otherwise stated, to be transported and delivered as provided herein.

The terms of the carrier's standard conditions of carriage (including those relating to pre-carriage and on-carriage and any reference to the Hague and/or Hague-Visby Rules as well as the applicable tariff) are incorporated herein as well as any international convention or national law which is compulsorily applicable, and, without prejudice to any explicit stipulation herein, any reference to "the Bill of Lading" in the standard conditions shall be construed as a reference to this SWB.

A copy of the carrier's standard conditions of carriage applicable hereto will be supplied on request at the office of the carrier or his principal agents. The shipper accepts the said standard conditions on his own behalf and on behalf of the consignee and the owner of the goods and warrants that he has authority to do so.

This SWB is not a document of title and the goods shipped hereunder will be delivered when they have arrived at the place of delivery to the party who demands their delivery and can identify himself as the person either named as Consignee or authorized by the Consignee to receive the goods.

Pre-carriage by*	Place of receipt*
Ocean vessel	Port of loading
Port of discharge	Place of delivery*

Container Nos., marks and Nos.	Number and kind of packages; description of goods	Gross weight, kg	Measurement, m¹

Particulars declared by Shipper

Freight and charges

NODISP

NOTE: Unless the word "NODISP" in the box has been deleted, the following shall apply:

1. The shipper has irrevocably declared that he has assigned his right to control the goods during transport to the named consignee.

2. The carrier has agreed to hold this consignment in security and as collateral for the named consignee subject to any lien in favour of the carrier.

Freight payable at

Place and date of issue

Signed for the Carrier

This form is approved by SWEPRO

* Applicable only when document used as a Through or Combined Transport Sea Waybill

As Agents only

Appendix N FIATA combined transport bill of lading. The standard conditions on the reverse side are not shown.

Consignor		Emblem of National Association	**FBL**	
			NEGOTIABLE FIATA COMBINED TRANSPORT BILL OF LADING	**ICC**
			issued subject to ICC Uniform Rules for a Combined Transport Document (ICC publication 298).	

Consigned to order of

Notify address

	Place of receipt
Ocean vessel	Port of loading
Port of discharge	Place of delivery

Marks and numbers	Number and kind of packages	Description of goods	Gross weight	Measurement

specimen

according to the declaration of the consignor

The goods and instructions are accepted and dealt with subject to the Standard Conditions printed overleaf.

Taken in charge in apparent good order and condition, unless otherwise noted herein, at the place of receipt for transport and delivery as mentioned above.

One of these Combined Transport Bills of Lading must be surrendered duly endorsed in exchange for the goods. In Witness whereof the original Combined Transport Bills of Lading all of this tenor and date have been signed in the number stated below, one of which being accomplished the other(s) to be void.

Freight amount	Freight payable at	Place and date of issue
Cargo Insurance through the undersigned ☐ not covered ☐ Covered according to attached Policy	Number of Original FBL's	Stamp and signature
For delivery of goods please apply to:		

Appendix O Dangerous Goods Note (1981). The conditions on the reverse side are also shown. This is one of a set of seven. The top two copies are for use as a Declaration and Permit. The permit is signed by the ocean carrier and returned to the originator. Any additional copies needed by the carrier have to be photocopied. The remainder of the set serve as the Dangerous Goods Shipping Note (colour flashed) and office copy.

DG.

DANGEROUS GOODS DECLARATION, SHIPPING NOTE
& CONTAINER/VEHICLE PACKING CERTIFICATE
© SITPRO 1987

DANGEROUS GOODS NOTE

Special information is required for (a) dangerous goods in limited quantities (b) radioactive substances (class 7) (c) tank containers and road tankers (d) in certain circumstances a weathering certificate is required

SHADED AREAS NEED NOT BE SHIPPER COMPLETED FOR SHORT SEA RO. RO./ RAIL

Exporter	1	Customs reference/status	2

| Booking number | 3 | Exporter's reference | 4 |

| Port charges payable by * | exporter | freight forwarder | 5 | Forwarder's reference | 6 |

| Consignee | 7A | other (name & address) |

| Freight forwarder | 7 | International carrier | 8 |

For use of receiving authority only

| Other UK transport details (e.g. ICD, terminal, vehicle bkg. ref., receiving dates) | 9 |

Consecutive no. or DG reference allocated by international carrier (if any) | 10A

| Vessel | Port of loading | 10 |

| Port of discharge | Destination | 11 |

TO THE RECEIVING AUTHORITY
Please receive for shipment the goods described below subject to your published regulations and conditions (including those as to liability)

Shipping marks   Number and kind of packages; description of goods †
SPECIFY: HAZARD CLASS, UN/ADR/RID/IMDG CODE (AS APPROPRIATE), FLASHPOINT °C. | 12 | Receiving authority use | Gross wt (kg) 13 | Cube (m³) 14 |
Net wt (kg) | of goods |

SYSTEMFORMS LTD 01-505 6125
SITPRO APPROVED LICENSEE No. 09
(2.88)

MUST BE COMPLETED FOR FULL CONTAINER/ VEHICLE LOADS:-

† PROPER SHIPPING NAME—PROPRIETARY NAMES ALONE ARE NOT SUFFICIENT.

CONTAINER/VEHICLE PACKING CERTIFICATE	15	**DANGEROUS GOODS DECLARATION**	Total gross weight of goods	Total cube of goods

It is declared that the packing of the container has been carried out in accordance with the provisions shown overleaf:-

I hereby declare that the contents of this consignment are fully and accurately described above by the correct technical name(s) (proper shipping name(s)), that the shipment is packaged in such a manner as to withstand the ordinary risks of handling and transport by sea, having regard to the properties of the goods to be carried, and that the goods are classified, packaged, marked and labelled in accordance with the requirements of the Merchant Shipping (Dangerous Goods) Regulations 1981 as currently amended. I further declare that if appropriate the goods are classified, packaged and marked to comply with the requirement of the European Agreement concerning the International Carriage of Dangerous Goods by Road (ADR) and of Annex 1 (RID) to the International Convention concerning the Carriage of Goods by Rail (CIM) or special arrangements made between the contracting parties to these Agreements.
The shipper must complete and sign box 17.

Name of company

Signature   Date
of person responsible for packing container

| Prefix and container/vehicle number | 16 | Seal number(s) | 16A | Container/vehicle size & type | 16B | Tare wt (kg) as marked on CSC plate | 16C | Total of boxes 13 and 16C | 16D |

DOCK/TERMINAL RECEIPT
Received the above number of packages/containers/trailers in apparent good order and condition unless stated hereon.
RECEIVING AUTHORITY REMARKS

Haulier's Name

Vehicle reg. no.

DRIVER'S SIGNATURE   SIGNATURE AND DATE

Name and telephone no. of shipper preparing this note | 17

NAME/STATUS OF DECLARANT

DATE

Signature of declarant

890   *Mark X as appropriate. If box 5 is not completed the company preparing this note may be held liable for payment of port charges
Non completion of any boxes is a subject for resolution by the contracting parties.

SYSTEMFORMS LTD 01-505 6125
SITPRO APPROVED LICENSEE No. 09

CONTAINER/VEHICLE PACKING CERTIFICATE (see box 15 overleaf)

It is certified that:

1 The container/vehicle was clean, dry and appeared fit to receive the goods.

2 No incompatible substances have been packed within the freight container/vehicle except where this is permitted by the Merchant Shipping (Dangerous Goods) Regulations 1981 as currently amended.

3 Where packages or receptacles have been packed into a container/vehicle they were in sound condition.

4 All packages have been properly stowed and secured and where necessary suitable securing materials used.

5 The packages are clearly marked with a distinctive label or stencil of the label and the container/vehicle is clearly marked with labels to indicate the nature of the danger to which the goods give rise. Where the vehicle is a road tank vehicle or the goods are contained in a portable tank or tank container the label or marking shall in addition indicate the correct technical name of the goods.

6 The Dangerous Goods in this container/vehicle are those accepted by the carrier against the reference as identified in box 3 overleaf.

7 Where this Dangerous Goods Note is used as a Container/Vehicle Packing Certificate only, not a combined document, a Dangerous Goods Declaration signed by the shipper or supplier has been issued/received to cover each dangerous goods consignment packed in the container.

8 Where the Dangerous Goods Note applies to a road tank vehicle, or tank container, closures and valves have been properly closed and the correct ullage space left.

THE SIGNATURE GIVEN OVERLEAF IN BOX 15 MUST BE THAT OF THE PERSON CONTROLLING THE CONTAINER LOADING OPERATION. AFTER THE CONTAINER/VEHICLE HAS BEEN PACKED THE CERTIFICATE MUST BE GIVEN TO THE DRIVER ON COLLECTON AND PRESENTED TO THE CONTAINER/VEHICLE OPERATOR UPON DELIVERY.

DECLARATION

The company preparing this note declares that, to the best of their belief the goods have been accurately described, their quantities, weights and measurements are correct, and at the time of despatch they were in good order and condition.

Appendix P   Standard Shipping Note (1981). This document is in a six part colour-coded set. The top and bottom copies are plain and the remainder are coloured pink, yellow, blue and green. The distribution of the copies is usually as follows, but the colour coding chosen will vary from port to port depending on the system being operated:

One retained by docks or terminal; one returned to ocean carrier as a 'received for shipment' return; one to HM Customs; one to lorry driver as his receipt; one to ocean carrier as 'shipped on board' return; one retained by shipper or supplier as an office copy.

ⓒ SITPRO 1987

STANDARD SHIPPING NOTE

Exporter	1	Customs reference/status	2

Booking number	3	Exporter's reference	4

Port charges payable by *   5   Forwarder's reference   6

☐ exporter   ☐ freight forwarder

other (name and address)

Freight forwarder	7	International carrier	8

For use of receiving authority only

Other UK transport details (e.g. ICD, terminal, vehicle bkg. ref. receiving dates)   9

The Company preparing this note declares that, to the best of their belief, the goods have been accurately described, their quantities, weights and measurements are correct and at the time of despatch they were in good order and condition; that the goods are not classified as dangerous in any UK, IMO, ADR, RID or IATA/ICAO regulation applicable to the intended modes of transport.   10A

Vessel/flight no. and date   Port/airport of loading   10

Port/airport of discharge   Destination   11

TO THE RECEIVING AUTHORITY – Please receive for shipment the goods described below subject to your published regulations and conditions (including those as to liability).

Shipping marks	Number and kind of packages; description of goods; non-hazardous special stowage requirements	12	Receiving authority use	Gross wt (kg) of goods	13	Cube (m³) of goods	14

For use of shipping company only

Total gross weight of goods   Total cube of goods

PREFIX and container/trailer number(s)	16	Seal number(s)	16A	Container/trailer size(s) and type(s)	16B	Tare wt (kg) as marked on CSC plate	16C	Total of boxes 13 and 16C	16D

DOCK/TERMINAL RECEIPT
Received the above number of packages/containers/trailers in apparent good order and condition unless stated hereon.
RECEIVING AUTHORITY REMARKS

Haulier's name

Vehicle reg. no.

Name of company preparing this note   17

Date

DRIVER'S SIGNATURE   SIGNATURE AND DATE

(Indicate name and telephone number of contact)

Appendix Q   Indemnity form.

ELLERMAN LINES plc

INDEMNITY

TO THE OWNERS AND/OR AGENTS AND/OR CHARTERERS AND/OR MASTER

Ship   Date Sailed/Arrived

* In consideration for your issuing to us or to our order duplicate Bills of Lading for the undermentioned goods.

* In consideration for your releasing for delivery to us or to our order the undermentioned goods of which we claim to be the rightful owners without production of the relevant Bill of Lading (not as yet in our possession).

We hereby undertake and agree to indemnify you and/or your principals fully against all consequences and/or liabilities of any kind whatsoever directly or indirectly arising from or relating to the said action and immediately on demand against all payments made by you in respect of such consequences and/or liabilities, including costs as between solicitor and client and all or any sums demanded by you and/or your principals for the defence of any proceedings brought against you by reason of the aforesaid action.

And we further undertake and agree upon demand to pay any freight and/or General Average and/or charges due on the goods aforesaid (it being expressly agreed and understood that all liens shall subsist and be unaffected by the terms hereof);

And we further undertake and agree that immediately the Bill(s) of Lading is/are received by us we will deliver the same to you duly endorsed.

* Shipper/Consignee – delete whichever is inappropriate before submitting to guarantor.

B/L No.	Marks and Nos.	Quantity and Contents	Shipper	Port of Shipment	Port of Discharge

INDEMNITIES WITH LIMITED GUARANTEES OR BEARING ANY QUALIFYING REMARKS WHATSOEVER CANNOT BE ACCEPTED

Dated_____

Shippers or
Consignees_____
Signature

We join the above Indemnity and Guarantee

Dated_____

Bankers
Signature_____

CUNARD ELLERMAN

LAB 77

LLOYD'S AVERAGE BOND.

To ....

Owner(s) of the ....

Voyage and date ....

        Port of shipment ....

        Port of destination/discharge ....

        Bill of Lading or waybill number(s) ....

Quantity and description of goods

In consideration of the delivery to us or to our order, on payment of the freight due, of the goods noted above we agree to pay the proper proportion of any salvage and/or general average and/or special charges which may hereafter be ascertained to be due from the goods or the shippers or owners thereof under an adjustment prepared in accordance with the provisions of the contract of affreightment governing the carriage of the goods or, failing any such provision, in accordance with the law and practice of the place where the common maritime adventure ended and which is payable in respect of the goods by the shippers or owners thereof.

We also agree to:

(i) *furnish particulars of the value of the goods, supported by a copy of the commercial invoice rendered to us or, if there is no such invoice, details of the shipped value and*

(ii) *make a payment on account of such sum as is duly certified by the average adjusters to be due from the goods and which is payable in respect of the goods by the shippers or owners thereof.*

Date ....   Signature of receiver of goods ....

Full name and address ....

AVERAGE GUARANTEE

For Signature by Underwriters of Cargo to avoid collection of Deposits

Vessel:

Accident:

DEAR SIRS,

    In consideration of the Delivery in due course to the Consignees of the Merchandise specified at foot hereof, without collection of a Deposit on Account of Average, We, the Undersigned Underwriters, hereby guarantee to the Ship Owners the payment of any Contribution to General Average and/or Salvage and/or Charges which may hereafter be ascertained to be in respect to the said Merchandise.

    We further agree to arrange a prompt payment on account if required so soon as such payment may be substantiated by the necessary documents and certified to by ………
…………………………………… the Average Adjusters.

Name and Address of Underwriters:- (Please quote Policy/Certificate of Insurance No. and Date)

Signature:-

Particulars of Goods referred to in this Guarantee

B/L	Marks and Numbers	Packages and Contents	Total Insured Value

Insurance Brokers: (Please insert)

Name: ....

Address: ....*Ref. No.:* ....

VALUATION FORM

To ....

Owner(s) of the ....

Voyage and date ....

      Port of shipment ....

      Port of destination/discharge ....

      Bill of Lading or waybill number(s) ....

Quantity and description of goods	Particulars of value	
	A Invoice value (specify currency)	**B** Shipped value (specify currency)
Currency		

1. If the goods are insured please state the following details (if known):—

   Name and address of insurers or brokers ....

   Policy or certificate number and date .... Insured value ....

2. If the goods arrived subject to loss or damage, please state nature and extent thereof ....

....

....

and ensure that copies of supporting documents are forwarded either direct or through the insurers to the average adjusters named below.

3. If a general average deposit has been paid, please state:—

    (a) Amount of the deposit .... (b) Deposit receipt number ....

    (c) Whether you have made any claim on your insurers

       for reimbursement ....

Date .... Signature ....

Full name and address ....

....

....

NOTES

1. If the goods form the subject of a commercial transaction, fill in column A with the amount of the commercial invoice rendered to you, *and attach a copy of thi* *invoice hereto.*
2. If there is no commercial invoice covering the goods, state the shipped value, if known to you, in column B.
3. In either case, state the currency involved.
4. The shipowners have appointed as average adjusters

to whom this form should be sent duly completed together with a copy of the commercial invoice.

Appendix S General Average Deposit Receipt.

ORIGINAL

No.

GENERAL AVERAGE DEPOSIT RECEIPT.

No.

General Average Deposit Receipt.

———

Dated at

19

Vessel

Depositors, Messrs.

Arrived Value
(provisional).

B/L No.

Amount of Deposit

Description of Goods:

NOTICE TO CONSIGNEE: If insured, send this receipt to your Underwriters for payment. If NOT insured, hold this receipt until the Adjustment is completed as Credit balance will not be paid over without its production.

NOTICE TO UNDERWRITERS: When payment of this Deposit has been made by you, kindly advise Adjusters and thus assist Final Settlement.

Dated at _____ 19

Vessel _____ from _____ to

Nature and date of Accident

Received from Messrs.

the sum of

deposit on account of General Average and/or Salvage and/or Charges, being _____ per cent. on _____ provisionally adopted as the net arrived value of the following goods, viz.:

Marks and Nos. and description of interest to be inserted here.

B/L No.

£

Trustees.

N.B.—The refund, if any, will be made only to the bearer of, and in exchange for this Receipt, and will be the whole balance of the deposit after satisfying the General Average and/or Salvage and/or Charges without deduction or set off of any other claims of the Shipowner against the Shipper or Consignee.

The General Average will be adjusted in the United Kingdom, and the Shipowners have given the necessary instructions to . . . . Average Adjusters

Index

Adler v Dickson (1954) 34
Agency clause 35
Arbitration 69
Ardennes v Ardennes (1952) 18
Arrospe v Barr (1881) 48
Australian Sea-Carriage of Goods Act 1904 5
Average Guarantee Form – Appendix R

Bills of lading
  application as document of title 19
  application as receipt 19
  BIMCO
    blank back, liner – Appendix K
    COGENBILL – Appendix J
    liner form – Appendix I
  Both-to-blame Collision clause 33
  claims 32
  clean, definition of 48
  combined transport – Appendix H
  common short form – Appendix L
  contents of 67
  conventional and through 18–35
  dangerous goods 31
  deck cargo 29
  definition of 5
  delivery of cargo 50
  delivery of goods without
    production of 20
  Demise or Agency clause 35
  evidence of contract 3, 18, 19
  FIATA combined transport –
    Appendix N
  Government form 44
  issue of 67
  issued under charter party 42
  issued by freight forwarder 43
  Jurisdiction clause 35
  New Jason clause 34
  received for shipment 9, 22, 23
  reservations and evidentiary
    effect 68
  shipped on board 9, 22, 23
  short form or blank back 44
  transhipment and forwarding 30,
    31
  Voyage clause 29
  War clause 30

Bills of Lading Act (1855) 2, 3, 5
BIMCO 24, 36
Birkley v Presgrave (1801) 77
Blockade 29
Blue Book 79
British Imex Industries v Midland Bank
  (1958) 48, 49
Book of Lading 1
Both-to-blame Collision clause 33
Bulk tank shipments (dangerous
  goods) 81

Canadian Water Carriage Act 1910 5
*Canadian Water Carriage of Goods Act
  1936* 5
Carriage of Goods by Sea Act 1924 5, 6,
  27, Appendix A
Carriage of Goods by Sea Act 1971 13,
  14, 21, 22, 27, Appendix B
'Caspiana' clause 29
CHEMTANKWAYBILL '85 47
Chapman v Peers (1534) 1
Claims 32
Clause Paramount 27
Clean bill of lading 48–9
COMBICONBILL 36
COMBIDOC 36
Combined transport documents 36–
  41, Appendix H
Compensation: combined transport
  38
Conference Form bill (1885) 2
Congenbill 42
Conlinebill 42, 44
Consignees impowered to sue 4
Consignor, guarantee by 74
Container/Vehicle Packing
  Certificate 80
Contract of affreightment 18
Conveyance clause 28

Dangerous goods
  special rules 11, 31, 76
  carriage of 79–81
  classes of 81
Data Freight Receipt 46
Deck cargo 29, 66
Definition of bill of lading 5

Delivery of cargo under bills of lading 50
Delivery orders, ships' 53
DGN (dangerous goods note) – Appendix O
Documentary credits 56–60
Droit Commercial Maritime 1

Electronic Data Interchange (EDI) xi
Endorsees empowered to sue 4
Endorsement 2, 3, 20
Enechem & others v Ampelos shipping (The Delfini) (1988) 3
Eurymedon (1974) 35
Evidence of shipment 4

FIATA (international federation of freight forwarders associations) 43, 44
  combined transport bill of lading – Appendix N
Fowler v Knoop (1878) 3
Freight 25–6, 32

GASTANKWAYBILL 47
General Average 33, 70, 77
  Deposit Receipt – Appendix R
Gold Clause Agreement 11, 13
Golodetz v Czarnikow-Rionda (The Galatia) (1980) 48
Grant v Norway (1851) 3, 24
Guarantees by shipper/consignor 68, 74
Guidon de la mer 1

Hague Rules 6–13, Appendix A
Hague–Visby rules 6, 13–17, Appendix B
Hamburg Rules (1885) 2
Hamburg Rules (1978) 5, 63–71, Appendix E
Harter Act 1893 (US) 5, 6, 9
Himalaya clause 16, 34

ICC Rules for combined transport documents 56
Increase of responsibility & liability 12
Indemnity form – Appendix Q
Inherent vice 10
Issue of bill of lading 67

Jurisdiction 35, 69, 76

Laws of Visby 13

Letters of Indemnity 11, 61–2, Appendix Q
Lewis v McKee (1868) 3
Liability
  basis of 64, 75
  of carrier 15, 17, 66
  of consignor/shipper 67, 76
  limits of 11, 65, 75
  loss of right to limit 75
  of servants/agents 74
Lickbarrow v Mason (1794) 3, 19
Limitation of actions 69, 76
Lloyd's Average Bond/Guarantee/Receipt 78, Appendix R
Lloyds v Grace Smith & Co (1912) 24
Loss, notice of 68, 76
Limitation Act 1939 61
Limitation on the application of Hague Rules 12
Lien 33, 40

Manifest, ship's 55
Margarine Union v Cambay Prince Steamship Co (1967) 53
Mates receipt 52
Merchant Shipping Act 1894 10
Merchant Shipping Act 1981 14
Midland Silicones v Scruttons (1962) 34
Model bill of lading 2
Monetary units 12
Multimodal transport document, issue of 73

National Standard Shipping Note 52, Appendix P
New Jason Clause 34
New Zealand Carriage of Goods by Sea Act 1940 5
New Zealand and Seamen Act 1908 5
Notice of loss, damage or delay 68, 76

Ordinance of Louis XIV (1681) 77
Ordonnance Maritime of Trani 1063 1

Package limitation 11
Petersen v Freebody (1895) 8
POLCOALBILL 43
POLCOALVOY, charter 43
Pomerene Bills of Lading Act 1916 (US) xi, 4, Appendix C
Port regulations 30

Renton v Palmyra (1957) 29

Responsibilities and liabilities
  of carrier 8, 64
  of shippers/merchants 40
Rights and immunities 9
Risks 7
'Rosa S' case (1988) 13

Saudi Crown (1985) 24
Scaramanga v Stamp (1880) 11
Sea waybills 46, Appendix M
Ship's manifest, see Manifest
Skibsaktieselskapet Thor v Tyrer (1929)
  50
Snee v Prescott (1793) 2
SOVORECONBILL, charter 43
Special drawing rights (SDR) 14, 65
Stagg Line v Foscolo, Mango & Co
  (1932) 11
Standard shipping note 52, Appendix
  P
Stoppage in transitu 4
Stumore v Breen (1886) 24
Surrender of rights and immunities
  12
SWEPRO Sea Waybill 47
Sze Hai Tong Bank v Rambler Cycle Co
  (1959) 50

Through carriage 66

Through bill of lading conditions –
  Appendix G
Transhipment and forwarding 30–1
Transport emergency information
  (dangerous goods) 80

Unit of account 15, 70
United Nations Conventions
  1978, the Hamburg Rules 63–71,
    Appendix E
  1980, International Multimodal
    Transport of Goods 72–6

United States, pomerene act, see
  Pomerene Bills of Lading Act
United States Carriage of goods by sea
  act 1936 5, Appendix D

Van Ekris v Rio Paraguay (US) (1983) 23
Variation of contract (combined
  transport) 41
Voyage clause 29

Weight, quality, marks etc.,
  acknowledgement of 28
War, Carrier's Liberties 30

York-Antwerp Rules 77, Appendix F
York rules (1864) 77